Trinity Mirror Media

THE ACCIDENTAL SOLDIER

Stephen Paul Stewart

This book is dedicated to all the servicemen and women who have fought so hard for so long in Afghanistan.

To absent friends.

For Mum, Dad and RMH.

THE ACCIDENTAL SOLDIER

Trinity Mirror Media

Written by Stephen Paul Stewart

Editing & Production by James Cleary
Cover: Lee Ashun

Copyright text: Stephen Paul Stewart

Published in Great Britain in 2014
Published and produced by: Trinity Mirror Media,
PO Box 48, Old Hall Street, Liverpool L69 3EB.
Managing Director: Ken Rogers
Publishing Director: Steve Hanrahan
Executive Editor: Paul Dove
Executive Art Editor: Rick Cooke
Sales and Marketing Manager: Elizabeth Morgan
Senior Marketing Executive: Claire Brown

Images: Stephen Paul Stewart.

Printed and bound by CPI Group (UK) Ltd, Croydon, CR0 4YY

ISBN: 9781908695932

CONTENTS

ACKNOWLEDGEMENTS

THANKS to Lynda for everything, especially all the home-cooked meals. My time at OP Dara would have been so much harder and more uncomfortable if it wasn't for the support of a large number of people. This includes Timmy Millen, Colin Robb, Tom Ross, Sharon Crozier, Sarah Jane Adams and Ryan Knox.

Staff at Trinity Mirror, Media Scotland and the *Daily Record* have been a great source of strength. My thanks go to Eugene Duffy, Allan Rennie, Murray Foote and Kevin Mansi and everyone on the *Record* newsdesk for their words of encouragement.

Organisations such as Treats for Troops and Support Our Soldiers do first-class work, sending out much needed items to soldiers on the frontline. I and my fellow Dara inmates enjoyed their largesse on a number of occasions. It warmed my heart to read notes from well wishers, some old, some young, who I would never meet. They had taken the time and effort to spend their own cash to send gifts to myself and fellow soldiers.

Thanks to Calum McLeod and everyone at Alba Military Fitness for the parcels and messages of support. They meant a great deal to me. Thanks also to Big Terry for his sage advice – who know who you are! Cheers to Duncan Bick for his brainstorming sessions – the shandies are on you next time.

Robert and Gerard kept me going. Although their patter

may be dubious, they have been like brothers to me.

This book would not have been possible without the fore-sight, patience and talent of Ken Rogers, Paul Dove and James Cleary. They have made this ride as pain-free as possible.

Also, I should not forget Leah for all those frenzied trips to the park and Dino's to take my mind off the craft of writing.

As always, I owe everything to my mum and dad.

"War is an ugly thing but not the ugliest of things. The decayed and degraded state of moral and patriotic feeling, which thinks that nothing is worth war, is much worse. The person who has nothing for which he is willing to fight, nothing which is more important than his own personal safety, is a miserable creature and has no chance of being free unless made and kept so by the exertions of better men than himself"
– John Stuart Mill

CALL OF DUTY

'Private S P Stewart – Notice of Compulsory Call Out. As you know, the British armed forces are involved in supporting a number of international military operations. The Government has taken the decision to call out compulsorily elements of the Reserve Forces in order to sustain deployments. They will deploy alongside the Regular Services in support of the UK's contribution to operations.

You have been called out because under powers conferred on him by the Reserve Forces Act 1996, the Secretary of State for Defence has issued an order authorising the compulsory call out of reservists from the Regular and Volunteer Reserves.'

PROLOGUE

IMAGINE your own death. In Afghanistan, I was most likely to be killed by a roadside bomb planted by the Taliban. Improvised explosive devices (IEDs) account for around three quarters of all coalition deaths. So, that's most likely how my end would come. I just hoped it would be quick. Thinking about spending months in a ward, missing arms and legs like a burst rag doll before succumbing to an agonising death, filled me with primal, nerve-shredding fear.

Then, on top of all that, try to get your head around communicating to your loved ones from beyond the grave in the form of a letter. Not easy is it? We all had to do it. My deployment to Afghanistan as an infantry soldier was looming. I sat down to pen a letter to my family to be opened only in the event of my death. Nothing in Army training prepared me for this. It remains one of the toughest things I've ever had to do, making the pain, discomfort and harshness of military life pale in comparison.

I had a few pages of writing paper to cram in a lifetime of love, saying all the things that all too often remain unsaid. It took weeks for me to get round to finally composing my 'death letter'. I would always find something else to do. There would always be tomorrow to do it. As the clock wound down, my deployment date grew nearer. I couldn't put it off any longer. I even toyed with the idea of not writing one at all, then I thought that would be too cruel. A missed opportunity to say what you need to.

I also had the surreal situation of posing for 'death pictures', snaps of me looking bold and brave that would be released to the press in the event that I got whacked, wasted, smashed, rubbed out. Soldiers have a lot of words for getting killed. I stood outside the battalion headquarters as another soldier took a couple of head and shoulder pictures of me. Do I smile or not? No-one really seemed to know. I got measured for my 'number twos' – the full Highland kit, in case I had to either come home in a coffin wearing it, or wear it to carry someone else's. I did have that horrible, complacent feeling of 'it won't happen to me' but that's just a facade, a coping mechanism. You have to hope for the best but prepare for the worst.

Why did I leave a good career in an air conditioned office to join the Army as a lowly private before going to the most dangerous country in the planet? At times, I asked myself the same question. What on earth am I doing signing up for military service? Afghanistan grabbed me by the throat when I went there as an embedded journalist. It wouldn't let go. That country changed my life.

Going there was undoubtedly one of the biggest formative experiences of my life. I thought the heat, among other things, would kill me but, in a perverse way, I rather enjoyed it. It made a refreshing change from watching my fingers turn blue as I drove into work in the depths of yet another savage Scottish winter.

Life on operations seemed to me to be life in its stripped down, unadorned, purest form. You did your job, you ate, slept then got up and did your job again. There was no office politics, no bills, no hassle, none of the flippant, unimportant floss that clutters our modern lives.

Afghanistan was a terrifyingly beautiful place. It seemed

ahistorical. When I was there as a reporter, I gazed out at the countryside in wonder. It could have been 2009 or nine years BC, this landscape was stark, unforgiving and timeless. It felt like I had travelled in a time machine back to the period when Alexander the Great wandered these lands. It felt almost like a love affair. I was captivated, I had to go back, this time to see what it was like as a soldier.

The anti-modernity of soldiering appealed to me too. Newspaper stories are full of high-tech derring do with stealth planes, laser-guided missiles and pilotless drones hitting our nation's enemies. An infanteer's role, though, hasn't changed much over the centuries. Weaponry, uniforms and such like come and go but the role of a foot soldier in 21st century Afghanistan would look familiar to a trooper from the Boer War. I found the collectivism of the Army to be a sharp contrast to the atomised society we live in today. Recruits are hammered with the benefits of the 'buddy buddy system', of looking out for one another. It's hard not to admire the determination and fellowship. And as every infantry sergeant major will tell you: it's still boots on the ground that win wars.

I never contemplated joining anything other than the infantry. To the civilian public, a soldier is a soldier. In the military, however, not all soldiers are created equal. All troops get a basic grounding in soldiering. It's only the infantryman, the grunt, the Jock, the Tommy, call him what you will, whose sole job is to 'close with and destroy the enemy'. He, and I use 'he' advisedly, doesn't train to do office work, cook or dish out supplies. He is what the public visualises when they think of a 'soldier'. They are trained to kill, and that's pretty much it.

At the time of writing, women are barred from the infantry in the British Army. They can support front-line operations in logistics, artillery and engineering teams but are banned from the infantry or tactical combat teams. In America, they are considering opening up all combat roles to women.

It had to be the infantry for me. This job alone would give me a priceless insight into the reality of soldiering in the most difficult circumstances the British Army have faced since the Korean War, or even World War II. I did not sign up as a grand, patriotic gesture for Queen and country. I did not sign up because my mates were doing it and I didn't want to be left out. I became a soldier by accident.

When the vast majority of troops pull out of Afghanistan at the end of 2014, it will be the first time Britain has been at peace after a century of constant warfare. Defence spending is being cut. Britain's reserve soldiers will form the backbone of the new armed forces. More teachers, bakers and binmen will give up their jobs to train and deploy to the frontline of wherever Britain is engaged.

Restructuring means that tomorrow's British Army will be much, much smaller. In 2010 the Army's strength was about 102,000 troops. By 2020 there will be a regular army of just 82,000 – half the size it was during the Cold War, complemented by 30,000 Reservists. In 1978 the Army had more than 163,000 troops.

Deploying to Afghanistan was tough. In some ways, coming back was even harder.

PROLOGUE

It was meant to be an adventure, an immersive experience throwing light on life on the frontline. It ended up coming far too close to home. Going back to work and civilian life was a struggle. After the novelty of running water and clean sheets wore off, normal life felt a bit flat. You were left feeling that no matter what you did, it would never be life and death important, as it was over there. As much as I couldn't wait for the tour to be over, I can now understand why people kept signing up for more and going back again and again.

My death letter sits gathering dust in a manilla envelope in a drawer, unopened, unread. The seal of masking tape that I put on the back of the envelope, to prevent my partner Lynda's curiosity getting the better of her, is still there. Maybe, one day, I'll let her read it but then again, maybe I won't. It may be better to just destroy it. I don't need it now, after all. She might not be surprised by the contents, she knows me too well.

In my letter, I told her what I had hoped to achieve by going to Afghanistan as a soldier, of how I wanted to take part in the campaign rather than just reporting on it from the sidelines. Deploying to Afghanistan killed many relationships. In fact, during my tour, in our tiny camp, at least two men split from their girlfriends. I told her that I thought my tour of Afghanistan would make us stronger. If we could cope with that, we could cope with anything.

I would find out a lot of things during my tour, about myself, the Army, Afghanistan. I discovered that families complete a tour of duty just as much as any soldier toughing it out in a tiny camp, eating cold rations and wishing that he was somewhere else.

We give an incredible amount of responsibility to our soldiers, many of whom are boys and who have never left Govan, Salford or Bermondsey before. We train them to kill, send them to the harshest soldiering conditions on the planet while telling them to adhere to strict Rules Of Engagement (ROE) governing when they can and cannot kill the enemy. In Helmand, I would hear many soldiers muttering: "Better to be judged by 12 than carried by six." In other words, it's better to kill someone and end up in court for it, rather than wind up dead yourself because you hesitated.

I discovered that there are so many contradictions about war in general, but especially Afghanistan. We call our soldiers heroes constantly, much to their embarrassment. Yet, we pay some of them just 18 grand a year for going to the frontline. Serving in the Army was a true eye opener. I would see war as it is — in all it's mundane, heroless glory.

This book is my account, a subjective one. I do not pretend to offer a complete history of Afghanistan nor a detailed panoramic view of the British campaign there. I kept diaries during my Army training and my tour. This is my story about what I saw and experienced before, during and after going to Afghanistan as a soldier.

My family were spared the horror of reading my death letter. I was fortunate. I came back. Some people would not be so lucky.

CHAPTER 1

DEEP END

*"Every man thinks meanly of himself
for not having been a soldier"*
– Samuel Johnson

"WHAT the fuck are you looking at!?" Welcome to the British Army, I think. I have wandered innocently into the office of a 6ft 3ins slab of muscle on my first day as a full-time soldier. My impromptu arrival in this cramped office is met with a fusillade of abuse. I was certainly hoping for an easier start to my budding military career. With veins in his forehead straining to the surface, the sergeant before me arches his eyebrows, pacing ominously ever closer.

My stomach has been pretty unsettled anyway, given that I am truly in uncharted territory here. I have hung up my pen and notepad as a professional journalist to join the Army as an infantry soldier. Today is the first step towards achieving my dream of serving on the front line. As the sergeant steps closer to me, I feel like an amateur boxer who is about to undergo his first pummelling. My guts fizz for the umpteenth time that morning.

'Why me?' I think, not for the first or last time. I curse my stupidity for walking into this guy's personal space. In most workplaces, fellow workers would ask if I needed a hand, or if I want directions. Obviously, not here. My eyes haven't left this military monster in front of me. "What are you doing here?" he growls. There isn't an ounce of fat on his body, his bulging forearms and inflated upper arms suggest he is a boxer or weightlifter. Every sinew looks finely honed and perfectly designed to inflict damage on the fragile human frame, like mine. I discover later that he is a mixed martial artist and a handy cage fighter.

Right now, he is just a walking, talking threat. "Why are you fucking in here?" he asks. I wasn't to know it at the time but I have just stumbled across one of the hardest men in the battalion. He is a specialist in reconnaissance, going behind enemy lines to gather intelligence, spearheading the way for the rest of the army. He also has the unmistakable air of a man who doesn't so much have a short fuse, as no fuse at all.

Like an awkward schoolboy, I mumble my heartfelt apologies to the V-shaped monster who I would eventually come to know as "Boab The Dug" and beat a hasty retreat, edging towards the safety of the office door. I am in the heart of Glencorse Barracks, near Edinburgh, to join 2 SCOTS, the Royal Highland Fusiliers. I will train with these men, and some women, before deploying to Afghanistan for a gruelling six-month tour of duty as a frontline soldier.

My Army career, humble though it may be, stands in stark contrast to most soldiers. I came to this soldiering lark pretty late. In fact, I am the complete opposite of the stereotypical fresh-faced, naive boy soldier. Many soldiers join up at 17 or maybe slightly older but I am a 38-year-old newspaper reporter who has given up the relative comfort and stability of the air-conditioned newsroom to join the Army Reserves before heading out to the Afghan badlands.

If someone had said to me a few years ago that I was going to give up my career and family life to be a trained soldier in the most challenging environment the forces have faced since the Korean War, I would have laughed at their outlandish imagination. My journey from observer to participant in the Afghanistan campaign began when I was embedded as a reporter with a historic battalion on Op Herrick, the military's name for the Afghan mission, in 2009.

It is not journalistic hyperbole to say that those three weeks with 3 SCOTS, the Black Watch, were a revelation which utterly transformed my life. I was in the newsroom at the *Daily Record* when I got a call saying that I had been cleared to go out to Kandahar to report on the battalion's work smashing Taliban bomb-making facilities and fracturing their lucrative drugs trade. I was blissfully unaware that this assignment would ultimately lead to me signing up to join the British Army.

Like millions of boys around Britain, and the world for that matter, I was obsessed with all things military. From sitting hunched over *Commando* comics devouring tales of derring do about grizzled fighter pilots and stiff upper lipped POWs, to spending countless Saturday afternoons watching war movies like *Kelly's Heroes* and *A Bridge Too Far*, I could not get enough. Never did I think, though, that I would end up joining the Army myself, particularly at nearly 40 with a perfectly comfy, more or less socially acceptable career in journalism under my belt.

I vividly remember quizzing both my grandfathers about their part in World War Two. My grandad on my mum's side served with the Cameronians, a legendary Scottish outfit that served with distinction with the Chindits, a British Indian force that fought miles behind enemy lines in Burma. He was one of millions of men who was conscripted at the start of the war and never returned home to my gran until the end of the conflict. There was no such thing as Rest and Recuperation or R&R in those days. He was a tall, easy-going man with a mop of silvery hair. Try as I might, I can never remember him raising his voice, no matter how badly I behaved or how daft my questions were. So I was amazed to find out that he went from private soldier to corporal, a rank that is carried by the toughest, no-nonsense men of any battalion. In my later Army career, I would find out that any corporal's word is law.

My grandad Robert was injured in the buttocks and legs – I never did get to ask him how it happened. According to family legend, when the war started he went off with a full head of mousey, light brown hair. Years later, my gran was in the garden hanging out washing when she spotted a tall stranger walking down the road in a demob suit. She watched as he turned up her path and said hello. It was her husband, my grandad, back home for good – but his hair had turned totally white. Was it natural ageing or was it because of the horrors of what he had witnessed around the world from Italy to India, and pretty much everywhere in between? Again, sadly, I never got to ask him.

He sported a large tattoo of a woman with the words 'Mother India' underneath. His skin art, which had turned a grey blue with the passage of time, was a permanent reminder of his time in the east. Army service had, literally, left its mark on him. He smoked fervently, with the passion a hobbyist has for stamp collecting or some other past-time. Smoking was his 'thing' – again, this I now know, was probably a relic from his Army days. I remember he would often have a basin wash – barechested at the sink, scrubbing himself. I would do the same in Afghanistan.

My other grandad, James, or Jim as he was known to his pals, was a Royal Navy man. As a boy of nine or 10, I was eager to hear his war stories but sadly I never kept any records of his chats. As a result, to my eternal shame, I can't recollect what ships he served on. In old pictures from the war, he was a trim, high cheekboned young blade. He was a junior seaman on one of the battleships that sank the famous Bismarck. That historic battle would change his life forever.

His face was ripped apart by shrapnel in the blasts that racked his ship. He lost one eye and was left with a skein of deep scars which pulled the skin taut on his face. He told me, as I sat in shorts and scabby knees in his front room, how they used metal wire to stitch his face up as the doctors had run out of catgut since there were so many horrifically injured men to deal with. His web of scars criss-crossed his scalp and face, etching white lines into his paper thin, pale flesh. I never knew him any other way so I was unfazed by it. I only balked at the thought of him taking his glass eye out, which thankfully didn't happen very often.

In his younger days, I was left with the distinct impression that my 'granda' had been a bit of a 'boy', a risk taking handful who certainly knew how to look after himself. He told me one vivid anecdote about how he smashed a fellow sailor in the face for referring to him as a 'Jock bastard'. He ruefully rubbed the grey stubble on his chin as he said: "Being called a bastard was a big insult in those days."

He had also been a boxer, although I think his flirtation with pugilism was brief. He loved telling me how he had a huge respect for the sportsmen on TV after he sampled the delights of the ring when he was in the Navy. He would don the gloves for three, three-minute rounds with a fellow shipmate and by the end neither he nor his pal could raise their fists, let alone throw a punch. "Their strength and stamina is unbelievable" he would tell me, as Frank Bruno bobbed about the TV screen in his living room.

To this day, I have an aversion to killing spiders after he told me how, while he was recuperating in hospital, he watched nurses telling off injured sailors for killing spiders which crawled around the decaying hospital ward. The nurses said the spiders were 'clean' insects which helped them keep diseases at bay by killing off 'dirty' creatures such as flies and cockroaches. Spiders, no matter how big and ugly, have been safe in my home ever since.

I remember perching on the edge of the sofas in their respective houses, quizzing my grandads about the war. "Don't you hate the Germans?" I asked, being totally bamboozled by their complete lack of bitterness. "Those German guys were just like me, they were doing what they had to. They suffered just like we did," was the gist of their reply. At the time, I felt angry and a bit miffed that I hadn't got more out of them. Now, I see that their answer says a lot about their humanity, empathy and wisdom.

Until now, my grandad's experience had been my only window into the military life. I certainly wasn't destined to follow in the footsteps of a glorious forefather who commanded a regiment at Waterloo or anything of that sort. My martial career until now went as far as playing with Action Man or shoving toy tanks around in the dirt at the foot of my garden as a kid. In my late teens and early twenties, I studied military history at university as part of a wider degree in modern history. Perhaps, my penchant for *Commando* comics had carried over into academe.

I loved the subject – one minute, studying the campaigns of Napoleon, learning about all the tactics and strategy of Napoleonic warfare, the next minute, you would be brought right up to date with the latest theories on the carnage and seeming futility of the Somme and Passchendaele in World War One. Still, though, I never developed the urge to don a uniform and enlist.

That all changed with my trip to Afghanistan as a journo. I now tend to think of my life in two halves – pre-

Afghanistan and post-Afghanistan. So here I am, clad in full Multi-Terrain Pattern, or modern camouflage to the military novice, and sporting a white hackle on my regimental Tam O'Shanter headdress, or bunnet as it's known to the 'sojers' or soldiers to non-Scots.

My white hackle is the distinctive emblem of 2 SCOTS, its white spray of feathers is meant to represent the white puff of smoke from the barrel of a fusil, a small flintlock musket popular in the 17th century. Each battalion in the Royal Regiment of Scotland has its own hackle: black for 1 SCOTS, red for 3 SCOTS, blue for 4 SCOTS, green for 5 SCOTS, grey for 6 and purple for 7 SCOTS.

Scotland's 'super-regiment', as it was quickly dubbed, was formed in 2006 from some of the most famous antecedent regiments in the Army such as the Black Watch, the Argyll and Sutherland Highlanders and the King's Own Scottish Borderers. Hackles, as well as being colourful and eye-catching against the usual military backdrop of Army issue greens and browns, serve a practical purpose. They are a direct, visible nod to the history of these regiments which were reduced in size to become battalions, forming part of the new 'super-regiment'. It was a controversial move at the time and Army chiefs were desperate to reassure the grumbling public that they would retain the 'golden thread' of history. No-one wanted to lose the hard-fought glory that these units had won in scores of conflicts in every part of the world over centuries.

Scots, like the Irish, have very long memories. I have heard people in the Army talk about the battle of Bannockburn or

Flodden as if it happened last Tuesday. History lies heavily on the British Army anyway, but arguably even more so in the Scottish battalions, where even the youngest recruit is supposed to be immersed in battle honours and regimental pride. Woe betide any 'crow', the derogative term for a new, inexperienced recruit, if he dares to call his coloured hackle a "feather". That would be tantamount to urinating in someone's cornflakes and would generate similar looks of utter despair and derision.

During my stint with the Army, I would pause open-mouthed to watch as grown men, some sporting mangled noses and cauliflower ears, took their hackles from their headdress carefully, in order to shampoo and blow dry them in a bid to keep them looking pristine. They were then stored inside the cardboard roll from a roll of toilet paper in order to keep them suitably fluffy and erect. I wouldn't have believed it unless I had seen it with my own eyes.

Even before my nerve shredding confrontation with Boab the Dug, my first day isn't going too well. I barely sleep the night before, spending the night lying in Redford Barracks, Edinburgh, as there's no room for us at Glencorse. Each day, we have a 15-minute commute by bus across the city at the crack of dawn from Redford to get to the camp where we will actually be working. Terrific.

I did some of my basic training at Redford, which is home also to 3 Rifles, who recruit largely from Yorkshire and north-east England. Let's just say that I am not enamoured to be back. I thought I had seen the last of this crumbling wreck of a place. To be fair, the Rifles are in the nice, new,

clean modern part while we fester away in the old, cavernous, cavalry barracks.

I am here, yet again to my eternal chagrin, at 0600 hours.
That's definitely, categorically, not 6am by the way. I am
pacing the parade square, waiting for everyone else. It's
Monday and I can just hear the distinctive rumble of the
Edinburgh bypass in the distance. I fight the urge to go to
the toilet again, as that will be the third time this morning.

My nerves and listless apprehension lift as I see a pair of
pals, Russ MacLean and Bobby Hetherington. I've got to
know Bobby especially well as his budding Army career
has mirrored mine. We completed both phases of our basic
training together and have been on training camps before
we arrived here.

He is nervous, I can tell from his high pitched laugh. He
only does that when he is stressing out. That's good, it means
I am not the only one fighting a sense of acute panic. We
stand around, waiting for something, anything, to happen
in age-old Army tradition. "Hurry up and wait!" has been
the unofficial war cry of the Army since at least the 1940s, I
will quickly find out.

The minutes tick by as we shuffle around, watching our
breath form in white puffs as we chat about anything but
our current situation. "What will it be like? What will we
be doing?" I want to ask but I know that I won't. I would
sound like a total 'crowbag', yet another derogatory Army
term for a newbie. 'Don't be that guy, don't be that guy,' I
think to myself.

There's a total of around 20 guys here, from 18 to 45 years

old. Some have jobs and families, some are single, footloose students or unemployed. We have been mobilised to go to Afghanistan, so we have left our reserve part-time battalion to join our regular full-time counterparts at 2 SCOTS.

No-one really knows what to expect as none of us have served with this battalion before. For Bobby, like me, this will be his first tour. It may be my last as this tour is my sole reason for joining the Army. I don't hold any desire to rise up the ranks. I am here for the experience and that's that, I tell myself.

As Russ lights up a fag as the sun starts to rise over the jagged roof of the barracks, I am already sick of my uniform, even though I've only had it on for five minutes. It feels like I am wearing pyjamas, the paper thin material doesn't keep the heat in. Good for Afghanistan maybe, not so great here in a Scottish winter.

"Maybe the bus won't come and we can just sack it and go home," says a skinny, fellow soldier with an Adam's apple the size of a golf ball. No sooner does he say this than the bus wheezes through the barrack gates. Here we go. Time for a last minute kit check: notepad, pencil, daysack, PT kit. I'm good to go.

Our destination at Glencorse is apparently the crown jewel in the Army's real estate empire. Millions of pounds have been spent doing up the accommodation and facilities. It boasts single rooms for the soldiers with all mod cons: ensuite showers, gleaming toilets and even Sky television. It's a shame we won't get to use them.

The first ride in to work is tense. I squeeze in next to Russ and Bobby at the back of the bus. There's a definite buzz of testosterone, mixed with queasy first-day nerves. Everyone is reasonably upbeat, as far as I can tell in the subdued atmosphere. Then, we are hit with a surprise and surprises are never good in the Army. I'll learn that the hard way.

We are going to have a few guests joining us on the bus today in the form of a horde of soldiers from 3 SCOTS, the Black Watch. Maybe I will see a few familiar faces as that's the unit I was embedded with as a reporter in 2009. My curiosity is tempered by the fact that, for some reason which I will never fully understand, every other battalion in the Royal Regiment of Scotland seems to have a visceral hatred of the Black Watch. To this day, I still don't know why. Soldiers are tribal, thanks in part to the regimental system, and the Watch aroused strong emotions.

'Great,' I think, 'it's the first day and we are turning up with a bunch of guys from a rival unit.' It is like turning up to a Celtic supporters' convention in a Rangers strip. We make a sudden detour to pick up the troops, all buzz haircuts and boisterous bravado. Our balding, paunchy driver looks out of his depth as the onslaught begins, with the soldiers scrambling on board.

To combat the bitter tang of nervous indigestion rising in my throat, I try to divert my attention by musing over the Army's innate tribalism. 'Why do other battalions hate the Watch?' I ask myself. Is it their eye-catching red hackles that make them stand out from the crowd, is it their place as the Queen Mother's favourite unit, perhaps their well publicised mission in Iraq's so called 'triangle of death' where three of their troops were killed by a suicide bomber? The deployment alongside US forces in a fearsome area south of Baghdad caused fury at the time in the UK. Whatever the reason, a bullnecked sergeant major once scowled at me: "They seem to get all the attention, it's as if they are the only ones ever to have lost people."

Whatever the cause, the enmity seemed to run pretty deep. I don't care, I feel a certain fondness for the battalion. They were my first real introduction to the military and they facilitated my first trip to Afghanistan. Who knows? I may even meet some of the guys I was embedded with then. That would be a great icebreaker, it might even help to see off my stomach percolating jitters.

It is no exaggeration to say that it's thanks to the Black Watch soldiers that I am here as a soldier myself. I have them to thank or blame, depending on how you look at it, for my military adventure, for giving me a taste of life on the frontline. As the troops pile on board our bus, I try to discreetly scour each man's face, hoping to see one of the guys I met in Afghanistan. Alas, there are no familiar faces.

As we start to drive off, a dark haired corporal wearing shorts and t-shirt in anticipation of a lung bursting early morning bout of Physical Training, lumbers towards our seats at the back of the bus. I am bracing myself for a burst of abuse, before he kicks us mere mortals off our seats, but he makes a point of studiously ignoring us. Instead, he grins at a Commonwealth soldier, shouts, "Alright, ya black bastard!" before grabbing his bleary-eyed buddy in a headlock.

This pair are clearly pals but the racial outburst shocks me at first, before I can see that it is taken in good humour. I realise, then and there, that I quickly need to shed any soft, civilian notions of decorum here. I definitely need a more robust sense of humour among serving soldiers, it seems.

The rest of the trip is uneventful. We watch the Black Watch corporal and his Commonwealth 'mucker' jog towards the parade square laughing. It will be interesting to see how a rival battalion, especially the Black Watch, will be received here at the home of the Royal Highland Fusiliers.

As everyone stands about, trying to figure out exactly where we are meant to be, I stand around chewing the fat with Bobby and Russ. The pair are inseparable, they both come from the same reserve unit and I have never seen one without the other in tow. When we first met during basic training, I was a bit stand-offish with Bobby but he and Russ share my dry, self-deprecating sense of humour. I have known them for two years now but, as with all good friendships, it feels as if I have known them forever.

In civilian life, Russ works as a postman while Bobby gave up his office job to go on this forthcoming tour. Russ has served in Iraq and Afghanistan before, so he quickly and justifiably sees himself as the veteran of our wee group.

Russ, with a shock of mousey hair on top of a close crop, very much looks the part as a soldier with a lean build and a smattering of tattoos. He leads the way as we form up under the stern eye of a regimental sergeant major who has just arrived on the scene to marshal us to our next rendezvous, or RV in Army-speak.

We head toward the Keep, a massive tower made of rough

hewn stone which dominates the landscape at Glencorse. A lot of 'high heid yins' dwell there so, in the course of time, we learn to avoid the place like the plague. Somewhere in the medieval-looking, dungeon of a building, we will receive our welcome to the battalion in the form of a condensed history of the unit.

After a brief march across the barracks, with me trying and failing to keep the step, we settle into a lecture theatre at the top of the Keep for our introduction. No sooner are we all settled when a sergeant major demands: "Right, who is the oldest Jock here then?" At nearly 40, that's me by some considerable margin so I hold my breath, sheepishly raising my hand. "What's your name?" "Private Stewart, sir" is my response. "Good stuff. Well now it's Fusilier Stewart as we don't have privates here. I expect you to screw the nut and be a good example to the rest of them." I seriously doubt it, I think to myself as I get back in my seat, trying to look as anonymous and inconspicuous as possible.

No-one does history and heritage quite like the British Army so for the next few hours, we are treated to an easily digestible tour of the battalion's glorious deeds. Thanks to my love of history, this actually turns out to be highly enjoyable. As the younger soldiers' heads start to wobble and nod, I actually scribble down a few notes and forget my nerves and irritable stomach.

I learn that Assaye Day, which marks the eponymous battle of September 23, 1803, is treated like Christmas Day, Hogmanay and the Queen's Birthday all rolled into one at this battalion. Assaye was one of Wellington's greatest victories and the antecedent regiments of 2 SCOTS were in the thick of the fighting.

Of all his battles, the Iron Duke is reputed to have said that Assaye was "the bloodiest for the numbers that I ever saw". It took place during the long period of imperial expansion when Britain was battling to maintain primacy over India's patchwork of tribes and petty fiefdoms. His infantry regiments, the 74th and 78th Foot, forerunner of 2 SCOTS, kitted out in their finest kilts and feathered bonnets, managed to smash through the lines of enemy troops, saving the day. This three-hour battle, yet again, bolstered the Scottish troops' reputation for bloody-minded courage and obstinacy. Wellington started the day with 6000 but by the battle's climax, 1600 lay dead or wounded. Waterloo is undoubtedly more famous among the general public but Assaye still resonates deeply with the men here.

Next, we are briefed on the importance of the 'Birkenhead Drill'. I thought I was quite well versed in my military history but this is a new one on me. HMS Birkenhead's sinking, I find out, was the biggest maritime disaster in British history until the Titanic. Sitting in that lecture theatre overlooking the parade square, I am amazed that I know so little about such a momentous event. I'm humbled to hear the extraordinary tale of sacrifice which saw British soldiers give up their lives to save women and children from certain death in shark-infested waters.

The sinking of HMS Birkenhead in the mid-nineteenth century became legendary for the first recorded order of "women and children first" to the lifeboats after the paddle steamer hit a rock off the South African coast. Infantrymen from the 91st Argyllshire Regiment and the 74th Highlanders – again forerunners of 2 SCOTS – stood to attention as the ship sank, with the tragedy being immortalised as the "Birkenhead Drill" by Rudyard Kipling in his poem *A Soldier An' Sailor Too*. The death toll was horrific: out of 638 people onboard, only 193 survived from the accident off the coast of South Africa on February 26, 1852.

"That's why youse don't move when you are on parade, right? If those men can stand to attention as that ship went down and not move a muscle, you can stand on parade and not flinch, even if it's pishin' wi' rain or there is a fly wheeching roon yer heid!" the sergeant major says. Fair point. I can never again moan about standing to attention as some officer drones on about an arcane order, which nobody knew about in the first place.

Finally, we reach the crescendo of the day, the moment we have all been eagerly listening out for. We are about to be told which company we are joining. I hope that I get landed in the same unit as Bobby and Russ as I don't know the rest of the reservists that well. As the list of names is read out by the sergeant major, I crane forward to hear who is going where. Halfway through the list, Bobby and Russ get called out and they almost hug each other with delight as they are going to the same company.

There are hardly any names left and still mine hasn't been shouted out. I curse my luck as I frantically look about trying to figure out who is left. Then, right at the end, it comes: "Stewart, Carling, youse are going to Fire Support Group."

And with that unexceptional sentence, the map of my next 12 months is drawn. I will be working with Gary Carling, a dad of two, from Perthshire who normally works on building sites as a labourer. We will go to the Fire Support Group, or FSG for short, which specialises in the use of vehicles and heavy weapons, such as the 50 cal, a massive lump of machinery that can spew out hefty rounds that can take down an aircraft. FSG companies in most battalions are normally reserved for older, more experienced soldiers. I breathe a sigh of relief that I have not been dumped into a rifle company with the young bucks, where a glance in the wrong direction can end up with you on the deck, banging out press ups for some zealous corporal.

We are dismissed and break for the door, to head to our respective company offices. Gary and I eventually find the FSG offices, where our arrival is greeted by our future platoon sergeant yelling: "Whit you daing here? Ahm waiting on two Gurkhas and youse don't look like Gurkhas tae me." Not the most auspicious start, especially after our tetchy meeting with Boab the Dug earlier.

After a day where we roamed the barracks uneventfully, spending more time in the Naafi than I imagined possible, I finally climb into bed. It's the first night back at Redford Barracks and I fear that I won't get much sleep. I am lying on a dubiously stained, blue vinyl mattress, feeling totally out of my depth.

I am amazed at how much my life has been transformed in such a short space of time. Just a week or two ago, I was a white collar professional with a nice car, a home, a partner.

I worked in a job where I could be interviewing chief executives or celebrities, or quaffing cocktails in some of the finest hotels in the world for free on a VIP press trip.

Now, I am listening to 20 other men fart, snore and scratch themselves in a dorm room with peeling paint and a fusty smell that never fades. Redford, with its 20-men rooms, freezing, temperamental showers and antique bunk beds that looked like they had been used in the Boer War, will be home for the next four months, before we head to Afghan.

I can't be accused of any half measures in my quest to serve as a soldier. I am in at the deep end. I've been attached to 2 SCOTS, who have a fearsome reputation as one of the hardest, fittest battalions in the British Army's infantry, which is recognised as the toughest branch of the Army.

My new battalion is known by a number of names: the Royal Highland Fusiliers or RHF are the more respectable ones. Lesser known are its nicknames: the 'Dug Eaters', the 'Jimmy Jimmy Fuck Fucks' and even more ominously, 'The White Mafia'. According to one version of the battalion folklore, the 'Dug Eaters' name comes from when the soldiers were based overseas. The troops found a dubious kebab house they liked. Later, it turned out that the meat they enjoyed each night was dog. They still went back each night for their snacks, so the legend goes.

I have never managed to get to the bottom of the 'Jimmy Jimmy Fuck Fucks' moniker. 'The White Mafia' name, one source tells me, comes from the fact that guys stick together, no matter what. They also adhere to the Mafia code of 'omerta' or silence. In other words, no matter what happens, don't grass to anyone.

I wonder how my civvy job as a journalist will go down in that type of environment. I console myself with an irony of history. Winston Churchill served with the Royal Scots Fusiliers, one of 2 SCOTS antecedent regiments. He was also a journalist before he went on to be one of Britain's best known, most loved prime ministers. The great man himself has maybe sent me an auspicious precedent.

It's 2300, not 11pm. I am still getting used to the idiosyncrasies of the military life, such as using the 24-hour clock. Our dorm lights are flicked off. "Lights out!" Now alone with my thoughts, I am unsettled by the growing realisation that the tour which we are here to train for will be the last fighting season in the final combat tour, before most British troops go home for good. Will the Taliban be determined that the campaign in Afghanistan concludes with a literal and metaphorical bang?

I lie in my rickety, flaking bunk-bed, staring at the underside of the mattress above me, jiggling around as the upper occupant twists, turns and farts. I have lost count of how many times today I have been asked: "Whit are you daeing here?" The question echoes around my head, unanswered. Inches from my nose, the sagging metal framework bulges ominously, as I conclude that I must be insane.

CHAPTER 2

THE ROAD TO AFGHAN

"No honest journalist should be willing to describe himself as 'embedded.' To say 'I'm an embedded journalist' is to say 'I'm a government propagandist'"
– Noam Chomsky

JOURNALISM turned me into a soldier. Literally. My decision to take the momentous step of joining the armed forces was triggered by going to Afghanistan as a reporter. Once I went there, a place with so much history and so much bloodshed, I knew my life would never be the same again.

And, boy, was I right about that. I have always been mesmerised by Afghanistan, even before it burst on to the West's collective conscience in the wake of the 9/11 bombings. Up to that time, some people had never even heard of the place. I was all too aware of its bloody history, having soaked up everything I could about its spellbinding heritage. Everyone who was anyone in world history has marched through the dusty plains of Afghanistan, from Genghis Khan and Alexander the Great to Churchill and the colossus that was the Red Army.

As the post 9/11 war picked up and dominated our newspapers and TV screens, I was obsessed. Again, history was being made in this nation that so few people in the west knew anything about. This time, history was being made before my eyes, so I vowed to go there to take part in history unfurling. This was our generation's war.

I was like a man possessed. I read and watched everything I could get my hands on about Afghanistan. Ross Kemp, dubbed by the newspapers a 'TV hardman', became my erstwhile companion. I stayed up all night watching back-to-back programmes detailing his exploits on the Helmand frontline and even forced myself to read his book on Afghanistan. As my girlfriend is an *EastEnders* fanatic, over the years I have been forced to endure my fair share of Albert Square shenanigans. Never did I imagine, however, that the bald-headed guy who I watched propping up in the bar in the Queen Vic would go on to be an acclaimed war reporter.

In his series *Return to Afghanistan*, he even ended up dodging bullets with one of my local battalions. In summer 2008, Ross, to his eternal credit, gets out on the ground in the recently captured town of Musa Qaleh. At that stage, the small collection of compounds and shacks was at the epicentre of some of the fiercest fighting that British forces have faced in years. He joined 5 SCOTS as they ventured in the green zone. Memorably, in one scene, he and his camera-man made an unceremonious dive for cover as AK47 bullets shrieked by, just inches from their heads.

Say what you like about the bald-headed 'tough guy', he certainly captured the imagination of a generation. I met a fair few soldiers who said their mind had been made up to join the Army by watching Ross's Afghan adventures.

I was working as a news reporter in a small local newspaper when the planes smashed into the twin towers on that clear, sunny day in 2001. There wasn't a cloud in the sky as I cruised around several small villages near Stirling in central Scotland, collecting snippets of news from our local correspondents. They tended to be older ladies, who would pass me handwritten notes about a local gala day or bric-a-brac sale. I was enjoying the tranquil bucolic splendour, just dodging the odd tractor or combine harvester, when the radio presenter said that a plane had crashed into the World Trade Centre in New York. I had visions of a small, light aircraft accidentally clipping one of the buildings. Later, there was news of the second plane smashing into the towers. 'Utter carnage', I thought as I pulled into a lay-by.

I fumbled around with the radio dials trying to get a station that could tell me what exactly was going on. I had been toying with the idea of stopping off for a sandwich but there was no way I could eat. I felt like I had been kicked in the stomach. This was big, unbelievably, horrifically big – and all too real.

How could this happen? Who would be so full of hatred, so driven, so organised to carry out this attack? My mind was reeling. Even when I saw the images on screen of the planes careering into the towers, and the building erupting into flames before collapsing in a sea of ash and metal, I still could not get my head around it. This feels like a movie: surreal, beyond comprehension.

Shortly afterwards, the US-led invasion of Afghanistan began. At first, the mission was to capture Osama Bin Laden but this soon metastasised into a wider economic, social, military and political project. Critics called this 'mission creep', condemning the way the mission has mushroomed well beyond its original scope.

At the time, though, in 2001, I was hooked. A country I knew from the history books was back on centre stage. I had to go. It would take me years but I would get there eventually. After leaving my local paper for a job at *The Herald*, from there I moved to BBC Scotland working across online, radio and TV. In 2008, I was on the move again to my current job at the country's biggest paper, the *Daily Record*.

My role gave me the perfect excuse to immerse myself in the latest twists and turns of the conflict in Afghanistan. British troops were there, scrapping away in their toughest campaign since World War Two, or the Korean War, depending on who you ask.

My work at the *Record* was a godsend. Unlike my stint at the BBC, where I was all too often tied to a desk, I was given free rein to go after exclusive stories. Time and time again, my focus was brought back to Afghanistan. The campaign had really kicked up a gear in 2006; with the West's focus on Iraq, the Taliban decided to raise the stakes.

Taliban leader Mullah Omar, aka the one-eyed Mullah, had vanished, so the campaign was being orchestrated from Pakistan, home to the Quetta Shura, a militant organisation which included the Taliban's top men.

Tactics began to change dramatically in Afghanistan. According to the BBC's figures, suicide bombings were a rarity in Afghanistan prior to 2004. That year, six such attacks were launched by the Taliban. The following year, there were 21 and in 2006 there were 141 suicide attacks, causing 1166 casualties. In September 2004, a rocket was fired at a helicopter carrying Afghan President Karzai. It missed its VIP target but it was the most serious attempt on Karzai's life since September 2002.

Taliban use of improvised explosive devices (IEDs) soared at an alarming rate. There were 530 IED strikes in 2005, but by the next year this jumped to 1297. Nato's International Security Assistance Force (ISAF) was the umbrella organisation under which British troops worked in Afghanistan.

ISAF's 'Operation Mountain Thrust' kicked off in May 2006, aiming to annihilate the Taliban in southern Afghanistan. This move triggered the bloodiest period of fighting since the Taliban were ousted in 2001. A multi-national force comprising Afghan and Canadian soldiers, as well as some 3300 British and 2300 US troops, took part in the blitz. More than 1000 Taliban fighters were killed and nearly 400 captured, while 150 ISAF soldiers died.

History has ultimately branded the operation a failure. At the time, United Nation envoy Tom Koenigs said: "The Taliban fighters' reservoir is practically limitless. The movement will not be overcome by high casualty figures." His words were prophetic as Taliban attacks multiplied, with the IED fast becoming their weapon of choice.

So, the stage was set. As the war heightened so did my interest in the conflict. After months of pestering the news-desk to get the chance to go out there to the badlands, I got my chance. A media embed was planned for summer 2009 and I was on it. A *Record* photographer and I were due to go out to work with 3 SCOTS as they battled it out with the Taliban. Summer is 'fighting season' in Afghanistan so it was a prime time to be there.

My reading on Afghanistan went from being a leisurely pursuit to an all-encompassing passion. Now that I was going there, I had to get my hands on as much informa-tion about the place as possible. This even involved probing colleagues who had been out before, for relevant pointers on the terrain, climate, history, you name it. I knew fitness was a big deal in the Army so seeing as how I would be working closely with them, I even started donning my trainers to pound the pavements in my evenings off. I knew the Afghan heat could kill me so I worked hard. I heard of a young journalist who almost died from heat exhaustion out there, so that freaked me out even more. It was certainly enough to get me out running, even in the incessant Scottish rain.

I was fascinated to read that Afghanistan, dubbed the 'Graveyard of Empires', had never been fully conquered. It was a crossroads for the ancient, medieval and modern worlds but has never submitted to any ruler; a sobering thought for any nation setting foot there. What makes

Afghanistan so indomitable? Terrain and climate are two main reasons as the country is incredibly mountainous, particularly in the east. The awe inspiring Hindu Kush mountain range also cuts through a large swathe of the country. Afghanistan's flatter plains are arid deserts with settled communities dotted around the more fertile valleys. Afghanistan's geography means it is a difficult place to attack but a great place to defend. Areas such as the Panjshir Valley and the Khyber Pass can be easily blocked by dedicated bands of men, who know the terrain all too well.

Persia was the first 'superpower' to set its sights on Afghanistan. Persia's kings failed to subdue the native tribes, so much so that Cyrus the Great had to invade the region twice. He died fighting there in around 530 BC near the modern Syr Darya river in central Asia, in a melee the ancient Greek historian Herodotus described as "the most violent of all battles ever fought by barbarians."

Next up was another historical heavyweight: Alexander the Great. He defeated Persia before pushing onwards through central Asia to try to crush Afghanistan. In 329 BC, Alexander defeated the region's remaining Persian governors before founding a fortified city that would become modern Kandahar. In fact, my late night reading revealed that the name 'Kandahar' is derived from 'Iskandar', a local version of Alexander, after the great man himself. His campaign came at a high price as he lost more soldiers there than in all of his other battles combined.

Another wave of invaders came in the seventh century, brandishing the sword and the Koran. These Arab warriors managed to convert the fearsome local tribes to Islam and their belief in Allah, "the one, true God". This belief would even survive the apocalyptic Mongol invasions of the 1200s. Genghis Khan wreaked havoc on the countryside, laying waste to entire regions, in his pursuit of power. After one of his favourite grandsons was killed attacking the city of Bamyan, he ordered that every living thing be massacred, even down to the local cats and dogs.

One of history's most brutal butchers, Tamerlane, who had enemies beheaded so he could build massive pyramids from their skulls, also rampaged through Afghanistan, I was to find. The 14th century ruler waged war against the rebellious tribesmen who tried to control the mountain passages.

My head was buzzing, trying to take in the weight of history in this country which I was about to visit. My mounting nerves took a turn for the worse as I learned more about the fairly disastrous British involvement in Afghanistan over the years. Britain in the heyday of empire, viewed Afghanistan as a vital piece of the geo-political jigsaw, a buffer state ideally situated to prevent Russia encroaching on India, the jewel in the crown of the British state.

In 1839, the British invaded to deny the territory to Russia, a period that would become known as the 'Great Game' when Afghanistan became a focal point for imperial rivalry in central Asia. It wasn't long before the local sullen looks turned into outright war, with rebels sweeping down from the mountains to decimate British outposts and columns.

By January 6, 1842, the British were forced to withdraw from Kabul. Some 4500 British troops and 12,000 civilians set out to march to Jalalabad, about 90 miles away. In what must be one of the darkest days in British history, the retreat fast became a massacre.

Historian Robert McNamara uncovered this excerpt from a contemporary magazine that vividly describes the fate of those on the march:

'On the 6th of January, 1842, the Caboul forces commenced their retreat through the dismal pass, destined to be their grave. On the third day they were attacked by the mountaineers from all points, and a fearful slaughter ensued...the troops kept on, and awful scenes ensued. Without food, mangled and cut to pieces, each one caring only for himself, all subordination had fled; and the soldiers of the forty-fourth English regiment are reported to have knocked down their officers with the butts of their muskets. On the 13th of January, just seven days after the retreat commenced, one man, bloody and torn, mounted on a miserable pony, and pursued by horsemen, was seen riding furiously across the plains to Jellalabad. That was Dr Brydon, the sole person to tell the tale of the passage of Khourd Caboul.'

More than 16,000 set out on this disastrous journey but only one man, a British Army surgeon called Dr William Brydon, survived. In later years, Rudyard Kipling would immortalise the conditions 19th century troops faced in Afghanistan in his poem *The Young British Soldier*. He wrote:

When you're wounded and left on Afghanistan's plains,
And the women come out to cut up what remains,
Jest roll to your rifle and blow out your brains,
An' go to your Gawd like a soldier.

My eyes burned with tiredness as I read these words, since I was staying up late every night to complete my research. Were conditions in Afghanistan still as bad as this? I would soon find out for myself.

I had no time to stew over these gloomy thoughts for long as I was off to London for a government briefing on the situation in Afghanistan. This was deemed a vital pre-condition of my visit by the MoD. Before we went out, we had to learn what was being done to deny the country to the terrorists. Photographer Lesley Martin and I met up on a crisp Monday morning on the steps of the forbidding MoD building in Whitehall. She had long, well tended chestnut hair and wire-rimmed glasses, looking more like a florist than a veteran snapper. I would soon find out, though, that she was no fainthearted prima donna but a gutsy perfectionist with a keen eye for detail.

We were tagged with security passes, swept with an array of metal detectors and herded along several corridors into the heart of the building. Lesley and I were then led into a conference room where we were greeted by an army of press officers and officials. A suited, middle-aged official from the Department for International Development kicked off the session, outlining how British involvement in Afghanistan wasn't just about bombs and bullets. Millions of pounds were being funnelled into the country to prevent it again becoming a failed state, a nest for international terrorism.

His PowerPoint presentation said: "We are in Afghanistan for one overriding reason – to protect our national security by helping the Afghans take control of their own. We are helping the Afghan Government to develop its ability to maintain security, so that it can prevent the return of international terrorists, such as Al-Qaeda, to Afghanistan.

"Preventing the return of international terrorists has been the most important part of our work and the terrorist threat to the UK from this region has been substantially reduced."

He added: "The UK has played an important role in developing and training Afghan security forces. UK support has also helped Afghanistan to become a more viable state; one that can provide basic services, improve the lives of its ordinary citizens and reduce instability. A range of international partners are also working in Afghanistan to develop security, governance, infrastructure, economy and the Afghan government's ability to provide essential services."

The message I took from this was clear: we wouldn't be leaving Afghanistan any time soon. I didn't know it at the time but it would be five more years and hundreds more lives, before Britain started to withdraw.

Next, we picked up a hire car and drove to an Army camp to collect our body armour. Without this vital, life-saving bit of kit we wouldn't be allowed into Afghanistan. A stout sergeant took us into a storeroom, packed to the rafters with supplies, and had us try on different sized helmets and bulletproof vests. I was totally unprepared for the weight of the gear. I felt like a life-size bobblehead doll as the cumbersome navy blue helmet seemed to wrench my neck from side to side. As I donned the blue flak jacket, complete with ceramic plates in the centre to cover my heart, I couldn't help but wonder what celeb had sweated their backside off in this gear. Was that the white armpit sweat stains of David Beckham or even the main man himself, Ross Kemp? As I waddled out to my car, underneath my cumbersome blue load with beads of sweat already forming on my forehead, I had to give credit to the men and women who worked in Afghanistan wearing gear five times as heavy as this.

After being 'suited and booted', the next bureaucratic hurdle was the ominous sounding 'signing of the Green Book'. Although, it had the air of signing a pact with the devil himself, this process was actually a bit more anodyne. The Green Book is an MoD document covering what can and cannot be reported by journalists. By signing it, I was agreeing that I would not do anything to compromise operational security or the safety of military personnel. According to defence chiefs: "It covers the practical arrangements for enabling correspondents to report on operations, including the MoD's plans for correspondents accompanying British forces and sets out what editors can expect from the MoD, and what the MoD seeks from the media."

So far, so good but one aspect of the document made me slightly uneasy. By signing it I was agreeing to let defence media relations-types check my copy. As a self respecting, impartial journo that was a hard one to take. If I didn't sign, I didn't go so I put my lofty principles to one side and signed on the dotted line.

Within weeks, Lesley and I were back together. This time, we were at a hotel in the outskirts of Brize Norton. Our flight out to Afghanistan was due the following day but we could get bumped off it at any time due to operational necessity.

As mere journalists, we were way down the pecking order and rightly so. Troops were risking their lives out there and if our flight got rescheduled or diverted to help someone out, we certainly wouldn't grumble. Our last night in Britain was subdued. We had an early curry dinner and a quiet drink in the hotel's bar, which was dotted with middle-aged locals in to watch Sky Sports.

I pushed my anemic-looking Thai green curry around my plate, wondering if we would get the green light to go. We spent a nervy last night checking satellite phones and wiring up satellite dishes as a dry run before we used them for real in Afghanistan. As Lesley tinkered with her laptop, I called RAF Brize Norton to check we were going tomorrow as planned. We were.

My destination, Kandahar Air Field, or KAF as it's known in the acronym-mad military, will be the catalyst for my decision to join the Army as a soldier. My Afghan trip was meant to last two or three weeks but its ramifications would dominate my life for the next four years.

CHAPTER 3

ON THE GROUND

"Afghanistan – where empires go to die"
– Mike Malloy

MY mind is racing through what could happen. Can I handle losing my legs, an arm or my testicles? I battle the urge to call the whole thing off. Forget Afghanistan and go back to my cushy job in the newsroom, where the worst wound you can expect is a nasty paper cut.

Mind you, it's a bit late for that as I am sitting among hundreds of squaddies on a creaking RAF jet as it lurches thousands of feet above the desert. I am running through the horrific realities of my first visit to Afghanistan. It's August 2009 and there has just been some of the worst fighting yet in the Afghan campaign.

ON THE GROUND

Operation Panther's Claw, or Panchai Palang in Pashto, has just taken place in the last few weeks. A total of 11 British soldiers were killed in a massive mission to seize canal and river crossings from the Taliban. Defence chiefs hailed it as one of the biggest airborne missions since World War Two.

This drive into a Taliban stronghold in Helmand was designed to squeeze out the enemy and pave the way for the Afghan presidential elections. Hundreds of British troops used a dozen Chinook helicopters to flood the area near the town of Babaji. Scores of other aircraft including Apache gunships, Black Hawk choppers, Harriers, Spectre gunships and unmanned drones were drafted in to help out.

Taliban chieftains didn't take too kindly to this mass excursion into their backyard but soldiers seized three key crossings at Lui Mandey Wadi, the Nahr-e-Burgha canal and the Shamalan canal. My hosts will be 3 SCOTS, aka The Black Watch, who were at the vanguard of this blitz.

Our flight plunges us towards Kandahar Air Field. I jerk, looking around me as the lights flicker and go out, plunging us into total darkness. Unknown to me this is the sign for us to don our unwieldy helmets as the ageing Tristar plane starts to dip and weave. Is this turbulence or a jittery pilot? I am never quite sure but I reassure myself by deciding that it must be some tactical flying to deter anyone from having a pop at us with a rocket propelled grenade.

In front and behind me, all I can see is row after row of helmeted soldiers. Silence is all pervasive, no-one speaks or even coughs. As a journalist, the thought of getting to Afghanistan to cover the war has appealed to me for years.

Now, I am not so sure.

In the gloom, I take stock of my decision to come here. My photographer, Lesley, and I are due to stay at Kandahar the whole time. There is no plan yet for us to go out on patrol during our weeks out here. How bad can it be inside an impenetrable superbase like KAF, which one squaddy pal described to me as: "Heathrow in the desert with guns"? The thought placates me, conjuring up images of acres of razor wire, machine guns and well armed Brits between me and any nasty Taliban types.

We are lucky. We manage to get on our flight at Brize after an interminable wait with hundreds of squaddies either returning from R&R (rest and recuperation) or going out to start their tours of duty. Our stay will be nothing compared to the six-month tours that the troops have to endure. The strain on the military of fighting such a vicious campaign in Afghanistan means that many soldiers are doing a tour of duty every 18 months or so.

Our approach into Kandahar is made at night, another tactic designed to frustrate any Taliban gunman determined to bring down the plane. We land with a minimum of fuss but nothing prepares me for the diabolical blast of heat once the cabin doors open. It feels like moisture of any sort has been systematically removed from the air.

A blast furnace comes to mind. Think of high summer heat in the Costa Brava or Morocco, then multiply it by 20, and you are still not close. We are shepherded on to local buses, each decorated with bells, trinkets and baubles on the front grill indicating the idiosyncratic panache of the driver.

Everything is coated with the infamous Afghan sand, from my laptop to my socks. This fine, dusty sand has the same consistency of talcum powder and catches the back of your throat. I will develop a hacking, spluttering cough for the duration of my stay.

Next day, we arrive at Camp Roberts, home of 3 SCOTS. A massive lion rampant flag next to the front gate tells us straight away that we are in the right place. The Black Watch, as the battalion is also known, is one of the most famous units in the British Army. In 1715, in the aftermath of the first Jacobite Rebellion, companies of Highlanders were raised from clans loyal to the ruling Hanoverian dynasty. They were set up to prevent fighting among belligerent clans, to stop raiding and help enforce laws banning the carrying of weapons.

Historians say the battalion's name comes from the dark colour of the unit's tartan and its original role, to 'watch' the Highlands. From Fontenoy, Fallujah and Ticonderoga, to Waterloo and El Alamein, the battalion has been at the forefront of pretty much every British conflict. We quickly learn that our hosts wear their red hackles with a certain swagger.

Camp Roberts is named after Major Alexis Roberts, who was killed in October 2007. Major Roberts is famed for his role as Prince William's platoon commander at Sandhurst military academy. The 32-year-old father of two is yet another victim of the roadside bombs that litter the country. His vehicle triggered a device on the way back to Kandahar after a successful operation. At the time, he was the most senior British Army officer to die in Afghanistan.

We are greeted by a loud "Huuulllllooo!!" as we squint into the sun after clambering down from our ramshackle minivan. It is our escort, a man mountain by the name of Captain Harry Hood. He will be our fixer and general guide while we are in the camp. I am more than six feet tall and yet Harry seems much bigger than me. He is a large presence in every sense of the phrase.

We find that he has made his way up through the ranks and commands the respect of everyone we meet. His pallid Scottish complexion, burnished by the scorching sun, adds to his fierce look. He is a barrel-chested officer who knows the job of soldiering intimately.

After the initial introductions, the lifelong Dunfermline fan seems a touch taciturn, as if he is fed up having to usher around nosey journalists. Once we get used to his thick Fife brogue and no-nonsense ways, he quickly becomes a pal rather than a mere military minder.

After a few hours in the camp, we notice that flags are at half mast. 'Op Minimise' is in effect, we are told. This is the normal procedure that kicks in when a soldier is killed in action. All communication between troops and the outside world is shut down for 24 hours. Harry explains that it's meant to stop the families getting the bad news before they can be formally notified.

We would hear the monotone drawl of "Op Minimise, Op Minimise" over the camp's public address system more times than I care to remember. Daily life at KAF was bizarre for the soldiers. One minute they could be munching on a footlong Subway sandwich, the next they could be dropped by chopper into a frenzied firefight with the Taliban forces, miles from civilization.

Deep within the camp lies the boardwalk – a wooden walkway lined with shops, restaurants and cafes. The only facility missing are pubs since Afghanistan is a Muslim, alcohol-free state. Most of the British soldiers I speak to prefer to be based at KAF before flying out on airborne assault missions and being whisked back again by Chinook helicopters, usually at dawn.

That way, the soldiers are guaranteed running water, proper toilets and other mod-cons at KAF, rather than having to stay in rudimentary Forward Operating Bases or Fobs. As I would find out in years to come, Fobs were luxurious compared to some of the smaller bases out there.

KAF is home to some 30,000 military and civilian staff, with a massive 24-hour-a-day security operation guarding its perimeter. We find, though, that it's still far from totally safe. My first whiff of danger comes after we have retired to the media operations office one night to file our stories and pictures. "Rocket attack, rocket attack" drones out of the tannoys dotted around the base. I turn and look goggle-eyed at Lesley, completely forgetting the drills we have been told to carry out in such a situation.

A Paratrooper and a female RAF officer, our media minders, take over, telling us to grab helmets and body armour and head into the corridor as far as possible from any windows which could soon become lethal, razor sharp projectiles. As we lie face down on the ground, I wonder how people cope with these sudden life-altering changes.

One minute, you are sitting at work bored, then the next you are staring death or serious injury in the face. 'This never happens at the *Daily Record*,' I thought.

There are no great thuds or bangs, and gradually everyone returns to their work after the all-clear siren has sounded. My legs feel wobbly, as if I am trying to walk across the deck of a ship in the middle of a raging storm.

Attacks such as this used to occur only once every few weeks, but they are now happening several times a night or at least every few nights. We are told that Taliban fighters fire rockets from the mountains to the north-west, giving the base just seconds before they start to hit.

Three nights later, we are back at the boardwalk for a concert for troops of the multi-national International Security Assistance Force (ISAF) which includes Britain, Denmark, Estonia and the US. Details of the concert have been kept secret to prevent any more attacks. Even so, within minutes of troops gathering in the sun-blasted wooden hub, sirens begin to wail. We hit the deck and eat dirt, literally, in my case. After the all-clear, we dust ourselves off, only for it to happen again. I become intimately acquainted with every grain of the ochre floorboards, wondering where these rockets will eventually land.

Some time later the concert ends, with soldiers scattering in every direction to smoke a fag, or haggle in the carpet stores, or head over to the huge American tax-free PX stores flogging everything from laptop computers to cigarettes, sweets, DVDs, magazines and clothing. I ask Lesley: "I wonder if that was just good luck on the Taliban's part? How did they know about the concert? It seems odd that they guessed the time and place of the concert. Someone working in the base could easily have tipped them off." The realities of living, working and surviving in Afghanistan are thrown into focus.

The next day, I am amazed to find that the old cliche is true – you can literally fry an egg on the armour of the Mastiff armoured vehicles that are parked inside the camp. A few of the troops we meet have done just that in the middle of the dasht, or desert. As we wander into the cookhouse, or canteen to mere civilians, I meet an old pal, Sergeant Major Paul Dargavel, who I got to know as he runs the Black Watch football team. I have covered their exploits for the newspaper a few times. He is a tall, athletic-looking 40-something with mousey hair, turned straw coloured by the vicious Afghan sun. He is friendly but his face is more angular and drawn than I remember. He tells me of their recent missions carrying weapons, body armour and 80lb packs crammed with water, food and ammunition.

After lunch, we go to a central area within Camp Roberts – an open space of parched dusty land that has been turned into a training area and a car park for dozens of Mastiff, Jackals and other armoured vehicles. As we crouch in the only shade we could find, behind a wall of Hesco Bastion – the ubiquitous fortifications that line every part of the landscape – we watch as military working dog Benji is put through his paces. With his tail wagging, Benji criss crosses the berms of the training area in search of his quarry – a small sample of explosives. Within minutes, he is on to the scent. He gets his prize, a favourite toy, after he passively indicates the correct site of the potential IED.

We don't have to wait long before we get the chance to see Benji working for real. Just days later, we are invited to sit in on a briefing for a mission called Op Tyruna, a surgical strike on a Taliban drugs factory deep in the Valley of Death, aka Sangin Valley.

After listening to the plans for the attack, I have an idea. Why not join the troops out there, go with them and see what really happens on the ground? Before I know what I am doing, I get a rush of adrenaline and stick my hand up: "Can I go?" An audible gasp greets my question. An officer tells me they will have to check with more senior officers before letting me know.

My pulse is racing when I get the answer "yes". Top brass have cleared us to go along on the operation. I am a cauldron of emotions, happy to be able to see life on the frontline but aware that I could easily die or get maimed. I have no idea what makes me go through with it – male pride, reluctance to lose face? I battle the urge to pull out; I can't bring myself to cancel now that we have permission to go out on the ground.

Later, photographer Lesley confides that she is nervous about going out on the op but still wants to do it. I spend the night pacing around the air-conditioned portakabin that is my bedroom. I feel like a man on death row as I spend the night checking and re-checking my kit. Water, sweets for energy, rations, batteries, do I have everything I need?

In the morning, Lesley and I meet Captain Hood, who drives us down to the battalion's training areas as his soldiers make final preparations. We watch as the troops practice their drills on how to clear compounds, check for IEDs and search for weapon stashes.

I feel like a melting ice lolly as the extreme heat batters down on our heads. I have no idea how the soldiers manage to cope with helmets, body armour and bergen as they spring between compounds. I feel the blood rush from my face as we are ushered to one side of the training area. Everyone here looks grim faced.

We are given a special crash course in emergency medical procedures in the event that we are shot or blown up. We are shown the different bits of kit – tourniquets, field dressing and an emergency syringe of morphine that will keep us alive. In a matter of fact way, the 20-year-old female medic from South Africa runs through what we should do. Nonchalantly, she says: "If your arm or leg is blown off, try to stay calm and attach the tourniquet above the point where it has been severed. Pull it as tight as you can, then tighten it with these twists to stop the blood flow."

I feel a knot in the pit of my stomach. This is real now. Captain Hood explains what to do if we get separated from the patrol, how to attract helicopters overhead without giving our location to the Taliban. The thought of being alone out there makes me want to be physically sick.

As the medic explains how to self administer morphine with the small syringe to ease the pain of a traumatic amputation in an IED strike, I feel faint. Is this worth it for the sake of a story? Once we return to our accommodation, to prepare for the mission, I seem to spend the bulk of my time in the toilet. I decide to take a North Face rucksack, bulging with a bladder and Camelbak drinking system with three litres of water, another five litres of bottled water, rations, jelly sweets (good for energy apparently) and a small compact camera.

This is only going to be a 10-hour operation or we would have needed much, much more. I struggle to get the unwieldy pack on my shoulders and marvel about how some of the skinnier soldiers manage to cope with much more gear. We are picked up in a small, white people carrier and taken closer to the landing strip. As a measure of the colossal scale of KAF, the drive takes us 10 minutes just to get close to our rendezvous area.

We can hear the roar of the engines as we approach. Dusk hits fast in Afghanistan so by this time, we are in pitch darkness. After a briefing, we join the soldiers as they sit around on their bergens, chatting and, in most cases – smoking. It reminds me of the old grainy black and white footage of the trenches in World War One, with seemingly every soldier smoking their cigarettes.

We get a first look at the chariot that will wing us into the badlands: a US Chinook helicopter. The double rotored choppers are the workhorse of Afghanistan hauling troops, beans and bullets over massive distances, as the roads are so dangerous. They are also one of the Taliban's most prized targets – the insurgents would dearly love to bring one of these aircraft down. One lucky shot could wipe out dozens of troops, destroy a multi-million pound helicopter and signal a colossal propaganda coup for the Taliban.

ON THE GROUND

After an interminable period of waiting, this is it: 22:22 hours exactly. Kick-off time. Soldiers trudge on board, placing their weapons downwards so that a stray round is not accidentally fired up into the rotors, which would potentially bring down the aircraft.

I will soon see first-hand the Sangin Valley – dubbed 'the most dangerous place in the world for British troops'. Sangin has long been a focus of coalition efforts, given its key role as an economic and transport hub in southern Afghanistan. The Taliban has other plans – they have fought tenaciously to maintain a stranglehold over the area. It is the scene of heavy fighting for British forces before being handed over to US troops in September 2010. At one stage of the war, the Sangin Valley alone accounts for almost a third of UK deaths since 2001.

A total of 18 UK, US and Australian helicopters are taking part in this raid. Nine Chinooks, three Black Hawks, two Sea Kings and four Apache attack helicopters tear up out of the darkness like deadly mosquitoes, before buzzing into the night. We sweep across vast, almost oceanic expanses of open desert. Some 300 Scots soldiers, a US Army engineering detachment and scores of crack Afghan troops are on this op. Our target: a heavily guarded Taliban fortress in the small hamlet of Malmand Chinah.

Everything inside our Chinook is bathed in an eerie, green light. Suddenly, Darth Vader looms at me from out of nowhere. After an initial wave of terror, I eventually realise that it's a young US Army gunner, skipping over boxes of equipment to take up his post. He is wearing a striking, black

Darth Vader-style dust mask as he grabs his machine gun, rattling off dozens of rounds into the darkness as we prepare to hit the landing zone. Lesley grabs my leg, terrified, as the bullets roar out into the night, just inches from us.

A shaven-headed soldier – complete with a tattooed angel glistening through the sweat on his neck – gives me a broad grin minus two front teeth. The dull glow inside the chopper illuminates a fearsome sight that will make the most bloodthirsty Taliban fanatic weep. I have never seen such an arsenal of modern weaponry crammed into such a tight space. The 'Jocks', as the Scots are affectionately known, are armed with machine guns, missiles, grenades, sniper rifles, high explosives and good old-fashioned bayonets.

It's hard to imagine being on the receiving end of this onslaught. With stomachs churning, thanks to a combination of nerves and the choppy ride, we are given the nudge and told to prepare to run off as the helicopter touches down at out target. I pull down my ballistic goggles, adjust my helmet and sweat furiously under pounds of body armour. The Chinook blasts down with the rear of the aircraft bucking wildly in the air, flinging the rear gunner to one side and nearly out of the door into the blackness.

Rotors whine and splutter as we run off the rear ramp onto the parched earth in the middle of a 80mph down blast from the engines. Lesley has grabbed the back of my body armour so that we don't get separated in the chaos. We fling ourselves into the furrowed earth of a ploughed field as soldiers burst out into a ring of steel around us. I am in danger of hyper-ventilating. I have seconds to catch my breath and take a swig from my water pack before it starts: an Apache helicopter's fearsome chain gun starts ripping into insurgent positions.

I hear another sound I will never forget – hundreds of crazed dogs barking as the massive column of troops begins to infiltrate the Taliban compounds. A crackle and pop sound, like giant sheets of bubble wrap being twisted and burst, signals incoming small arms fire. The Taliban know we have arrived. We make our way through a maze of sun-scorched compounds, all the time making sure we follow directly in the footsteps of the man in front.

My heart seems about to leap out of my chest as I round a corner, only to have a huge, rabid dog leap towards my face. Staggering back across the solid ground, I fall into a clump of needle-sharp bushes. The growling terror has no ears, they have doubtless been hacked off by the owner to make him even more fearsome. This is one of the infamous fighting dogs of Afghanistan, brutally maimed and then occasionally used as guard dogs. I recoil with my arms flailing as a chain, which I haven't noticed in the pitch darkness, takes hold and drags the devilish-looking dog back to earth.

A white flash erupts, followed by a bang which shakes me to the core and nearly knocks me over. The Afghan crack units have just made their way into another suspicious home. This time, they decide to go through the wall by blowing a gaping hole in it. Sporadic gunfire breaks out followed by suppressing shots. Cracks and pops of bullets soaring over our heads pierce the breathless valley for the entire mission that lasts almost nine hours.

As the night wears on, we clamber to the top of a compound to have a look at the sentry positions. We have to climb up on to a wall, walking along the top on a surface that is big enough for just one foot at a time. On either side is a sheer drop into inky blackness. We make it to the top, chatting with the troops who are keen to get a break from their 'stag' or sentry duties. On the way down our escort, a burly Northern Irish officer, careers off the side, twisting at the last moment to ensure that he lands on his cushioned bergen. He is unhurt but could have easily broken his neck, a reminder, not that I needed it, that there is more than one way to get killed or seriously injured in Afghanistan.

After a brief rest, we gather our kit, which includes the remainder of our surprisingly tasty rations and seven litres of water, and move out in single file. We start to make the two-and-a-half-hour march out to the helicopter landing zone, through a field dotted with boobytrap bombs, always fearful that the next step could be our last.

We are all silent, which gives me the chance to lose myself in the landscape. It's an eerily beautiful place, riddled with mountains and ravines. It feels like walking on the surface of the moon as choppers whoosh over us. Eventually, the moonlight fades and the sun gradually begins to appear from behind the awe-inspiring mountains of the Sangin Valley.

We pass an eerie site as attack helicopters in the air behind us launch a series of chaff and flares, designed to deflect any heat-seeking missiles. We are threading our way past an old cemetery. In Afghanistan, the dead are buried above the ground, with rocks piled over them to keep away predators ready to scavenge on the corpses. As dawn gets closer, this feels like a strangely tranquil place.

Rags used as markers above the stone cairns flutter in the dry wind that sweeps down from the mountains. I spot several small stones stacked up into a small pyramid – a tell-tale marker used by locals to indicate IEDs or old Soviet-era landmines. There are too many IEDs or mines, a legacy of the Red Army invasion, to clear so they are left where they are. The Taliban too use these stone markers to show where they have placed IEDs to locals. It would be a propaganda disaster for them if they killed local kids.

My eyes are burning with fatigue but still I plod on, always checking I am following in the footsteps of the man in front. We have no time to worry about the possible dangers as we must be at the landing site just after 6am for our extraction.

We make it to the LZ or landing zone, kneeling down to await the churned up rocks and sand which will herald the Chinooks' arrival. We feel horrifically exposed as we slump on the flat ground at the foot of several mountains. Time seems to telescope as a minute feels like an hour.

Soldiers spark up their fags and an American soldier asks me: "Could you kindly take a photograph, sir?" as he and his buddies slump on their backpacks. Then, a thunderous "whock, whock" noise signals that our taxis have arrived.

Our fleet of Chinooks roar in, slamming down a few hundred feet in front of us. Grabbing cameras and rucksacks we run for the rear doors, diving into the chopper which speeds off in an undulating, defensive move to deter any watching Taliban snipers.

It is a rewarding night's work. Soldiers discovered a massive haul of 250kg of wet opium, worth more than £1m, as well as a cache of deadly weapons that would have been used to target British soldiers. Seven Taliban fighters are killed during the night's firefights. One by one, soldiers on the flight slump on their weapons, drifting into a deep and well deserved sleep.

After a small detour to drop off Taliban suspects captured during the raid, the Jocks swooped back into Kandahar. I get back to my bunk bed, throw off my gear and slump on to my sleeping bag. I feel as if I have won a prize. I've had the most intense, awe-inspiring experience of my life and come out the other end unscathed. I want more.

CHAPTER 4

A LIFE LESS MILITARY

"As a rule it is circumstances that make men""
– Napoleon Bonaparte

I WAS born at a minute to five in the evening in a small town near Loch Lomond to a mum who was a primary school teacher and a dad who was a stocktaker. My earliest memory is of climbing the white, wooden cot next to my mum and dad's bed like it was the north face of the Eiger. Dawn's murky grey light was just starting to poke through the bedroom window when I would balance on the side of the cot before leaping over to my parents' bed. I had it planned to perfection and would land right in between them. The startled look of sleepy shock on their faces was priceless. I have no idea what age I was but I must have been very young.

Those days before I went to school seem so idyllic now.

In my mind's eye, my mum and dad seem so strong and full of life. I was obviously a handful as I also remember collecting pots, pans, basins and tubs of all shapes and sizes before spreading them around me. I then found an old pair of Chinese takeaway chopsticks in a drawer and proceeded to use them as drumsticks. It's a mark of my parents' loving indulgence that they let me clatter away happily for hours. Even now, I don't have a musical bone in my body so God knows what the racket must have been like.

My mum, Anne, was very easy-going and as a child, I knew that if she raised her voice or got flustered then I must have been really out of line. She had long, fair hair which she usually wore pulled back with ornate clasps. She always moaned about her hair, as she felt hers was too fine and not as thick as she would have liked. I would wind her up by saying that women just loved to complain, that if her hair was thick she would have wanted fine hair, and vice versa. Her skin was like marble, dotted with the occasional spray of freckles. As a student, she had lived and worked in Spain and loved all things Spanish, although she never was one for basking in the sun. Her pallid Celtic complexion was topped off with high cheekbones and crystal blue eyes.

My dad, James, or Jim to most people, in his younger days looked like a young Dennis Waterman with collar length, reddy-brown hair. His stubble had a weird bluey-reddish tinge if he hadn't shaved for a few days. When I got into my teens, I was taller than my dad but in my childhood he always seemed like a man mountain. When I fell asleep in the back of the car after a day trip to Dunoon or Largs, he would bundle me up and carry me gently into the house.

He was more highly strung than my mum, but he still spoiled me rotten. No matter what he was doing, if I asked him to take me out to practice my football skills, he would drop everything to drive me down the park or go for a kick about in the back garden. One day, I was out playing 'wallsy', kicking the ball off the wall and then retrieving the rebound. My lack of ball control was evident though, when I leaned back kicking the ball way too high.

Time seemed to go into freeze frame, moving so slowly as the peeling white Mitre football arced towards the kitchen window where my dad was doing the dishes. He ducked as the ball smashed through the window, with shards of glass exploding in every direction. I thought my heart would stop, I couldn't breathe. As time began to move at normal speed, I felt the urge to run, anywhere, just run. But, lo and behold, my dad got up and said: "Jings, what happened there?!" He didn't lose his temper, he just regained his composure and got me to tread carefully as he picked up the glass. I was told not to play football near the kitchen window and that was it. He must have had the patience of a saint.

He loved gardening and when the weather was good, which was thankfully rare, he would get his shorts on and start digging the garden, placing plants in neat rows and spreading manure. Much to my despair at the time, he would do this minus a t-shirt so the world could see his curly chest hair. One Christmas, I got a pair of boxing gloves and put them on to spar with him. I flung a playful left hook, catching him on the lip. As a bead of blood blossomed on his lower lip, I burst into inconsolable tears.

It is a universal of human nature that nearly everyone remembers their childhood as being carefree and happy. I am the same. I don't remember any tears on my first day at school, in fact primary school felt like a second home as my mum taught there. She was never more than a few feet from me in the small red brick bungalow which was my school. We often walked to school as it was only five minutes walk from our front door.

As a red-cheeked, bowl-cutted youngster, only one thing traumatised me. Bizarrely, I hated the *Happy Birthday* song at any family gatherings. I dissolved in a flood of tears and bolted for the back garden during my seventh birthday party. For some reason, the tones of: "Happy Birthday, dear Stephen, Happy Birthday to you" even now sounds like some funereal dirge to me.

Education was a big thing, unsurprisingly, since I had a teacher for a mother. When asked about what I would do when I grew up, I would invariably mumble something about "going to college", as that's what I had heard young-sters talking about in American television shows. Every time, my mum would correct by saying: "You will be going to university, Stephen." I was left with the impression that college just wouldn't do.

The only time I remember my mum losing her temper with me was during a primary four test. I spent too long whispering and joking with a pal, so I had to stay behind to finish the maths questions. Somehow, on the school grape-vine, she got wind of this and I was pulled aside and told in no uncertain terms that I better get a wriggle on. I never dallied during a test again.

After high school and a brief flirtation with the idea of going to art school, I went to study modern history at university. It was an enjoyable, relatively carefree time punctuated by the odd bout of study amid loads of boozy jaunts to the union to play pool into the wee, small hours.

My love of books was fuelled by university. In fact, one of the joys of graduation was that I could now read whatever I liked, rather than the titles I was told to devour as part of the course curriculum. My uni career gave me the chance to indulge my love of military history from Alexander the Great and Hannibal to Napoleon and Patton.

Soldiers are often asked if their families are supportive of their decision to join the Army and go off to the frontline. I have a confession to make: mine were not. Or they certainly wouldn't have been if they had still been alive when I took the Queen's shilling. My mum hated the Army and would never have dreamed of me donning a uniform of any sort. If my mum disliked all things military, my gran, who had considerably more direct experience of the military, totally despised anything to do with the forces.

Little wonder, considering that thanks to the Army, and Hitler, of course, she had been separated from my grandfather Robert for nearly six years during the war. She would often tell me how everyone would anxiously watch the postman, waiting to see where he would deliver the telegram with the bombshell news that a loved one was lost.

In photographs of the time, my gran sports wavy collar-length auburn hair, clear unblemished skin and a nose which she always complained was far too big. She had an opinion on most, if not all things, and was never shy in telling you what she thought. From politics to her beloved Celtic, she always vociferously defended her position. As a bus conductress during the war, she often had to square up to drunken sailors and soldiers. Knowing my gran, they would always have come off worst.

I had always been very close to my gran but after my parents' death, she was like a second mother. She must have had woman's intuition because when a story about the Army came on the TV news or she read an article about the military in a newspaper, she would say to me: "If you ever join the Army, it'll be over my dead body." She was the type of woman who would have dragged me from the recruitment office if she ever got wind of me signing up.

When I went to Afghanistan as a reporter in 2009, I knew she would be worried so I had to construct a 'white lie' about going to Spain on an assignment for the paper. I told her I would be out of contact with her for a while, but she wasn't to panic. I even had to arrange for my uncle to hide the paper from her so she wouldn't see my antics with the Black Watch. She passed away in 2012, the year before I was deployed to Afghanistan.

My universe came to a grinding, crashing halt in 1998 when my parents died, just a few months apart. In both cases, it was natural causes. They were only in their forties. That year was truly an 'annus horribilis', one I will never forget. It amazes me that it all happened 16 years ago as it feels so vivid, the tears, the nervous knot in the stomach that stopped me from eating.

My dad's health had deteriorated very quickly and he was admitted to hospital. My mum at that stage was also unwell so I went to visit him alone one day. As I approached his ward, a nurse saw me and asked me to step into a side room. That's when they told me he had died just shortly before. I then had to go home and tell my already ailing mum.

I drove home choking on the tears. Another family member must have broken the news because she just cried and held me when I got to her bedside. Just a few weeks later, her health would take a turn for the worse and after a spell in hospital, she would pass away too.

I met a pal and came home with him just to hang out, playing music and relaxing. After a while, I heard my mum thrashing about in bed. I rushed in to check what was happening. It was obvious, her face was contorted as she writhed around, trying to say the word: "Strrrrroke". My heart felt like it was leaping out of my chest as I quickly dialled for the ambulance.

That was the beginning of the end. Her funeral was one of the worst days in a year of horrific days. It had been horrendous in the few weeks before but that event was as bad as it gets. The lowest point of my life. At both my mum and dad's funeral, my legs wobbled and I thought I would collapse when the hearse rolled up with their coffins in the back, wreathed in flowers.

No sleep, precious little food, a gnawing sense of helplessness. At the age of just 24 my mum's funeral, shortly after my dad's, meant it was official: I was an orphan. I had joined the ranks of the motherless and fatherless. Like it or not, my world would truly never be the same again.

In the weeks before she died, I had been sleeping in my car outside the hospital as I didn't want to be far when the worst happened. It made me even more worn out and irritable. In the hours before she passed away, a priest turned up to give her the last rites. When he came in to her room, she started to moan and thrash about on the bed.

She was only just conscious but she knew the end was coming. He was there perched at the end of the bed like an old crow. God knows what she thought he was, a menacing, black-clad harbinger of doom. Even I was taken aback at the ferocity of my outburst. "Get out of here, just go!!" I was almost hysterical and I could hear my own voice booming off the walls. The priest saw sense, took to his heels and disappeared down the hospital corridor, never to be seen again. Just as well.

After the hospital paroxysm came the funeral, the platitudes and the emptiness. People behaved strangely. They would either avoid me or be scared to raise the subject. It was as if they thought I should try to forget and that bringing up the subject would remind me of it. Far from it, loss like that is something you never forget.

Her death was due to natural causes so there were no car crashes, no flowers by the side of the road. I sometimes watch news reports of fatal road accidents or such like and ponder what would have been worse: to lose them suddenly or in the manner of what actually happened – creeping illness followed by premature death?

Either way, it was never going to be easy but I just didn't quite expect it to be that hard. It is a difficult, harrowing thing to see someone who was your universe wither and die before your very eyes. The speed of the entire, wicked process amazes me to this day.

You have good days and bad days, mostly bad. After a long time, the good days outnumber the bad and you can look back on their lives with a freshness that wasn't there before. I am an only child and I still don't know if that made it even more difficult. At least if you had a brother or sister there would have been someone there to share the grief, not to mention the myriad of other mundane things that never cross your mind in normal life: what to do with their books, or my mum's dusty Rod Stewart video collection.

When it happened, everything was a struggle. It was hard to get out of bed some days and just the thought of tidying her room filled me with dread. When I looked through my mum and dad's things, I became aware that I was loathe to throw anything out. Every old picture, every old receipt stirred the memories and felt like somebody was twisting the knife stuck in my soul.

Bereavement puts things in perspective, that is it's only remotely positive aspect. You think you are having a bad day when it pours with rain, or you get a flat tyre, or you run out of money before pay day. Now, I realise all of that pales into insignificance. I now have perspective, an ability to see the bigger picture.

Bitterness still creeps in from time to time: why me? Why

her? Why him? I see people throw their lives away on drink, drugs, so-called fast living. Some people seem to have an unfulfilled death wish while those that gave so much and had so much to offer, are taken all too quickly.

At my mum's funeral, I was literally dumbstruck at the turnout and the way some people touched the coffin with tears in their eyes. I had no idea that she knew so many people, and that she had touched so many people's lives. A wee boy from her school stood, looking as forlorn as I felt, as her coffin was carried past. The rest of the ceremony was a bit of a blur. Prayers, the hymns, the sorrow, the rain, the half remembered faces from years ago. I threw a blood red rose in the freshly dug grave and walked shakily away through the clay and mud.

No experience with the Army, whether eating cold rations in a rain soaked poncho or jogging up vertical hills with my shins ready to burst up through my knees, could be as bad that. Of that, I was sure.

I did some serious soul searching after going to Afghanistan. My conclusion: if I wanted more than just a taster of life on the frontline, I had to sign up, be a soldier, doing the job out there for real. It was a momentous decision, especially as I had no previous military experience and no idea of even how to go about it.

One experience gave me the strength to go through with it. For many, joining the Army is the toughest thing they will ever do. It was not the hardest thing that I have done. Watching my parents die was harder. I am an only child and I lost my parents young. Seeing them fade away before my eyes was the worst thing that has ever happened to me.

Thinking of my loss got me through a few hard times, when I was lying in a shell scrape in the pouring rain at Catterick, or sweating bullets in the middle of Afghanistan. Nothing was as bad as that. It gave me an inner strength and a kind of mental robustness that is vital for a career in the military, especially on the frontline.

CHAPTER 5

IMMERSE THYSELF

*"I still believe that if your aim is to change
the world, journalism is a more
immediate short-term weapon"*
– Tom Stoppard

LOSING mum and dad gave me the inner resolve to join up. My decision was not taken lightly. I did my homework. I was convinced that the best way to experience the war in Afghanistan, without the barrier of media relations-types and endless bureaucracy, was by being a soldier.

My work colleagues had reacted in wildly different ways when they heard about my decision to become a soldier. One wag nudged me as he walked past me in the canteen: "Hey, how's mummy's wee soldier?" Others saw it less as an excuse for a joke, and more of a reason to question my mental health. A respected middle-aged reporter, who had friends in the armed forces, took me aside one day. He said: "Are you sure you know what you are doing?" I explained my reasons: I wanted to complete a full tour of duty, I wanted to see the campaign from the bottom up and inside out, I really felt a deep need to get back to Afghanistan. I knew it was almost irrational. His last words to me: "You must be off your feckin' rocker."

Sometimes, people's profound ignorance of Afghanistan specifically and military matters generally, made my temper flare. I had to suppress my urge to walk away from people who had no idea at all about Army life. A 40-something secretary was standing in the kitchen area, just off the newsroom floor one day, quizzing me about my decision to join the Army. I had explained that as a reservist I trained on certain weekends and in my free time before hopefully deploying to Afghanistan later as a full-time soldier. I would need to give up my reporter job for a year, before returning after my tour. A military sabbatical, if you like.

She scratched her highly conditioned, blonde bob: "Do you get paid for it?" Yes, they pay you for your time, obviously, I replied. "So, do you just, like, run about with paintball guns and all that?" I sighed, before making my excuses to go somewhere, anywhere else. Another chap asked me: "What are those big mad hats you wear in the Army?" After a few minutes of quizzing him about what in God's name he was talking about, it transpired he was referring to helmets. Some people didn't know the difference between

Iraq and Afghanistan despite the fact they are countries with totally different societies, economies and cultures in separate continents. Sadly, for way too many people, even supposedly educated ones, these countries were just dusty, remote places where soldiers were occasionally killed.

It was sad to think that just a few decades ago, everyone had some sort of connection to the military – a dad, brother, sister, uncle in the Army, RAF or Navy. Now, it appeared that precious few people had a clue about the forces. No wonder some of the senior soldiers I met had a healthy dose of contempt for 'civvies'.

My bosses had been very supportive of my Army manoeuvres. It was a no-brainer for them, as I did all the training in my own time. I made a point of never having to ask for time off or special treatment.

A typical morning at my newspaper could be very busy. I speak to the news editor about any stories I have that are ready to go in the paper. I also have to chat with colleagues on the picture desk to make sure we have images to go with my words. I also scour the newspapers to see if there are any stories to follow up on, and importantly to make sure any exclusive stories I am working on haven't appeared in a rival paper.

At roughly 11am, the department editors meet to discuss what's going into the following day's paper. I then get cracking on whatever I have been tasked to do, whether it's a crime, defence, entertainment or consumer story. No two days are ever exactly the same, which is one of the joys of journalism for me.

Depending on the story, I can be out trying to contact a family, interviewing a politician or researching and writing pieces for future editions. It can sometimes be intimidating to have to assimilate loads of information, write 800 words and generate ideas for pictures, all on a subject you may not be familiar with such as wind farms or welfare benefits. It can be rewarding – some stories stay with you, such as the piece I wrote about some Good Samaritans who transformed a young disabled girl's bedroom into a Princess fantasy room after her dad was killed in action in Afghanistan.

It's not a normal nine to five job where you just leave at the end of your shift. We leave when the job is done, but on most nights I leave for home by early evening. The job has its frustrations. Many is the time I have written a story, arranged for pictures to be taken, only for the person to get cold feet and refuse to be photographed at the last minute. Patience and persistence are the key. In a random week, I could be covering a murder case, writing about a remarkable football team comprised of refugees or telling the tale of a family who were saved from a huge house fire by an eight-year-old girl.

A typical Friday night would see me finishing work at around 6pm, before bolting to my car. My uniform was freshly ironed and hanging in the back as my headdress sat pristine in the boot. After a quick change in the Army reserve centre's car park, I was ready to board the bus for a basic training weekend at Redford Barracks.

Some of these bus drives were fraught affairs. I would be stressed from the running around, trying to get back in time, making sure I had packed the right equipment. Then, as I settled in for the hour-long drive couped up in the back, my phone would bleep. It was invariably my girlfriend, Lynda. She was getting more unhappy as my Army activity increased as she knew from the start that my goal was to deploy in Afghanistan.

I had noticed that as another training weekend loomed, she would become irritable and quick to snap at me. I decided to stop even mentioning the Army or my training progress, as she would often frown and ask: "Why don't you just leave the Army?" It was easy to see why so many marriages and relationships fall apart in the forces.

On one particularly stormy training weekend, she bombarded me with texts as I headed off to Edinburgh. She had been quizzing my choice to be a soldier even more than usual in recent days as she now knew this was no passing fad, but a real concerted effort to become a deployable soldier. Our text exchange ended with her tearfully texting: 'You are desperate to go over there to Afghanistan to die! What will I do!?'

I had to call her from the minibus, quietly reassuring her, as my fellow recruits slipped off their combat boots and went for a snooze. I hoped her sobs and gasps wouldn't be overheard. She had been trying to put me off the idea of going to Afghanistan from the day I first mentioned it. She said I wouldn't be able to get insurance, or be able to get the time away from the newspaper. Anything to put me off. She had even argued that I was too old to train as an officer but I explained that I wanted to go as a private soldier anyway, to see the job from the ground up rather than the top down.

My budding Army career put a tremendous strain on our relationship. We met years ago on a night out and we had never really looked back. Before we knew it, we had been together more that 10 years but it felt more like 10 minutes. We had travelled the world together, visiting Berlin, New York, Barcelona, revelling in each other's company. We planned to marry but hadn't yet got round to it.

She must have had Irish genes somewhere in her family history. She had wavy, rusty brown hair that hung down to her chest. Her skin was so white it was almost translucent, with a dusting of freckles. Her eyes were a deep, hazelnut brown colour and when we held hands, I was always amazed at how fine her fingers were, like those of a pianist.

We, like all couples, had our testy moments and our share of arguments, but my involvement with the Army was the only subject which consistently caused ructions. No matter how many times I explained my reasons for signing up, Lynda was never satisfied. She thought I was a fool to risk everything to do this. To be fair, she had a point.

But it was an itch I had to scratch. If I wasted any time at all it would be too late, my chance would be gone forever. When I was down, fed up with juggling a journalistic career and trying to be a soldier, I knew better than to mention it to her. If I complained, I would get a terse: "Ah well, it's your own fault for volunteering for it and putting everyone through this." I was fighting my own constant battle on the home front, just to keep things civil between us.

There were more than a few times when I was ready to call

it a day, return my kitbag to the stores and forget that I had ever been involved with the Army. Even in the run up to my first weekend of basic training, I was racked by self doubt. We had been given a 'kit list' with the equipment we were supposed to have for basic training. I felt a creeping sense of despair as I looked at the list – what were 'bungees'? Why did I need them? I apparently needed a ball of green twine. Where the hell would I get that at 6pm on a Friday night? Even if I got it, I would have no clue what to do with it. I was used to knowing what I was doing but as basic training unfolded, I felt out of my depth.

I was inspired by the technique of 'immersion journalism'. What better way to get to the heart of a story than by totally submerging yourself in the subject? America leads the way in this style of journalism, where writers try to 'walk in the shoes' of the people they are trying to cover.

Two authors stood out for me and reaffirmed my need to be a soldier. After years of battling to get inside the prison system in the US and trying – and failing – to shadow a prison officer, writer Ted Conover took a radical step. He became a prison guard at Sing Sing, one of the most notorious jails in the world.

He put his life on hold for a year to work as a prison guard at Sing Sing. *Newjack: Guarding Sing Sing*, his account of that experience, is a milestone in American journalism, and an inspiration to me. He never hid his journalistic background when he applied for his prison job. No-one scrutinised his application or queried it and before long he was inside New York State's most troubled maximum-security facility.

His book about his experiences was riveting and showed the benefit of getting out there to set a new benchmark for courageous, in-depth reporting. Conover went to work as a gallery officer, working gruelling shifts in which he supervised scores of violent inner-city criminals. He soon learns the impossibility of doing his job by the book. I was gripped by his storytelling, by reading what he did when he got the hair-raising tingle telling him a fight was about to break out, how he coped with being punched by a prisoner.

His characters leapt at me from the page: there was a no-nonsense supervisor called Mama Cradle, mentally ill prisoners or 'bugs', outrageous transvestites and even the odd philosophical inmate who ponders over the future of America's penal system.

In the weeks after I returned home from my journalistic trip to Afghanistan, I also stumbled across another book which further inspired me to throw myself into the military world. Alan Emmins wrote *31 Days* after he slept on the streets of New York for, unsurprisingly, 31 days. His journalistic classic was prompted by a feature he was writing about murals painted under the pavements of Manhattan by homeless artists. During the research for this article, Emmins was challenged by a homeless dancer to try homelessness himself to understand what he was writing about. Like all good 'immersion' journalists, he rose to the challenge. His chronicle of life on the streets shone a light on a previously hidden world.

Immersing myself by becoming a soldier before going off to fight on the frontline in Afghanistan was clearly dangerous. Journalist Stephen Browne summed up the dangers of these immersive techniques:

"There's always the possibility of danger while chasing a story a bit too enthusiastically. Intending to advance his career, investigative journalist Lee Halpin, 26, decided to acquire background in the problem by pretending to be homeless. He borrowed a sleeping bag and, waving aside the concerns of friends and family, he set off into the streets alone. 'I will sleep rough, scrounge for my food, interact with as many homeless people as possible and immerse myself in that lifestyle as deeply as I can,' said the journalist, three days before freezing to death in a boarded up hostel."

In traditional newspaper journalism, the reporter is always an impartial observer, he is never part of the story. The more I read, the more I became convinced that I had to have a major re-think to get the inside tack on what was happening to our troops. To see Afghanistan warts and all, I had to get involved and become part of the story.

It was a Eureka moment. My mind was set − the time for reading was now over. To be a better journalist, I had to become a soldier.

CHAPTER 6

THE QUEEN'S SHILLING

*"O why the deuce should I repine, And be an
ill foreboder? I'm twenty-three, and five feet
nine, I'll go and be a sodger!"*
– Robert Burns

IT'S August 24, 2011. My nostrils are filled with a heady
mix of furniture polish, the rich aroma of creaking leather
sofas and freshly laid carpet. So, this is what it is like in the
holy of holies, the inner sanctum, otherwise known as the
officers' mess. I am deep in the bowels of my local Army
centre, in a place where few are privileged to get access.
The walls are festooned with pictures of the battle of Balaklava – a notorious battle of the Crimean War in 1854 where
Scottish soldiers formed a 'thin red line' to see off Russian
cavalry charges. Richly brocaded flags along the cream
walls flank a stern looking portrait of the Queen in all her

monarchical, blinged-up finery.

It's a fitting location, with Her Majesty looking down on me as I am about to swear my oath of allegiance to her, a pivotal moment in my transition from civilian to soldier. This is known as an 'attestation' in the Army. My voice sounds hoarse and my lips stick to my teeth as I try to stumble my way through the oath to the assembled audience of a Captain and a recruiting Colour Sergeant. The pair nod appreciatively as I manage to say: "I, Stephen Paul Stewart, do solemnly, sincerely and truly declare and affirm that I will be faithful and bear true allegiance to Her Majesty Queen Elizabeth II, her heirs and successors, and that I will in duty bound honestly and faithfully defend Her Majesty, her heirs and successors, in person, crown and dignity against all enemies and will observe and obey all orders of Her Majesty, her heirs and successors and of the Generals and officers set over me."

And so it begins. I am now a member of the armed forces but, and it's a big 'but', I now have to get through basic training to become a fully trained soldier ready to deploy on operations in Afghanistan. Phase 1 doesn't sound too bad but Phase 2 will be held at the headquarters of the infantry – Catterick, a name that has struck fear into soldiers for generations. My grandad would have known the place well.

It has already been an interesting journey to get this far. I am amazed that there are so many hurdles to jump over before you even get near basic training. In the run up to my attestation, I had to attend a pre-selection day so that the Army could size me up and see if I had what it takes to be a full-time soldier.

My heart sank as I arrived at a TA centre in Paisley, outside Glasgow for my pre-selection ordeal. I was at least 15 years older than every other candidate there. My fellow fledgling soldiers, judging by the acne and Dayglo shell suits, were aged from 18 to 20. 'I have absolutely nothing in common with these kids' I thought, as I was briefed about the day's activities by a sergeant with a mouth like a razor slash.

"Right," he said. "Youse lot will do yer icebreaker first, so ye will stand up, address the rest of the recruits telling us who ye are, why ye want to join the Army, what ye want to do if you get in and aw' that. Then ye will get changed for some team building exercises so we can see if ye will work well in a group. Efter that, youse are aff to the local park for your mile-and-a-half run to see if yees are fit."

My advancing years had obviously been noticed as the sergeant singled me out and said: "Right, Stewart, son, you are up first." I had prepared a few words in advance but my nerves meant that the speech went out of the window. I had prepared a few 'bon mots' about my home town, my hobbies, my chosen cap badge, my ambitions, the qualities I had to offer the Army, my expectations of basic training, and even my most memorable moment. I had pencilled in my embed in Afghanistan as my finest hour, hoping to impress the recruiters.

As it turned out, I just adlibbed, throwing in a few lies: "My girlfriend is very supportive of my bid to join the Army (not true) and I really want to sign up so that I can serve as an infantry soldier in Afghanistan (true)." My days of studying military history, at university and in my own time, came in handy so I threw in a few respectful nods to regimental history – El Alamein, Normandy, the Somme, Cambrai.

The sergeant nodded sagely as I rambled on. I must have done well. Some of the youngsters, who were hoping to join regular Army units, seemed to have done no preparation at all. One pale lad scratched at the furious spots on his neck, stared at the floor and mumbled for about two minutes. Another recruit, a bright, bubbly girl with long golden brown hair who must have been on the cusp of 20 years old, suddenly went catatonic when it was her turn to speak.

Next up, team building tasks. I had no idea what this would entail. Out in the car park, an empty oil barrel and a length of rope sit accusingly, awaiting our attention. We are told that we have to get the barrel, which sits in the middle of a square formed by four cones, out of the area without touching it with our hands. Around the barrel, according to our sergeant, is a minefield so we can't just blunder in there. "Youse have got five minutes, GO!" he blasts.

I devise some method of looping the rope around the barrel and then getting one of my colleagues to grab the other end of the rope as we both twist it so that it tightens around the circumference. My attempt is not entirely successful as the barrel bumps around, triggering the imaginary mines that would have killed us all instantly. It becomes apparent that there are no right or wrong answers in this task, it's more about being part of a team, communicating and interacting with your fellow comrades.

Some of the young would-be soldiers stand around on the

sidelines, looking perplexed and shrinking into themselves, frightened to speak out for looking daft. That's the worst thing to do – the recruiters are after people who want to get involved and can get their ideas across to others.

Next, we are moved to a small patch of grass where we will have some role playing, military style. A corporal from the Royal Scots Dragoon Guards is in charge of us, he is 20-something with brilliant white teeth, despite his penchant for Lambert and Butler fags. He has his grey blue beret pulled tight down over his right eye, making him look even more rakish. He grins as he tells us the scenario: "Right, you are all in Afghanistan and you have taken a casualty. This kinda shite could happen so don't mess aboot."

We have what is called a poncho in the army – it's a large rectangular tarpaulin-type sheet which is often used to make a shelter. We are also given some thin rope. We have to get the casualty from one end of the grass field to the other using the materials. It sounds simple but, needless to say, it wasn't. Our corporal picks me as the casualty, presumably as I am the biggest person there, thereby ensuring the task isn't easy. I actually enjoyed this task as I get to lie about, playing dead. Simple.

It was a good laugh although I receive a few bruises as my team attempts to manhandle me all the way to the finish line. Our corporal took great pleasure in shouting, "Taliban!" which was the signal for everyone to hit the deck as if deadly rounds were whizzing past their heads. Our efforts to complete the task were interjected with shouts of: "Hey you there! Get tae that fence and back, move it," as some tracksuited boy is sent off jogging as a punishment for having his hands in his pockets.

In a lull in proceedings as we waited for our next 'tasking', I get chatting to my compadres. Joe, a sallow skinned 18-year-old with a nasal whine, told me his brother was in 5 SCOTS, aka the Argylls. "I thought it would be a good job, to go to Afghan an' aw that just like ma brer," he said. He seemed convinced that I was some sort of ex-regular who was now joining the reserves. I think that was his polite way of saying that he thought I was an old fart.

My mind is on other things as I know what is on the horizon. It's do or die time – we are shepherded into vans and taken to a local park to do our mile-and-a-half run. Fail this and you will not go forward. I look around the van and I am shocked at what I see. Some creatures have turned up wearing casual, dress trainers rather than proper running shoes, while some sport heavy metal sweatshirts and hoodies. Not the best kit for a timed mile-and-a-half sprint.

Fitness is massively important in the Army. The official British Army fitness guide, my Bible since I had decided to join the Army, told me: "The British Army has long been a pioneer in developing fitness plans for its soldiers. More than 150 years ago, following the Crimean War, it set about building the first 'Army Gymnastic Staff'. The benefits of the training it offered, which included boxing, fencing, gymnastics and general physical activity, were soon apparent. A good level of fitness ensures that soldiers can cope with the physical and psychological demands of the job, as well as reducing the time it takes for them to acclimatise to extreme conditions and recover from injury."

My journalistic jaunt to Afghanistan had confirmed to me how important fitness was in the Army. In preparation for that, I had bought decent running shoes and dragged myself out to pound the pavements. The first time I ran around the block before limping home, collapsing on top of my bed with my lungs rattling and my eyes burning.

My fitness had improved thanks to hours of road running and gym work, but I was still nervous about this mile-and-a-half. If I messed this up, I would have to go through this rigmarole again. My plans to pass out as a soldier then deploy to Afghanistan would be seriously scuppered.

Our track was to be a couple of laps of a public park. As we arrived in the car park, the mid-afternoon sunshine was still coating the place in a warm glow. As I tightened my running shoe laces for the umpteenth time, my lungs were filled with the oaky smoke of barbecues and the sweet tang of candy floss. There were ageing, cotton-headed dog walkers, young families with garish push chairs, kids skiving off school. Our fitness test was to be a very public spectacle.

We have a walk through the course, trying to dodge the prams and toddlers desperate to see what we are up to. Our corporal, with his headdress at a jaunty angle, explained that we have just over 10 minutes to get around the course. "It's only a mile-and-a-hauf, it's no' that bad, and you better get used to it, if ye go oan tae basic training, ye will be daeing a lot o' runnin'" he said.

Each candidate's age and sex is taken into account when it comes to the standard they have to meet to pass the run. So

I am left feeling vaguely insulted that I have about 11-and-a-half minutes to get around the course.

At the start line, the crowds of day trippers have thinned out enough for us to get formed up, ready to head off. We are sternly warned that the public has right of way and that we should not, under any circumstances, elbow an old granny out of the way as we charge around the course.

"GO!" We get the order and sprint off. Many of my spotty teenage pals, including one skinny guy who I notice has a smiley face tattooed on his knee, bolt off at suicide pace. I start streaking along beside them and then think, 'no, ease up' before dropping back a bit. As I suspected, after about three quarters of a mile, some people start pulling up, clutching their side and giving up.

It's unbelievable, some are 20 years younger than me and can't run a mile-and-a-half. The young girl who went catatonic during the icebreaker talk looked confident at the start of the run and was well turned out in proper sports gear. She, however, has 'piled in' in Army speak. I trot past as she lies sprawled on the grass, her hair soaking and strewn across her face.

My strategy was to do a mile in about six-and-a-half to seven minutes, then to get the head down and absolutely gun it over the last 500 metres. I eventually get round the course in a credible time of around 10 minutes. I am given a debrief later which told me that I had passed, paving the way for my oath taking.

Back at my local Army centre, I am enjoying my post-attestation glow. My military career has begun. I have taken the

Queen's Shilling. For many years a soldier's daily pay was the shilling so the expression "to take the Queen's shilling" or the King's shilling, meant that a man had agreed to serve as a soldier or sailor. In the 18th and 19 century, recruiters used all sorts of tricks, most involving strong drink, to press the shilling on unsuspecting victims. In a nod to this history, the Army would pay a day's wages into my bank account for signing up – an electronic money transfer payment was the modern equivalent of taking the Queen's shilling. I loved this kind of anti-modernity and the real sense of history.

My military musings are brought to an abrupt halt when my girlfriend, Lynda, draws up in her Corsa outside the Army centre. I tell her what happened and how this is a milestone on my Army journey. She looks at me, grimaces, and says: "You have really done it now!"

CHAPTER 7

GREEN BOILERSUITS AND GRENADES

"Military men are the scourges of the world"
– Guy de Maupassant

MY final hurdle before basic training was held at the Army Development and Selection Centre, or ADSC in the acronym-mad military world. Within a couple of hours of arrival, I had my pants around my ankles while a bespectacled, middle-age female doctor cupped my testicles, ordering me to cough. Quite an introduction to the selection process.

I got up at dawn that morning to get a lift through to the centre, near Edinburgh, where we would undergo two days of tests to see if we had the right attributes to succeed in basic training. Yet another obstacle to overcome before the real training finally kicked off.

I had heard so much about the infamous Army concept of 'hurry up and wait'. I was now seeing it at first hand, in all its hideous glory. According to Wikipedia, the phrase refers to "the situation in which one is forced to hurry in order to complete a certain task, or arrive at a certain destination, by a specified time; only for nothing to happen at that time, often because other required tasks are still awaiting completion." Very apt.

I was up at 5am, checking my kit, before running around to the local Army centre to get a lift in a minibus to the selection centre some 50 miles away. It was a mad dash to get there in time – once there, I sat around aimlessly in a waiting area, surrounded by tracksuited recruits for hours. Why the crazed panic to get here?

As a flatscreen TV blazed away unwatched in the background showing the latest series of Ross Kemp's adventures in Afghanistan, I surveyed my surroundings. We were sitting in small groups dotted around a large rectangular hall as we awaited our medicals. Public health posters, Army recruitment ads and other clinical bumf was festooned across the bright, white walls. A hatchet-faced nurse sat at a computer screen, her bosom like a wet sandbag, perched on the desk.

A pale, pimply, ginger haired English corporal earlier met me at reception before giving me a fleeting guided tour. He showed me where the toilets and showers were before taking me up to the dormitory above the reception area. He told me to pick a bedspace (in the Army, beds are known as bedspaces for some reason) and a wardrobe and told me to ditch my bag and suit. He then gave me what was clearly a well rehearsed speech: "Right, listen in, two stripes is corporal, three stripes is sergeant, pips and/or a crown is sir or ma'am. Got that?!" "Yes, corporal!" was my diligent reply as I eyed his two stripes.

As I sat in reception, I noticed the ginger corporal and a bald Scottish sergeant looking in my direction and whispering away. It came as no great surprise because, within seconds of my arrival, everyone in the place seemed to know that I was a journalist. I really was the talk of the town. Eventually, the sergeant trooped over to me as I sat outside the medical room and said: "Here, is it true you are a journo?"

I confirmed his worst fears, causing him to explode: "Jesus! That's a turn up for the books. Christ, you are in for some stick. We once had an undercover journalist sneak into basic training wi' us. He got caught though. They shoulda just kept him in. He had signed his papers an' everythin'."

He then jokingly announced to the whole room that he would have to keep checking me for any hidden cameras. Thankfully, he bounded off to deal with another bunch of new recruits. I felt increasingly self conscious as I sat outside the doctor's office, fumbling with my badge which said "No. 66" in bold type. I felt even more of a pillock thanks to my choice of ensemble of shellsuit with shorts underneath, running top and trainers which I was directed to wear in my pre-arrival briefing pack.

A nurse handed me a 'piddle pot' which I then had to go to the toilet and fill with my urine sample. After returning with my still lukewarm sample, handing it to the nurse and taking a seat, a mousey-looking woman doctor opened the consultation door to my left, peered around and shrilled: "Number 66, please." *Here goes.* I trotted in, indulging in a flurry of meaningless small talk in a futile bid to calm my nerves. She knew I was a reservist and asked about my day job as a journalist, the phone hacking scandal, the demise of the *News Of The World* and other weighty matters.

After a few minutes, she came out with the inevitable: "Ok, lie back on the couch and take your shorts down, please." She had asked if I wanted a 'chaperone' – *why would I want another person to witness this?* She felt around a bit at the top of my pubic mound, to use the technical term, then cupped my testicles and asked for "two good coughs." It was actually far less traumatic than I expected. The doc was very clinical and professional. Once I had dropped my trousers, I had been fighting the urge to say: "At least buy me dinner first."

She then asked me to walk around the room on tip toes, on my heels and on the side of my feet. I then had to crouch and walk around in that position. I was then told to do press ups on the cold lino floor. The whole process took about 10 minutes but there was a lot riding on these tests since certain medical conditions precluded you from joining the army. Next, I had a hearing and sight test with a no-nonsense nurse who clearly wasn't up for any small talk.

I was put in a small soundproof booth and given a clicker topped with a red button. I was meant to press this every time I heard a sound ranging from a buzz to a high-pitched whine, moving from one ear to another. At some stages, all I could hear was the pounding of my blood in my ears. After the test, which I somehow passed, I was given an orange bib with my number on it, a sheet with the icebreaker questions, a pen and a clipboard.

There were a few tough nuts in my group including one guy who had brown cropped hair, a stocky build and the mangled nose of a boxer. He seldom spoke, but when he cracked a joke, everyone laughed. Due to work commitments, I was here during the week so it meant everyone here, bar me, was planning to join the regulars. I was the sole reservist there, and the oldest candidate by a mile. We sat in rows waiting for something, anything to happen.

A black haired corporal sporting the red hackle of the Black Watch in his headdress appeared. He was top heavy with muscular arms laced with a spidery network of tribal tattoos. As he spoke, he also had a speech impediment which made his voice sound nasal. He announced that he was taking us off to a side room to have our 'icebreaker' – our opportunity to talk about why we wanted to join the Army and an opportunity to sell ourselves.

As we trooped off, the corporal spied me. "Fuck sake!" he said. "What age are you? You are old enough to be my da'!" This was supposed to inspire hilarity but everyone just looked shellshocked, afraid to laugh. He then said something else which I couldn't make out. I replied: "Pardon?" He then shouted: "Oh, so you are effing deaf as well!"

He took us into the room, where we arranged ourselves along the walls on cheap, plastic chairs. The corporal and his sidekick, another corporal from the Royal Artillery, sat in front of a whiteboard at a desk. He went round the room, starting to my left, asking people to begin. The Black Watch corporal removed his headdress, rubbed his mop of sleek black hair and yawned, regularly and theatrically as the candidates droned on about their love for the Army.

There must have been 20 of us in the room. Each of our 'icebreaker' speeches seemed to follow the same broad outline: what regiment we wanted to join, why we wanted to join, how supportive our families were, what skills we had and so on. It was very formulaic.

As it came to my turn, the corporal asked his sidekick to "pull his finger". As his mate pulled his finger, he let out an ear splitting fart. He then picked up my icebreaker form, detailing my skills, aptitudes and desire to serve on the frontline, and tossed it to one side. "I hate this guy," he announced to no-one in particular.

I was off to a great start. I hadn't even said a word and this guy hated me. I cleared my throat and started: "My name's Stephen. I am 36 years old and I thought I looked good for my age until I met you." I mentioned that I had been to Afghanistan with the Black Watch in 2009. The corporal laughed, and said: "Ah, I thought I recognised your face."

I must have talked for a good 10 minutes, adding in the odd anecdote and mentioning, truthfully, that I was desperate to get to Afghanistan, this time as a soldier. Chris, a 28-year-old from the Midlands, who looked like a bodybuilder, got up to give his talk. He worked as a supervisor in a crisp factory but was desperate to join the Army. He was also into mixed martial arts and was an ex-rugby player. He talked affably about his four kids, his desire to have purpose in his life and to have something more than just a nine to five job. His talk was the best by a mile.

After this ordeal, the corporal took us outside into the car park where he told us to get into three ranks. We then marched, or more correctly shuffled, our way to the 'cookhouse', the old Army term for the canteen.

It was lunchtime and the place was buzzing with people, in and out of uniform. We were lined up while the corporal said: "Right, get a tray and move around the hotplates. When you are taking food, be careful and don't splash it aw over the place!" I was slightly perturbed that people would need to be told how to keep food on their plates.

After getting my pie, chips and beans, I walked into the dining hall. There was a strict hierarchy in here obviously. Recruits sat on the left of the cavernous hall, which was the length of a football pitch, while corporals sat on the right behind a large partition. A long table at the top of the hall, presumably reserved for officers and VIPs, was carefully set with glasses, napkins and polished cutlery. We got plastic cups, chipped plates and paper napkins.

One thing struck me throughout the meal: no-one spoke. I tried to make small talk with the guys around me but it was like pulling teeth. Any chit-chat got a grunt in response. I gave up, chewing my pie as I stared into space. A wall-mounted 40-inch TV was switched on but the awful reception meant that no-one watched it.

Following a march back to the main office, we sat in the TV room waiting for our lunch to digest. A towering red-headed Physical Training Instructor (PTI), with a trademark blue tracksuit top emblazoned with the crossed swords of the Royal Army Physical Training Corps, barrelled in to brief us. He had a strong Glaswegian accent: "Form up ootside, we are going to the gym fur the strength tests then ye'll git a PT session to show ye whit to expect in the Army. Any questions? Naw, that's guid."

As we trooped down half-a-mile or so to the bottom of the barracks, I was amazed. I had never seen this guy before and yet, he already knew that I was a reporter. I was at the front of the squad where he grilled me about what I wrote, which paper I worked for, where I had been in Afghanistan, what I thought about the Army so far. No-one else dared speak. He was from 5 SCOTS, the Argyll and Sutherland Highlanders, a famous unit that traditionally recruited from Glasgow and the west of Scotland.

In the gym, we faced a number of tests including a 55kg static lift, which was supposed to simulate flinging ammo boxes on to the back of a truck. We were also given a back extension test. I was strapped into a harness and then had to pull back as hard as possible. PT staff then took a reading from a gauge on the harness. This was supposed to tell them if our frames could handle carrying heavy loads, a must for infanteers. Then we moved across to the pull up bar to bang out as many as we could.

We were then taken into the main gym hall for a PT taster session. This consisted of circuit training with lots of running. After half-an-hour, my legs were like jelly but the session was over. After we were escorted back to the main building, we sat in the TV room for hour after mind-numbing hour. More 'hurry up and wait', the Army speciality. By the end of the afternoon, I had seen enough *Deal or No Deal* repeats to last a lifetime.

Our evening meal in the cookhouse was uneventful, munching away in silence. As I cleared away my plate, my pal, the ginger PTI, blasted: "Aye, ahm watching you! Ah bet ye have got a camera hidden in yer laces or sumthin'" as he waved two fingers in the direction of my shoe.

After dinner, there was more aimless hanging about in the TV room or playing pool in the upstairs recreation area, which had all the ambience of a young offenders institution. I phoned Lynda to let her know I was okay. Ginger, the PTI, piped up again: "Haw! Is that you awa' tae phone the *Record* and tell 'em we've been rodgering young boys!?" Cue much hilarity from the staff and recruits.

Everyone was in bed for about 10pm. Lights out came half-an-hour later. I never slept a wink. A chorus of snoring started from approximately 11pm. I've always preferred my own bed and find it hard to get settled in new surroundings. I was made even more anxious by the fact that tomorrow was the day when we did the mile-and-a-half run and a series of arduous team building tasks.

At 5am, I got up from my vinyl nightmare of a mattress and shuffled off to the showers. There were five showers, as one was broken, for roughly 50 guys. After a wash and breakfast back at the cookhouse, we were soon taken out into the car park for a warm up which consisted of running from one distant fence to another. At one point, our flame-haired PTI saw a rabbit bouncing into the undergrowth.

"Get efter it!" he growled, prompting us to tear after the bewildered bunny.

We donned green boilersuits and what looked like skate-boarder helmets for the next task. We had been given a brief lesson on types of hand grenades the night before and now, we would put that into practice. We had to run through a small-scale assault course, then crawl through a waterlogged concrete tunnel, drag ourselves through a muddy stretch of grass before picking up a grenade and launching it at a target. Thankfully, these were dummy grenades as my lack of sleep and nerves wouldn't have stood me in good stead with the real thing.

I scrambled to the end of the course, my body coursing with adrenaline as two officers stood watching me from the side of the course. They were standing nonchalantly grip-ping dog leads, watching proceedings as their black Lab and Golden Retriever snuffled around. I located the dull silver grenade in the long grass, screamed "grrrreeeeeee-naaadee!!" and launched it towards the target. I missed by a considerable margin but the officers grunted "good effort" as I trotted past.

After everyone had a shot, we formed up and jogged down through the camp to the playing fields next to the gym. There were a number of obstacles, each of them next to a sign emblazoned with the name of a famous battle such as Assaye and Waterloo. We got a briefing before each task but they all seemed to consist of moving ammo tins from one side to the other without touching the ground, which was supposed to be a minefield.

We had a couple of planks, to be placed on top of the oil drum that acted as platforms for us to stand on. My adrenaline-fuelled, sleep-deprived, fuddled state meant that strategy was out of the window. I just decided to brass neck it by being vocal and looking enthusiastic. It must have worked because at the end of the task, the supervising staff said we had completed the tasks in record time. I beamed with pride as the sweat slowly dripped off the inside brim of my helmet.

We had little time to change out of our boilersuits, let alone rest. It was time for the big, do or die, run. Once we were stripped down into our PT gear, the warm-up started. Our friendly ginger giant PTI showed up to lead the session. He took us out to the football pitches, where he would shout a body part and we would have to touch the ground with said part of our anatomy. He had made sure we were in the muddiest, slimiest part of the field when he bellowed "left baw!" followed by "right erse cheek!" I was covered in filth and the run hadn't even started.

We formed up in three ranks under the PTI's watchful gaze before running down the hill at the back of the camp towards an old, disused railway track. The start line for the run was in an old, crumbling railway tunnel. The setting resembled the final scenes of Von Ryan's *Express* where Frank Sinatra fights off the Nazi hordes.

It hadn't rained at all but the path we were to be running on had been churned into a muddy swamp. We all jockeyed for position at the start line before plunging off down the muddy track, splashing through six-inch deep puddles and nearly losing a shoe in a foot-deep pool of cloying mud.

My breathing was all over the place, not just because of the physical exertion. I know that if I fail this run, I will be 'back squadded', meaning I would drop out and have to return here at a later date.

At the halfway stage, we had to go round a gate and return the way we had come. It was like a scene from *Passchendaele*; mud clogged my eyes, my running shoes were like lead weights encased in foul-smelling filth. Some officers were standing at the side of the track with their dogs sitting at their feet, nonchalantly observing proceedings.

I sensed we were getting near the finish line so I tucked my head down and tried to up my pace. I stumbled over the finish line, and I knew I must have passed as the Black Watch corporal ushered me into a line of recruits gleefully high-fiving each other. I watched as after a few minutes, a lanky bald Yorkshireman and a blond Londoner trudged over the finish line. They had failed to make the run in time and were told to turn their bibs inside out, before being hurried away to get the bad news and be sent home.

Once all the runners were back in, our ginger Glaswegian PTI jogged up to us. He looked immaculate in his white vest, budgie smuggler shorts and £120 trail running shoes. 'How did he manage that?' I thought, as I wiped the sheep dung and mud out of my eyes to look at my ruined trainers and sodden t-shirt and shorts.

He then spat into a nearby bush, wiping the drool from his chin, as he turned to us and grinned: "Well done, brers! See – what did ah tell yeez? It pays tae be a winner. We will get youse up the road in a minute where you will have a quick chat wi' the commanding officer. Ah'll gie yeez some questionnaires as well so you can put whitever ye want, how things were organised, how the scoff wis an' aw that. Ye can even put: 'ah hope ah never see that big, annoying ginger fanny again!'"

My motley crew of mud men roared in appreciation. An intoxicating mix of sleep deprivation, muscle fatigue and pure relief meant that I laughed so hard I thought I was going to puke.

CHAPTER 8

BRASS, BAYONETS AND BLOOD, BLOOD, BLOOD

"The soldier is the Army. No army is better than its soldiers. The soldier is also a citizen. The highest obligation and privilege of citizenship is that of bearing arms for one's country"
– General George S Patton

I WAS trembling. Snowflakes floated out of the gunmetal grey skies before drifting down the back of my neck with soul destroying regularity. However, my shakiness had nothing to do with the sub-zero conditions. My arms quivered as I struggled to keep my loaded rifle aimed at the target. I was so far out of my comfort zone that the whole situation seemed unreal. A veteran combat infantryman's rifle is meant to feel natural, like an extension of himself. It felt more like a cumbersome, metal, high-tech club to me.

109

It seemed as if my basic training had only just started and here I was, about to fire live rounds. One slip up and there was every chance that I could blast my brains out or kill someone else on the range.

If I messed up by switching the rifle to automatic fire, a deadly fusillade of bullets would spray hundreds of metres into the air or, even worse, into my nearby comrades. I tried to relax, ignoring the flurries of snow that kept drifting across the range, blurring my line of sight to the wooden targets which depicted a cartoon-like image of a helmeted soldier gripping a rifle.

It was a Saturday morning at Dreghorn Barracks, Edinburgh. Less than 24 hours before, I had been sitting in an air-conditioned office in a pressed suit, a shirt with French cuffs and a silk Gucci tie. Now, I was clad in combat trousers, jacket and Army-issue smock, slushy snow soaking through my trousers as I lay prone on the ground trying to hit a target 25 metres away.

We had been given an introduction to the SA80 rifle, the Army's standard weapon, in a draughty classroom before being let loose on the ranges. My right arm was stiff and sore after an hour of lugging the weapon about, taking aim and practicing getting into firing positions. We would have to pass a weapons handling test before we would be allowed anywhere near a live range.

I had to show I was able to make sure the weapon was safe with no bullets lurking inside. I had to strip the weapon, rebuild it, clear any stoppages and convince the staff I was going to be safe while working with real, live ammo. I was quietly proud of how quickly I had learnt to use the weapon. This was a new world to me, as the last weapon I'd touched was a Lone Star cap gun when I was about eight years old.

As I lay in the prone position on the range, I went through all the things I was supposed to remember: "Gently squeeze the trigger, don't snatch it, control your breathing, remember your marksmanship principles." My head throbbed under my helmet – it was barely 8am. I wouldn't even be up yet if I was at my civilian job. I normally started work in the newsroom at 10am.

Despite my feeling of impending doom on the ranges, my first experience with a deadly weapon had been a success, a small victory which slightly boosted my confidence. I managed not to kill myself or anyone else. As we checked the targets and patched them up with small flesh-coloured stickers, who would have guessed it? It turns out I was actually a pretty good shot.

Every live firing session ended with the age-old joy of 'picking up brass'. Any soldier knows this procedure all too well. Once the shooting is over for the day, everyone then starts picking up the brass cases which have been ejected from the side of the rifle when firing. The range should be immaculate for each group coming through so after an exhausting day's shooting, we would then have to get down in the slushy mud to pick up the brass with freezing, numb fingers. Sweet joy. We would then scour every inch of the range to make sure no casings had been missed when all anyone really wanted was a cup of tea and a sit down.

Every time, I crouched down to analyse every square inch

of the ground in front of me, I would find yet another errant casing lodged under a stone or half embedded in the stinking mud. So much for the Boys' Own images of a soldier hunting for glory in some foreign field, facing death with a cheerful smile, engaged in a bitter battle with the forces of evil. Instead here I was, picking up manky brass casings and stuffing them into my upturned sweaty helmet, wondering what my life had come to.

There were some brighter moments among the soul searching and the frenzied bouts of PT. I met fellow recruit, Bobby, who went on to become a good friend. At first, we never really took to each other. I felt he was a bit aloof and stand-offish and I know he felt the same about me. When I first saw him, I thought he was a rugby player or some type of athlete due to his build. I later discovered that my hunch was right – he was actually a great lacrosse player, even representing his country in the sport.

He loomed over the others, a big physical presence with a flick of incongruous grey hair, standing out among the chestnut brown. He looked clean cut with a sharp, well defined jawline. His boots were always highly polished, his uniform pressed and sitting perfectly. When our paths first crossed during basic training, I always noticed, over the throng of recruits, that Bobby looked sullen, as if he was ready to snap at the first pimply youth that tripped over his rifle.

That's maybe why we ended up being such good pals, because that was exactly how I felt. I had a good 10 years on him as he was just in his 20s but as we began to see each other on the training weekends, we discovered a lot of common ground. He had been to university, gaining a degree in environmental geography, where he had entered the officer training corps.

He was totally focused on serving in Afghanistan, as was I. As we grew closer, he confided that he would probably complete a tour then leave the Army, perhaps going to America to live with his girlfriend. Of course, I was in a similar position. I had no Army plans beyond getting out there on to the frontline.

I didn't see him around for a few weekends as it turned out he'd had a hernia operation. We were sitting in the cook-house when he showed me the scars and the swelling. He said: "It's pretty sore but if I tell the PTI, he will still let me train won't he?" He, like me, was desperate to get through basic training and get out to Afghanistan to do the job for real. All this training was just a stopgap, a means to an end.

One of my funniest moments in the Army was with Bobby. We were split into smaller groups to do our Chemical, Biological, Radiological and Nuclear or CBRN training, given the Army's acronym obsession. Bobby and I were in the same group as a young, gawky Aberdonian, whose accent was so thick few people understood him when he spoke. Colin, a porcelain skinned, fair haired white collar worker from outside Glasgow, was the other candidate.

We were preparing to enter the 'Gas Chamber'. Everyone had heard about the horror stories of soldiers choking, froth-ing at the mouth as they failed to get their gas mask back on. We stood in a huddle awaiting the call to go into the chamber, which looked like a small, concrete Portakabin at the top of a steep hill. Bobby was laughing, with his head back, in a high-pitched giggle. I knew he was nervous, we all were. Colin said: "It'll be fine, it's just CS gas, we aren't gonna die or anything." Our Aberdonian comrade retorted: "Fit ah dinnay ken argghgh arghagaha" – or that's what it sounded like anyway.

We wore thick camouflage coloured biological suits, carrying small packs with our rubbery gas masks. A sergeant gave us the nod that everything was ready so we got the masks on, using the 'buddy buddy' system to check each other, making sure there were no gaps in the hood around the face where gas could seep in.

We trooped towards the chamber like a row of condemned men. It was early morning in the depths of winter and I was sweating, not fully knowing what to expect. Once my eyes got accustomed to the gloom, I could see the small CS pellets smoking away in the middle of the room. "How bad can it be? It's only meant to sting a wee bit. They aren't actually going to kill us, are they?" I mused. Thankfully, team building at the *Record* was never like this.

We had to march round in circles with gas masks on to get accustomed to our surroundings. Then, the fun really started. We had to take a deep breath, remove our mask, keeping eyes and mouth tightly shut, to complete a number of tasks like changing the canister attached to the mask. In retrospect, it was all about controlling your fear, being able to act under pressure.

After we carried out all the drills satisfactorily, the sergeant briefed us on the grand finale. We were to remove our masks, one by one, take a good few gulps of the CS gas laden air, before reciting our full name, Army number and rank. Only if we managed it in full, would he then let us out of this noxious chamber.

Our Aberdonian mucker was first. He looked hesitant, but after a moment's doubt flashed across his face, he whipped off the mask. "He managed: "Prrrivate Ander...hack....sooon....hack...3..0 1...." before he collapsed in a coughing fit, with tears pouring from his eyes. He was writhing in agony as the sergeant opened the door and shoved him outside, into the waiting arms of a stocky corporal.

Bobby and I exchanged glances as we both guffawed nervously. I was next, it was my moment of truth. I felt as if my heart was throbbing in my throat as I fought to keep calm. I was tempted to just leg it out of the door, forget the Army, forget Afghanistan. I stood in front of the sergeant, trying to focus on the job in hand. My brain was in meltdown. I rehearsed my name, number and rank over and over in my mind, I didn't want to make a mess of this.

I stood in front of the sergeant, tore off the mask and looked him in the eye as I took in a few gulps of air. I think I got about halfway through my surname, before I completely lost control of my body. I could hear Bobby laughing at my paroxysm as I was gagging, coughing and spluttering. It felt like someone had rubbed Tabasco into my eyes, while pouring molten lava up my nostrils. I couldn't see at all but I could feel fluid pouring out my nose, merging with my tears before cascading down my face.

Once out in the fresh air, as instructed, I flapped about to get all the fumes out of my clothes. My urge to rub my eyes was tempered by the warning the sergeant gave us that this would actually make the stinging worse. After a few seconds, my eyes began to stop watering and the horrific, acrid smell, which seared into my nostrils, started to fade.

Just as I wiped an eight-inch bead of mucus from my stinging nose, I looked up to see Bobby, doubled up, falling out of the flung open chamber door. He staggered like a late night reveller before collapsing in a heap next to me. The CS gas was debilitating for a while but ultimately harmless. I had recovered sufficiently to watch him for a few seconds before bursting into helpless laughter.

We survived. Maybe it was relief, the ongoing sleep deprivation or just the sight of your mate covered in snot and gibbering like a baby but it was the funniest thing I had seen in years. Once we had cleaned ourselves up, we staggered to the cookhouse for lunch. I couldn't eat my pie and mash for laughing at Bobby's convulsive impression of me trying and failing to blurt out my own name in the gas chamber.

It was a great team building experience. It was supposed to test our CBRN skills and equipment but really it was all about facing and overcoming our fears while gelling as a team in the process. I would never have believed CS gas could be so versatile.

Bobby was superb at taking the piss out of me, whether it was tying knots into the straps of my daysack or giving me a 'dead leg' in the middle of a lecture on the laws of armed conflict that was so boring it could have made a hardened combat veteran sob. Bobby also almost managed to snap me in two. We had just finished an eight-mile tab, also known as a speed march, which involved a steady run for most of the distance while carrying a fully loaded pack and rifle. It was the climax of our physical training and yet another pass or fail test.

We were privileged to have elite soldiers overseeing our bid to get Army fit. Both of our PTIs were members of the elite Special Air Service (SAS) regiment. They had monitored our physical development all through basic training. Although they had the unmistakable air of men who shouldn't be messed with, I was just surprised that they looked like mere mortals. I was expecting them to be black clad Jedi Knights, capable of appearing from out of nowhere ready to deal death to the enemy.

One instructor, who I will call 'Jim', sported a cleanly shaven head which glistened like a cue ball as we ran around the camp. He had been a champion weightlifter, with the bowling bowl shoulder muscles to prove it. Despite his menacing look, he was the most mild-mannered instructor we had. I often had to crane forward in my seat to hear him as he lectured us on health and nutrition.

His pal and fellow instructor 'Georgie' was another SAS man. He was a ferocious runner, thinking nothing of travelling around 20 miles into work on foot, doing his shift as a fitness instructor, donning his backpack and then running the same distance home at night. Both men were close pals who clearly loved staying fit and the Army life. Their enthusiasm was infectious.

Bobby and I were with Jim as he trotted at the head of

a line of soldiers on this final, pass or fail, tab. We had discussed our strategy before we set off. We would both try to keep up with Jim as dropping behind meant you would have to then 'double' – or run in Army speak as in "on the double" – all the way back to the front of the column. If you dropped too far behind, you would be spotted by one of the supervising staff who would then tell you to get on the 'jack wagon'. This was the ultimate shame. The jack wagon was the Army slang term for the ambulance or minivan which followed the soldiers to pick up people who were injured or too unfit to keep up.

We would do whatever it took not to suffer the ignominy of being told to "get on the effing wagon!" Bobby was in front of me chatting to Jim as we swung our rifles from side to side as we tabbed up a hill which never seemed to end. I chucked in the odd question about life in 'The Regiment', as it was known to the cognoscenti, more to slow him down rather than anything else.

We rounded the shores of a reservoir at a fair clip before returning down the path we had just climbed. A couple of miles later, we were through the camp gates minus one or two stragglers. I hoisted the dead weight of my bergen on to the grass before sitting on top it, slurping water from my black issue bottle.

My ignorance lead me to believe we had completed the task but I was very, very wrong. Our PTI Jim had other ideas. We had another series of military tasks to complete before we had officially passed. We had to complete a 'casualty drag' with a fellow soldier lying on the ground as each recruit manhandled them over a set distance. I grabbed my casualty by the shoulders, my thighs bursting with the ache of lactic acid, as I hauled him towards the finish line. Next, we had to sprint 100 metres from a prone fire position, lying flat on the ground. This had to be done 10 times.

Last but not least, it was the fireman's lift. Jim told us to pick someone of similar height and weight to carry. In a millisecond, everyone tried to grab the smallest recruit they could find. I ended up with Bobby, who was about four inches taller than me and a few stone heavier. He, of course, carried me over the uneven grass, dotted with tufts of earth and long grass, with the minimum of fuss.

Then it was my turn to carry Bobby. I bent over as he leaned over my shoulder, grabbing my belt at the base of my back. I straightened up and tried to walk. I was on the verge of collapse, sweat pouring from every pore, as I felt my vertebrate strain. After a few halting steps, I was ready to stop but Bobby kept willing me on: "Come on, keep going, it's harder if you put me down and try to start again!"

I stumbled like a drunk man towards the line of bergens which marked the finishing line, deposited Bobby, fell over and tried to breathe. We had finally finished the first phase of basic training. Nine weekends of phase one training meant that the next stop was Catterick, the infamous HQ of the infantry.

Recruits would talk about Catterick in hushed, fearful tones as if invoking the place's name would be a bad omen. I wasn't looking forward to going there – a senior soldier had told me: "Look, it's gonna be shite but it's only for two weeks, you can handle that." The camp in North York-shire was built during the First World War and remains the biggest Army base in the UK.

I scoured the internet and my bookshelves for more information about this place, the military holy of holies. It seemed like Catterick had always been a purgatory for budding soldiers. A number of complaints about the place even made it to the House of Commons in May 1956. One MP said: "For a long time I have had a continuous stream of complaints from young men at the camp and from their parents. It is unnecessary to reiterate all the complaints, but they include too many bosses, too many orders, indifference to reasonable complaints, additional duties which keep men occupied the clock round, sweeping the roads outside the camp and carrying coal by hand from place to place. One parent spoke of non-commissioned officers standing over his son all day long to ensure that he did the right thing the whole time. That sort of thing has a psychological effect upon these young men which is very disturbing for them."

I am pleased to report that 50-odd years on, little has changed at Catterick. The infantry prides itself on being the fittest branch of the Army and Catterick certainly lived up to its reputation as the toughest place to train. I became thoroughly acquainted with the notorious 'steeplechase' – a two-mile run through swamp-like conditions, water obstacles and trenches before hitting a full scale assault course. It made the *Krypton Factor* look paltry in comparison.

Bobby was with me at Catterick although he was in a different platoon. I would see him in the cookhouse occasionally where he would fill me in on his latest horror stories. His platoon was full of crazed corporals who emptied water bottles over the heads of recruits for minor indiscretions, or made him and his muckers do press-ups until their arms collapsed after someone failed to clean their rifle. My platoon was more mellow but not much.

A Mancunian sergeant, who never smiled and called everybody "feckin' crows", threatened to cave my head in because I had the temerity to ask him a question. I managed to keep a low profile most of the time, avoiding the fury of all-seeing corporals ready to pounce on any transgression, no matter how minor.

The climax of my time at Catterick came on the last day: bayonet training. Our Manc sergeant told us: "War fighting hasn't changed – it's about blood and steel, it always has been, always will be. If your dad or grandad was in the Army, ask them, we teach you lot the same things that they got taught years ago."

Frost laced the ground as it was so early that the sun still wasn't up. We were formed into three ranks for a run around the camp with weapons and webbing, which held our water canteens and ammo pouches. After what seemed like an hour of sprinting in a pack all over the camp, we were finally lead into a fenced-off area.

We were told to 'mark time', marching while stationary and not stepping forward. "Get yer knees up!" cried one of the watching corporals. One of them would shout: "What makes the grass grow?!" and we would scream: "Blood! Blood! Blood!" Then it was: "What makes the blood flow!?"

We bellowed: "Kill! Kill! Kill!" This went on for an unholy length of time, so long that I started to lose my voice.

After what felt like hours of being whipped up into a frenzy, we were deemed to be suitably steely eyed and ready to slaughter anything that moved. We were herded across a small stream into a massive rectangular field which was dotted with wooden frames, holding sandbags that looked vaguely human shaped.

After leaving our rifles on the ground in a neat line, we then ran at full pelt from one nearby landmark to the next. Every 10 seconds or so, a sergeant from the Royal Irish would shout: "Grrrrrenaaaadee!!!!!" This was our signal to dive to the ground, then leopard crawl with our faces pushed into the muck. A flock of sheep must have been in the areas as my lips tasted something which wasn't mere mud.

As I crawled along, waiting for the sergeant to yell: "Clear!" which meant we could scramble to our feet and start running, he booted me in the backside, saying: "Get on yer feckin' belt buckle!" I never made that mistake again, keeping as low as I could as my muscles and ligaments throbbed with bruises yet to come.

We then ran into the middle of a huge puddle which looked more like a lake. Murky, foul-smelling water was up past my knees. No sooner had we stopped then it was "press-up position, down!" and we were banging out press-ups followed by sit ups and other exercises. For an encore, we then ran into a freezing stream at the opposite side of the field where we swam upstream to the shouts and jeers of watching corporals. I got an occasional boot in the face from a recruit bobbing around in front of me.

This, remarkably, was just the warm up. We grabbed our rifles, tipped with bayonets, and trooped into the main training area in front of the sandbag dummies. We roared: "En garde!" before ramming the steel into the hapless sandbags. At one point, we had to grab a battle buddy, staying by his shoulder to 'encourage' him as he closed in to finish the dummy off. I swore so loud and so hard, my voice cracked and rattled with the strain.

Bobby looked like a man possessed. His face was smeared with camouflage, mud and sheep shit, as he bayoneted a dummy lying on the ground. He used his soaking boot to hold it down as he ripped the bayonet out, only to plunge it in again. He was made for this job.

Despite being covered in cuts and bruises and suffering the much lamented loss of a toenail, I managed to pass out in the top third of my intake at Catterick, the position that all recruits aim for. After a period of probation, at the first available opportunity, I volunteered to go to Afghan. It was a Tuesday night in my local Army Reserve Centre, when I fired up my arm as they asked if anyone wanted to go on Op Herrick – the Army's name for its mission in Afghanistan.

An officer asked us: "Right, have we got any volunteers for Herrick 18?" This was the chance I had been waiting for. I shot my hand up without hesitation. Mobilisation is still voluntary in the Army reserves although this may change in years to come as the government continues to reform the armed forces. I always thought: 'Why join the Army if you don't want to deploy?'

My path crossed Bobby's again a few months after Catterick. We were in Warcop, Cumbria, for a battle camp, another training exercise deemed vital for our bid to get to the frontline. One of the directing staff was a colour sergeant from the Black Watch. As soon as I saw him, he broke into a broad grin. I had interviewed this guy in Afghanistan. He stuck out in my memory for an amazing feat of marksmanship – he fired a £70,000 Javelin missile at a Talib sniper, managing to get the missile through a tiny murder hole. There was nothing but bloody rags left of the insurgent.

He had recognised me instantly and we got chatting. Bobby grinned as I said: "Long time no see, you can't get enough of this soldiering game eh?" The colour sergeant puffed pensively on an e-cigarette: "I just fucking love killing cunts." At the end of our fortnight's training, we headed back to Scotland in an Army mini-bus. As he got off the bus at his home, the colour sergeant winked at Bobby and I. He said: "Well boys, enjoy Afghan, and make sure you don't forget to come back with your legs" as he slammed the door and walked off.

CHAPTER 9

CHRISTMAS IS CANCELLED

"He might go far away out of the sound of the tramp of marching, away from the smell of overcrowded barracks where men slept in rows like cattle but he would still be one of them"
– John Dos Passos

MY life was on hold for a year. I was leafing through my mail when I spotted an official-looking brown envelope. Without opening it, I knew that it was my mobilisation papers. My heart rate soared, leaving me almost breathless for a second.

As I cradled the papers in my hands, speed reading the details, I knew I was past the point of no return. I was leaving the Army Reserves, formerly the Territorial Army, to become part of a regular battalion. This would mean giving up my reporter job for a year.

I would be a member of the 'White Mafia', the Royal Highland Fusiliers, 2 SCOTS, call it what you will, it was now my battalion. I would train for a few months with my new unit before hitting the ground in Afghanistan in March 2013 for a six-and-a-half month tour. By law, the newspaper had to keep my job open for me while the Army had to match my civvy wages. That was all assuming that nothing went wrong in that time.

I tried to leave the *Record* in November 2012 with the absolute minimum of fuss. If I could have sneaked out of a back door, I would have. My entire military journey was daunting enough – I didn't want to compound the feeling of irrevocable change by saying goodbye to the people I had worked with for years. It would feel far too final. I would be back, wouldn't I?

It felt as if I left the paper on a Friday evening and was being lambasted by Boab the Dug on my first day at 2 SCOTS, as described earlier, on the Monday morning. I barely had time to contemplate the full ramifications of what I was doing. As I re-read the small print on my call-up papers, leafing through every acronym-laden page, I felt a knot in my stomach as if I was lurching around on a roller coaster. This was real, there was no messing about now. If I felt this dark sense of dread about 12 months with the Army, what must my grandad have felt as he disappeared for six years to fight the biggest war in history?

After a jumpy start with my new battalion, I started to get used to the routine. Each week began with me tearing myself from my bed at home, eyes glued together, at 4am to drive through to the barracks in Edinburgh for 6.30. Every time I saw the camp gate, complete with a soldier in high visibility vest manning the barrier, I felt a bit queasy.

In the civilian world, a soldier is a soldier. Within the stratified, tribal culture of the Army, however, no two soldiers are the same. Among troops, there is a real snobbery about which branch of the Army a soldier represents. Infantrymen consider themselves the top of the tree, the tip of the spear, the apex of Britain's armed forces. They do the dirtiest, toughest job in the worst conditions imaginable so as a result, a lot of infanteers look derisively down their noses on other soldiers in logistics or other branches of the Army. I lost count of the amount of times I would hear other branches referred to as 'remfs' – an acronym meaning 'Rear Echelon Mother Fuckers', which dates back at least as far as the Vietnam War.

Part of this tribal spirit that imbues the infantry is their inherent pride in their reputation as the fittest in the Army. So, it came as no major shock to the system that most of my days started with PT, which involved running everywhere at suicidal speed.

Everything I had ever read about physical training emphasised the necessity of a gentle warm-up before exercise. Obviously, our instructors had never read the same books. We bolted out the front gate as if we had ram-raided a shop and were trying to leg it with our ill-gotten gains. We usually careered down a road at the side of the camp, plunging headlong into the dawn mist.

Big Boab the Dug was like a man possessed as he tried to

turn us into action men. He would sometimes lead us into the hills around Glencorse Barracks for a sweaty training session. Fitness is the top priority for the infantry as they will be the ones slugging it out on the frontline – so Boab was never far away, trying to make sure we were up to scratch.

On an average session, the sun would be just rising when we were off, sprinting out of the barracks gate. After a few miles, we would get to a seemingly vertical slope, sprinting up it again and again until we thought our quadriceps would burst. At the end of this torture, we bolted back to barracks. On a typical day, we might then be told to get down and bang out 100 press-ups. On one memorable occasion, I looked over my shoulder in mid press-up to see a beetroot-faced private flamboyantly throw up down a drain.

After PT, there was the occasional parade, where we would be formed into three ranks while 'Queeny', our platoon sergeant, puffed on a Lambert and Butler and told us who was to report to the medical centre or go to the stores to get kit. He spoke from the side of his mouth in a Glaswegian wide boy drawl, with every announcement starting with: "Awright, troops!" These pronouncements were mercifully short and never involved me.

In fact, Queeny could never even remember my name. In hundreds of books about the elite SAS regiment, Andy McNab and his cohorts describe their experience of selection, the unit's infamous recruitment process designed to weed out everyone but the best, most robust soldiers. McNab tells readers that the best policy is to be the 'grey man', never too far up ahead, never too far behind, never

Nervous wait: The author and photographer, Lesley Martin, sit at the back of the Chinook helicopter that will take them into a night time surgical strike on the Taliban called Operation Tyruna

(Above left) Getting to grips with my pen and pad on another assignment at Kandahar Air Field or KAF – as it's known to the troops – in 2009; (above, middle) Lesley, festooned with cameras, gets ready for another day's work during my embed with 3 SCOTS, The Black Watch; (above, bottom pic) RAF ground crew give the thumbs up next to a Tornado jet at KAF

Take cover: Soldiers hit the dirt on the Boardwalk — a wooden walkway — in the centre of KAF during a Taliban rocket attack

War games at Warcop: (below, left) Fellow reservists Bobby and Russ (front left and centre) join the author (back right) on a pre-deployment exercise in Warcop, Cumbria as they gear up for Afghanistan

Board stiff: Gary Carling polishes up his chess moves on a break. The board game was a popular way to kill time in camp; (left) a selfie days after arriving in the splendour of OP Dara

Pipedreams: Even in the remotest outpost in Afghanistan, a Scottish battalion needs its fix of the bagpipes...

Press up: (Top) Working out was one of the few distractions at Dara. Even the furious desert heat didn't stop the workouts; (above) time for a quick snapshot among the surprisingly well-equipped gym at Dara; (right) note on the bed...

On duty: On sentry watch looking out into the desert and the Green Zone in full Personal Protective Equipment including body armour, helmet and ballistic glasses

Graveyard shift: Peering out of a sangar's camouflage netting towards a local graveyard, complete with gaudily covered flags to mark the graves

True colours: Garry John (far right) and his fellow Paisley buddies strike a pose for the camera in front of the ubiquitous camp football flags

Blessed rain: Soldiers strip down to enjoy the unseasonal night time rain at OP Dara; (above right) reclining on a cycling machine during a break. Note the obligatory t-shirt, shorts and flip flops. Dara was remote enough to have more relaxed dress codes

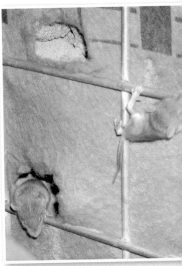

Scrubbed up: Garry John helps scrub the pots and pans after another Dan feast cobbled together from ration and welfare parcels; (above) bab desert mice make a break for it afte gnawing through the Hesco wa

Great cook off: Gary Carling helps prepare a lovo – a Fijian earth oven – where meat is wrapped before being buried with hot stones that cook it over a few hours. Delicious

Local hero: Garry John shows off his favourite tattoos – featuring song lyrics from his idol, Paolo Nutini

One for the ladies: Wee Paddy poses in a pic which went alongside a number of 'hometown stories' that the author wrote for the Army, which were then filed to local press; (right) Big Sean poses for a mugshot in full uniform, again for a 'hometown story' about his time on the frontline

(Top) Biblical storm: A sandstorm looms over the main sangar at Dara. Moments later, it would plunge the whole area into total darkness; (above) Behold! As the sandstorm races towards the camp, it resembled scenes from the Hollywood horror movie *The Mummy;* (right) posing for the camera minutes before everyone is 'stood to' in case the Taliban attack

standing out too much. Apparently, I had managed this with my new platoon without even trying.

From the first day we met, Queeny would always look at me with his best, most vacant expression. "I am Stewart", I would remind him. He could never distinguish between my fellow reservist Gary Carling and I, no matter how many times we told him. He knew I was a journalist so he would just call me "grass" or "snitch", or some other term designed to wind me up.

Queeny was actually younger than me but he seemed much older, more like an old, grizzled war-weary veteran. With his creeping middle-aged paunch, he didn't seem the stereotype of the tough infanteer. He had certainly paid his dues on past tours, sometimes lamenting: "Getting shot at and blown up isny aw it's cracked up tae be." He was naturally dishevelled, managing to look slightly untidy even in a well-pressed uniform.

To say he was forgetful and disorganised would be like saying Adolf Hitler was a touch right wing. On the first day at the battalion, Gary and I went into his office to introduce ourselves and find out what exactly we would be doing. We eventually convinced him that he wasn't getting two new Gurkhas, as he seemed to believe. We were the only two new attachments to his unit, prompting him to grab his fags, mumbling "fuckin' stabs..." before staggering into the car park for another smoke break. Stab is a derogatory army term, standing for 'Stupid Territorial Army Bastards', and one that I was going to hear a lot.

I expected everything to be regimented, with every minute

accounted for but, in fact, we were left to our own devices for hours at a time. Younger soldiers would disappear off to their rooms to play their Xboxes or watch Jeremy Kyle. Unfortunately, our accommodation was miles away, as they couldn't find space for us in this barracks. There was a Naafi lounge in the camp where we would go to hide for hours. As a result, I can safely say that I have never drank so much coffee in my life. I ended up on first-name terms with each of the chatty, middle-aged women that worked there.

The time honoured Army tradition of 'hurry up and wait' was also in evidence. My self-control was put to the test so many times as we trudged to the armoury for a bout of weapon cleaning, only to have to stand for two hours in the cold because the guy with the keys couldn't be found. On one memorable occasion late on a Friday afternoon, Queeny told Gary and I to make sure we were at the guard room for 6am on Sunday. We were going down to Wales for a week of heavy weapon training.

Visions of relaxing at home with Lynda after a fine meal and a few drinks at our local faded before my eyes. I flung my kitbag into the boot of my car, slammed the door heavily and drove home in a rage. Seemingly in a flash, it was 4am on Sunday and I was already driving back to barracks. My weekend had effectively been non-existent. I arrived at the guard room just before 6am, met Gary and waited for our transport to turn up.

We expected at least another 20-odd soldiers to have turned up but we were the only ones there. None of the soldiers knew anything about a bus turning up to take us to

Wales. As the clock in the guardroom ticked, we got more nervy. Calls to Queeny's mobile just rang out. What was happening? Were we in the wrong place? If there's one thing the Army teaches you, it's don't be late...for anything, ever.

We managed to get a phone number for the barrack's transport office. They had no idea what we were talking about, there were no buses booked for that day. There was, however, one booked to take soldiers to Wales the following day. Queeny had told us to turn up on the wrong day. I had curtailed my weekend, lost time with loved ones, driven all that way, for nothing. To add insult to injury, we had to do it all over again the following day. Thank Christ, at least I only had to put up with this for a year rather than the rest of my working life.

My mood picked up a bit when we learned Pashto, one of Afghanistan's main languages and the one most used in Helmand Province. Our teachers were Afghan men in their 20s, well educated, worldly, Westernised. They had come to the UK to escape the strife in their own country and build a new life or further their education. To some of my classmates, they were just "choagies", another term that I had never heard until I joined the Army.

Insider attacks by Afghan forces against British and US troops seemed to spike as our training progressed. I wondered if this had triggered some of the snide remarks about Afghans. That year, 2012, had been one of the worst for rogue 'green on blue' attacks, where Afghan soldiers had turned their weapons on their supposed British or US allies.

One killing was very close to home: a former soldier at my

new battalion was killed as he played football with his Afghan comrades. Captain Walter Barrie, who once served with 2 SCOTS, was shot dead at close range by a rogue member of the Afghan army while playing in the game on Remembrance Day. Captain Barrie was playing alongside members from the Afghan National Army (ANA) at his base when he was killed in the Nad-e Ali district of Helmand. The gunman was dressed in full ANA uniform when he approached the pitch and fired nine shots using an M16 rifle. Intelligence officers had warned British troops of insider attacks after a similar incident in western Afghanistan.

The news sent shock waves through the barracks as many of his close pals still worked with this battalion. I never knew the man but I was shocked that such a soldier, who was respected and valued so much by so many brothers in arms, would be killed by an erstwhile 'friend'. It gave added impetus to my bid to learn Pashto. Maybe, if I learned the language, I would be able to talk down any lone Taliban fanatic who decided to throw off his mask of comradeship, before coming at me all guns blazing.

A lot of the younger soldiers seemed to view the Pashto lessons as an opportunity to skive. As we sat in the harshly lit classroom for another session, one soldier, who looked about 15 with a snub nose and a wall of hair which seemed to start just above his eyebrows, stared out of the window. When asked to read out a passage from our textbook, he would mumble and, almost painfully, trip over the words. Even the attentions of a strict officer, who sometimes attended the classes literally breathing down his neck, never managed to spark his interest in the subject.

Things were changing in theatre, we were told. The newest development was the use of 'Guardian Angels'. Tensions betweens Afghan forces and the Brits were high, despite what Joe Public might think. Guardian Angels were now being used in bases to try to counter the insider threat – soldiers would guard their sleeping buddies, or join an officer as he liaised with his counterparts, lurking in the background with a loaded weapon, ready to come out fighting if things went wrong. Camps were being altered to prevent access by Afghan soldiers, soldiers were being posted as guards to protect themselves from their 'allies' working next to them inside the wire. The war in Afghanistan was often termed as unconventional because unlike World War 2, for example, you did not have two clearly delineated sides fighting it out. This certainly was war in its most unconventional form.

We were warned that sometimes these insider attacks were not always perpetrated by sneaky Taliban fighters infiltrating Afghan forces to wreak havoc. Sometimes, they were carried out by disenfranchised Afghans sickened by seeing their religious or cultural standards being ignored. One incident related to us was triggered by a towel, as incredible as that may seem.

Apparently, a British soldier was using a towel emblazoned with Afghanistan's flag to dry himself after coming out of the shower at a camp. A passing Afghan soldier took offence to the fact he was rubbing his backside and privates with the Afghan flag, which to make matters worse, has the words of the Shahada on it stating that "there is no God but Allah, and the Prophet Muhammad is his messenger."

This flashpoint was quickly averted by a number of profuse apologies and an explanation about the soldier's ignorance of Afghan sensitivities. It was easy to see how these confusions would arise, which is why we were subsequently bombarded with 'cultural sensitivity' training. We were guests in the Afghans' country and we should not forget it, was the overarching message.

Weeks dragged by. Long periods of drinking milky coffee in the Naafi and hanging about in the Fire Support Group's offices waiting for Queeny to tell us to do something were punctuated by the odd bout of more 'warry' training. We were to get a 'cadre', Army speak for a course, on the Heavy Machine Gun, better known in Hollywood popular culture as the 50 cal.

Our tutor was the camp's flashiest operator, Garry John Urie. He sported a spiffy Gucci digital watch under his camo shirt, got his eyebrows tinted and was rumoured to get tanning injections. On a meagre Lance Corporal's wages, he always drove into barracks in a series of slick motors whether it was an executive looking Merc or a sporty Golf GTI. Everyone in the place knew him. Watching him glide down the corridors was a joy as he glad-handed everyone, high-fiving some Fijians, patting a young recruit on the back before shouting: "Awright, brer" to a junior officer. He was like the Army's answer to Del Boy.

His teaching methods and his pally, cheerful demeanour certainly worked as Gary Carling and I had never touched a 50 cal machine gun in our lives, but we managed to pass a test on the weapon after just a couple of days of his tuition. The weapon was nearly as long as I was tall, firing rounds that were the size of big bingo marker pens. We were told that a single round could go through a wall, then take 10 people's heads off if they were lined up right.

I saw Bobby nearly every day, invariably bumping into him in the Naafi as he bought a bacon roll and I got my daily latte fix. We had both been down to Chetwynd Barracks, near Nottingham, for pre-deployment training. Bobby, Russ and I had perched at the back of cavernous hangars as we sat through lectures covering everything from how to fit our body armour together to how to spot a boobytrap bomb.

During one PowerPoint presentation about the effects of IEDs, images of soldiers with horrific injuries flashed up on the screen. One poor soul was missing half his face after the pens, scissors and other tools attached to the front panel of his body armour became deadly projectiles after a blast, spraying up into his chin. As we watched a presentation about a motorbike that had been rigged with explosives by the Taliban, Bobby leaned over to me as he gasped: "Christ, there's so many ways to die in Afghan."

He always had a dark sense of humour but he started cracking jokes about getting hit in an IED strike. He would make a buzzing noise "Zzzzzzz", before saying: "That's the last sound you hear when you get whacked, as the metal rods in the pressure plate connect just before the IED goes off." It was funny at first but after a while I stopped laughing. It sounded too real, too knowing.

Back at Glencorse Barracks, the original tally of nearly

30 reservists had been cut to about eight or nine soldiers. We were told that 2 SCOTS needed fewer soldiers to join their ranks than expected. My heart went out to the guys that were sent home, they had put their lives on standby to come here before hopefully deploying to Afghan. Some of them had sacrificed jobs, college courses and relationships to deploy. Then after all the self sacrifice, they had to slink back to their reserve units. Army chiefs did go out of their way to try to look after them: some were given other deployments to Cyprus or the chance to go on training courses. It never made sense to me why the Army didn't know well in advance how many soldiers they would need.

Anyway, I was glad to have made the final cut. Bobby, Russ and Gary Carling had made it too. We would be going to Afghanistan. I never realised it would be such a tortuous struggle to get out there. There were so many obstacles to negotiate, all so that you could go and get shot at or blown up in Afghanistan.

We were constantly on and off white anonymous looking contract buses, buzzing up and down the length of the country for a training exercise or a briefing. Christmas passed in a sweaty, nervy blur. Every day of leave was a day closer to leaving home to start the tour. At New Year, just before the bells at midnight, I got my training gear on and went for a run through my local town. Tipsy, beer bellied men watched me slack jawed as I sprinted down the street while the rest of the world partied. When I thought of going to Afghan as my time at home ran out, my nerves reared up, feeling like a steel fist crunching into the small of my neck.

Running helped me forget it, for a while.

Christmas and New Year were actually a non-event. Our festive leave was cut short for another training 'package' in Lydd, Kent. This major military exercise was called 'Pashtun Dawn'. It was designed to fully prepare us for our deployment in March. We travelled down in the first week of January to take part in a gruelling series of live fire exercises. While other people slept off their festive hangovers, I was enduring 12 hours on a bus with aromatic squaddies.

Bobby and Russ were down here as well. A Facebook picture from the time shows us sitting on the ground outside a troop shelter on the ranges, wearing our headdress, our heads just poking out above our new Osprey body armour. Minutes before the picture was taken, Bobby and some other soldiers had been messing about, lobbing small stones onto the roof shelter so they would slide down onto our heads.

There were loads of times like this, sitting about, chewing the fat, waiting for something to happen. Maybe that's why so many soldiers seemed to smoke, it gave them something to do as they savoured the old 'hurry up and wait'.

I was now confident with a number of 'weapon systems' as they are called in the Army. We had used 50 cals, grenade machine guns and the standard infantry weapon, the SA80 rifle, was now a familiar friend. My heart almost missed a beat, though, when after hiking miles across the Lydd ranges, we were told we were to get our first taste of using live hand grenades.

Horror stories were common of inexperienced soldiers dropping a live grenade or getting the pin snagged on tree branches during exercises, resulting in a swift and horrifically gory death. Beads of sweat slowly traced their way down my back underneath the heavy body armour, despite the sub-zero temperatures.

After all the safety briefs and dry runs, we waited in a troop shelter to take our turn. Hollywood movies do not really do justice to the sound of a high explosive grenade going off. People think they make a loud, rumbly noise because that's what they hear in films. Vibrating speaker cones can't even begin to come close to the reality. If you have never heard a large explosion go off close by, imagine a big firecracker which you see in Chinese New Year festivals then multiply it 10,000 times. It's a sharp, scary, loud noise which you feel as well as hear. It always seems way, way too close.

As I clutched my deadly grenade to my chest before hurling it at a shrapnel-shredded target, I could not help but think how different this job was to my *Daily Record* post. The odd papercut and an occasional elbow in the ribs during a packed press conference were the biggest hazards I had to contend with in my previous line of work. I removed the safety clip, pulled the pin, lobbed the grenade before ducking into cover with the instructor. Once we heard the boom, I walked shakily into another adjoining troop shelter. I must have been good at it because rather than throw one or two grenades as planned, I ended up flinging about six of the innocuous-looking green orbs.

I was pleased that I had, for the umpteenth time it seemed, faced my fears and got the job done. As I dozed at the back of the bus as we meandered back to Scotland, I knew my

Army career was without doubt the most mentally and physically challenging thing I had ever done.

But my biggest ordeal was still ahead of me. No training could have prepared me for it. I had to say goodbye to Lynda and my family as I headed to Afghanistan.

CHAPTER 10

I WILL ALWAYS LOVE YOU

"In the pain of death, spoken words often fail.
Words written down, last forever"
– Sian Price

"DEAR Lynda, If you are reading this, I am so sorry that things have not turned out the way I planned." This was the first line of my death letter to my girlfriend, Lynda, to be opened only if I was killed in action in Afghanistan. Those 21 opening words took me weeks to write.

Writing the letter, in fact, was one of the toughest things that I had to do. Trying to condense years of love into a few pages is an experience that I never want to repeat. I was not alone. Hundreds of fellow soldiers in my battalion were doing the same thing, leaving a note to their loved ones in case the worst happened.

We had been advised to leave a sealed letter to our families to help them come to terms with their loss if we weren't lucky enough to come back from the tour. I had put this moment off for weeks, finding a dozen other things to do instead of writing the letter.

When Lynda was safely out shopping, I sat on our double bed with a fountain pen and four sheets of cream foolscap paper. Rain battered off the bedroom window as I had a chilling moment of clarity, thinking: 'What am I doing?' The stark reality of being a frontline soldier suddenly hit me like a tidal wave.

I had a lot to lose: a partner, a family, a career, a full life. All my pals were the same. I didn't have to be in this position. I could have enjoyed my embed in Afghanistan in 2009, then just moved on, chalking it up to experience. Not me, I had to go the full way. I was regretting my decision now. I knew better than to mention it to Lynda though, she had enough on her mind.

It would have been easier to write this letter if I had some grandiose reason for going to Afghanistan, whether it be fighting for Queen and country, making a personal stand against global terrorism or just trying to make Afghanistan – and the world – a better, safer place.

My reasons were more mundane: I wanted to fully experience a war which I had only previously sampled. After the adrenalin subsided following my journalistic stint on the frontline, I reflected on how much I had enjoyed the experience. It had been stressful but to face your fears and get the job done was one of the most rewarding experiences of my life. I *had* to go back to do a tour of duty in the toughest role the Army has to offer as a combat infantryman.

Lynda would never understand or agree with my reasons for going, I knew her too well. She viewed the whole thing with a mixture of bewilderment and sadness. "Why would you want to go to such a dangerous place?" she would ask. She once asked me if I was going because I didn't love her any more. Her questions cut me to the bone. At least the letter gave me a chance to address some of them.

I told her that, for me, Afghanistan was like an itch that needed to be scratched. I didn't want to be an old man lying on my death bed, wondering what a tour of Afghan would have been like. It's better to regret something you have done, than something you haven't. This was the only way to experience the reality of the most gruelling conflict of our generation. Rather than sit on the sidelines and write about the campaign in Afghanistan, I would be an active participant in the war.

It felt confessional writing the letter. There was a need to show my love, gratitude and to try to offer solace. But, writing from beyond the grave, was not an experience I would want to repeat. Once I was finished, I put it in an envelope and hid it in a drawer. I made sure to mark the envelope so that I would know if she tried to open it on the sly. Later, before we got on the flight for Afghanistan, I would call Lynda to tell her about the letter's existence, why I wrote it and how she was not to open it unless I wasn't coming back alive.

Our 'death letters' were just another stark reminder of how dangerous this tour was going to be. Our 'death pictures' had been taken a few weeks before. A photographer took a snap of me as I posed, hatchet faced, in full uniform, outside battalion headquarters. This head and shoulders snap would be sent out to the media in the event of my death.

Even with all the death letters and pictures, I still had the feeling of 'it will never happen to me'. I was wary of this mind-set though, I didn't want that to slip into complacency. Treat every day in Afghan as if it's your first, I told myself. Complacency kills out there.

It was imperative that I tied up any loose ends before I went overseas. I didn't want to have anything hanging over me, playing on my mind as I tried to work in Afghan. My days were taken up finalising my will, arranging for insurance cover and a million other things that you don't even think of. Lynda told me not to even talk about going away as it depressed her too much.

I was ridden with guilt and remorse for putting my loved ones through this. I had condemned them to six months of emotional torture, dreading a sudden knock on the door to tell them I had been killed or maimed. My experience was about to give me a soldier's eye view of the front line but I had already learned that wives, girlfriends and families serve on a tour of duty as well. They are just as deeply involved as the frontline troops.

My decision to join the Army was not taken lightly. Going to Afghanistan with the Black Watch had been a transformational moment in my life. I felt privileged to have been given a real flavour for life on operations – I was going into this experience with my eyes wide open.

Before I left, I went to see an Army pal of mine. He was a sergeant major in another unit, a beast of a man with tattoos creeping out like the tendrils of a plant from underneath his collar and shirt cuffs. Some people seemed to fear him but I knew him as a confidante and a great laugh. His brown eyes would twinkle like a jackdaw's when he told me a funny story about a fellow soldier.

Terry consumed dozens of eggs, pounds of steak mince and mountains of chicken breast each day to sustain his passion for weightlifting. He had the physique to prove it and even his hands looked muscular and pumped. He was in his thirties but still had the youthful exuberance of a teenager and a visceral love of soldiering. He talked with a Glaswegian twang at a hundred miles an hour, almost without pausing for breath.

He wanted to know if I was sure about what I was doing. I said I was but it was academic anyway, it was way too late to back out now. He had completed four tours in Afghanistan and was involved in Operation Panchai Palang, aka Panther's Claw.

He said: "It should be safer for you now. We did a lot of fighting in the area you will be going, so hopefully conditions will be better." On July 4 2009, he stood on a pressure plate on the advance in at the start of Op Panchai Palang. The IED was big and was meant to take out a vehicle. It went off behind Terry.

He told me: "There were two bodies – one of them was my 'terp Nas. I was in a daze and thought I was already dead. I took my helmet off and was just wandering about, despite the fact we were taking rounds. It sounds weird but I was actually looking for my own body. My mate was shouting: 'Get down, Terry!' and I was amazed that he knew I was there. I asked him if he could see me and if I was alive – he shouted: 'Yes, but for Christ's sake, get down!'"

Nas was 24 years old and had an 18-month-old kid. He was lying in a ditch, I could just see that he had his hand up. I ordered the troops to put down suppressive fire when I ran over to him. I tried to grab his left arm but when I looked there was just four inches of bone sticking out from his shoulder. One of the other guys with me was sick as we tried to move him.

"He was basically sliced in half – his organs were hanging out. The medic was crying and I just told him to go away. Nas was still gasping for air, it was as if his body was shutting down. I just held his head in my arms and told Nas to let himself go."

On another occasion, an IED had blown up an armoured vehicle in one of Terry's patrols. He grabbed a guy who he was sure was dead and got a shock when he lurched over and grabbed him. His right leg was gone and the other one was hanging by strips of skin and tendon. His eyes were white and he had actually bitten his tongue clean off. Terry found it and stuck it in his shirt pocket – before leaving a note so that the medics could find it.

As he battled to get tourniquets on to what was left of his

leg, the limb came off in his hands. He managed to get the casualties on the chopper but the ANA soldier died in Camp Bastion from his injuries. He murmured: "I still have dreams about that one."

Listening to Terry's experiences, I knew without any shadow of a doubt how bad things could get over there. He asked me how Lynda was coping, offering to take his wife round to see her to make sure she was ok. "It's funny," he said, "a tour can make or break a relationship. Couples either get stronger through it or they drift apart, having affairs when their man is away an' aw that." I was sure my relationship would survive this tour.

I planned to make my departure for Afghan as low key, relaxed and painless as possible. In that, I failed miserably. In a cruel twist of fate, I had to say goodbye to Lynda not once, but twice. It felt like I was stabbing her in the back, then twisting the knife to add to her torment.

It was torture beyond belief. I travelled to Edinburgh on Sunday night as we were due to leave the following day. However, on Monday lunchtime, we were told there had been a change of plan. Now we would leave on Thursday. I had to go home and do it all over again later in the week. Welcome, yet again, to the notorious army concept of 'hurry up and wait' where we rush to a location, only to wait hours or days for something to happen.

On my way to the barracks, I checked Facebook to see if Bobby and Russ had got away on time. They were leaving before the rest of us. Bobby's final post was the Royal Regiment of Scotland's prayer: "God of our fathers, whose hand shapes the coastlands and hills of home, fashion likewise our lives. Guard the Royal Regiment of Scotland; keep us brave in battle, resolute in adversity, loyal to comrade and Crown; that inspired by the faith and cross of Saint Andrew, we might secure lasting peace and eternal rest, through Jesus Christ our Saviour."

At first, I thought he may have posted it as a joke. I had never heard him talk about religion and he seemed, like me, to be fairly sceptical about priests, ministers and spiritual stuff. There it was, though, in black and white. Gary Carling and I joked about it, how he had suddenly 'found God' at the start of the tour, vowing to wind him up the first chance we got. He would have been arriving in Afghanistan in the next day or so.

After a long drive with Lynda, experienced in silence for most of the way, we pulled up to the overspill car park, outside the barracks. We wanted somewhere quiet for our last few moments together. We shared a few whispered words and a hug before I really had to go this time. In the past few days, she had been tense, losing her temper with me over small things such as washing lying on the floor or forgetting to do the dishes. I knew what was really behind it. Her way of dealing with things was to get stressed then lash out over seemingly unrelated events. It was my fault for putting her through all of this.

Her eyes looked like two black pools in her face as streams of mascara dribbled down her chin. She was wearing a black faux fur jacket against the winter chills but her body shivered and convulsed as I held her as close as I could. There was no time for any cross words now, in less than 24 hours I would be on my way to Afghanistan.

I felt a gnawing sense of guilt in the pit of my stomach for putting her through this ordeal. I knew that she would be on tenterhooks for the entire six-month tour. A sense of selfishness washed over me for choosing to join the Army. My decision would mean that, through no fault of her own, Lynda would be condemned to a nerve shredding six-and-a-half months.

Sitting day after day during my tour, she would be at home waiting for a visit from Army officers to say that I wouldn't be coming home.

As I grabbed my kit bag and headed into the barracks for my last night in the UK for a long time, it was daunting to think this could be the last time I ever saw her.

CHAPTER 11

THE SHOCK OF CAPTURE

"They defended the grains of sand in the desert to the last drop of their blood"
– Gamal Abdel Nasser

THIS is far worse than I ever imagined. A toxic blend of cheap fags, melted plastic and an undertone of human excrement fills the air, searing the back of my throat with each breath. A guided tour of our camp takes a minute or two, as the place is so small.

This was Observation Post Dara, my new home for the next six-and-a-half months. Nearly 30 of us are rammed into a space no bigger than a five-a-side football pitch. Once I ditch my bergen and daysack, I wander like a mute, shell shock victim through the camp.

After entering through the ramshackle gate under the eyes of a watchful sangar, I first walk into the 'dining area' which amounts to two tables and some benches underneath a roof of wriggly tin, or corrugated iron to civvies. Just a few feet away, lies the kitchen which is an ancient field stove, covered in a crusty shell of ancient grease. One of our first tasks is to refurbish the kitchen. Pots are scrubbed, surfaces wiped clean and Scotland flags are carefully draped from the servery area.

My eyes again feel like I have rubbed Tabasco in them, due to a combination of tiredness and squinting through the overpowering sunlight.

Surveying the ground, I notice that millions of small stones have been spread across every inch of sand, presumably to deter insects and keep plumes of dust sweeping over the camp every time anyone walks about. A row of decrepit, blackened diesel generators create a deafening roar and a smog of fumes as I walk up a small path, leading from the front part of the camp to the rear sleeping area and the operations room, tucked away in an iso-container.

Outside a tent, which would be my home for the bulk of the tour, there is a makeshift gym. Rows of bulky dumb-bells, barbells and kettlebells sit in rows next to a plywood platform with a weights bench. Three cycling machines and a rowing machine, sat in the shadow of the main guard tower, otherwise known as Sangar One.

A few feet away is the ops room with all the communica-tions gear, maps festooned across the metal walls. This place is in constant contact with the sangars, the eyes and ears of Op Dara. It's also Queeny's lair.

Machine guns are dotted around the tops of the walls

made of Hesco, large wire and hessian baskets that are filled out with tonnes of sand and rock. Hesco has replaced sandbags as the fortification of choice for modern armies. There is still plenty of mileage in the old fashioned sandbag though as I will soon find out.

There is no running water. We have shower bags, large plastic sacks attached to an overhead nail, with a nozzle that emits a sprinkle of lukewarm water. There are a few aluminium bowls to use for brushing our teeth or a quick wash. An old, cracked car wing mirror, so thick with grime it's hard to see your reflection, stands on a table in the washing area for shaving. Privacy is out of the question.

A length of rusty, wriggly tin connected to an old plastic pipe in the wall is our urinal. A wooden booth is our toilet. Inside, a bench has a hole cut in it with a toilet seat. We place a sani-bag, a silver foil sack, over the seat, with the bag unfurled below to catch our waste. These 'shit bags' are then taken out to the burns pit each day. A lucky chap then has the honour of pouring diesel on the pungent poo parcels before igniting them. Our lives will come to revolve around bags: we sleep in them, eat from them and now, we even defecate in them. A lance corporal, who is strolling around with us, sums up the mood: "Ach, what a total shite hole of a place, man!"

Even a seemingly innocuous trip to the burns pit, a large metal brazier where all the camp's rubbish is destroyed, is fraught with potential danger. Just days before we arrived, a soldier at a nearby base had his legs blown off by an IED on his way to the burns pit. Taliban fighters had noticed that soldiers followed the same path each day. They had bided their time, planting a booby-trap bomb that had almost killed this unsuspecting soldier.

Dara is perched on a rocky outcrop, midway between the Green Zone, the fertile area around the Helmand river and Route 611, one of the only paved highways in Afghanistan. In military terms, we are here to provide 'overwatch' and 'force protection' for Route 611 and our much bigger neighbour, Forward Operating Base (Fob) Ouellette, which lies to our rear.

Dubbed the Valley of Death, the road runs through the Upper Gereshk valley linking Gereshk to Sangin. Taliban checkpoints were once strewn across this area where locals were taxed for money and items bought at a local bazaar. Taxation became so serious that the local economy was affected, causing prices of goods to soar. Burnt out shells of cars and lorries, some of which have been sown with IEDs, litter the route, the nation's main north-south road.

Dara is the most remote British base in Afghanistan, and it feels it. Everything – water, rations, mail – must be flown into Ouellette before being brought out to our fragile foothold in heavily-armed convoys. These patrols are our only lifeline to the outside world.

We have five luxuries: a dilapidated fridge, Wifi, a welfare phone which is limited to 30 minutes a week, a dusty TV and a Playstation 3 that has seen better days. A large bunker, with four-feet thick Hesco walls and a roof which is supposed to be able to withstand nine direct hits, serves as our TV room. We have to run in here if we come under rocket or mortar attack. I would come to know every inch of this claustrophobic den in the next few months.

We arrived at Dara after a week or so at Camp Bastion to get acclimatised and complete our final training. This Reception, Staging and Onward Integration (RSOI) training had become a running joke among us. Each time we raised questions, about when we would be fully trained with Vallon metal detectors to find IEDs or when we would get our hands on a specific weapon, the answer would come back: "Don't worry about it, you will get it on RSOI." RSOI had become a panacea for any worries we had about our training. It seemed a bit late in the day to be cramming so much into a week's worth of training.

This reception phase at Bastion is compulsory for all soldiers entering Afghanistan. It is the last chance for troops to hone their skills in the conditions they will face out on the ground. One of the main aims is to get men and women used to the extreme temperatures of Helmand. We were drinking as much as eight litres of water a day and were taught to look out for signs of dehydration among our comrades. With acclimatisation very much in mind, we completed a number of speed marches in full body armour and patrol kit.

RSOI was an eye-opener, although it didn't ease all my concerns about the training. It was comprehensive, covering everything from escaping from an overturned Mastiff armoured vehicle in a massive simulator to carrying out a fingertip search on a Taliban suspect. I never, however, got to feel comfortable using the Vallon. I was also never properly trained on the General Purpose Machine Gun,

(GPMG), or 'Gimpy', one of the main weapons in the British Army and ubiquitous in Afghanistan.

An Afghan National Army officer, who looked like a swarthy Hagrid from the Harry Potter movies, took us for the most interesting lessons on cultural awareness and Afghan history. He talked of Afghan history, manners and customs in a booming voice. He told us about Afghan customs, what to do and what not to do. Do shake hands with your right hand, never the left, as that's used to clean your backside. Never ask an Afghan man about his female relatives. Even a good natured inquiry about the health of his wife or sister is a major no-no. I also discovered the significance of the Afghan flag's colours – black for the darkness of the nation's history, red for the bloodshed the people had suffered and green for the bright, fruitful future of the Afghan people.

It had been hammered home to every rank, from private to colonel, from day one, that everything had to "have an Afghan face on it". We were here as facilitators, not as invaders. We were here to allow the Afghan National Security Forces (ANSF) to eventually take over and run the country once the allied withdrawal started in earnest.

En route to Dara, we had flown into Fob Ouellette by Chinook. We were given another informative briefing minute on local "atmospherics and the pattern of life", the military euphemism for the prevailing social, economic and cultural conditions in our new home. If we were in any doubt that this was a bad area, a sergeant major matter-of-factly tells us that the three major conurbations facing OP Dara are called Taliban Town 1, Taliban Town 2 and

Taliban Town 3.

We didn't stay long at Ouellette. After the briefing we had a hot shower, our last for a long time, then went to sleep on some rickety camp beds. It was an uneventful but freezing night. A chill air forced me to get up, don my trusty head torch and put my trousers and hoody on as my body jerked and shivered with the cold. An advance party had already headed out on the rocky road to OP Dara to take over from the Scots Guards who were due to head home to the UK.

Now, as I sit on a shaky bench in Dara's al fresco 'dining area', I can't help thinking how my life has transformed. A few months ago, I was a white-collar professional who, among other things, went on all-expenses-paid press trips to some of the most glamorous locations in the world to review hotels and write travel features, from the QE2 to the Waldorf Astoria hotel in New York and the famous Guggenheim Museum in Bilbao.

A constant drone from the generators which power the communications, television and fridge, assails my thoughts. Flies buzz around my ears while ants try to crawl up my leg. A sense of gloom, which is more than just normal homesickness, begins to kick in.

Most of my fellow soldiers are from the west of Scotland although there are some guys from Fiji, Mauritius and St Lucia. Within minutes of our arrival, the race was on to make the place into our own version of 'Little Scotland'. Celtic, Rangers, St Mirren and Scotland flags and banners appeared as if from nowhere and were draped across every available inch of space. This will be an all-male environment, the nearest women will be roughly a mile-and-a-half away. We don't have a medic on site and we won't have a chef; instead, we will have to cook for ourselves.

It will be like running a home. Queeny is the unit commander, the daddy, and we work under his direction. Gary Carling, who is sitting across from me, barechested despite the white hot midday sun, lights up his twelfth fag of the day. Shaking his head, he says: "Sorry to piss on yer parade but you are on sentry duty in less than an hour." I have still got to unpack my black kit bag and bergen before trying to make my bedspace habitable.

A bubble of despair wells up from the base of my spine before blooming across my chest, gripping me like a vice.

CHAPTER 12

THE ONE THAT GOT AWAY

"It is vain for the coward to flee. Death follows close behind. It is only by defying it that the brave escape"
– Voltaire

A HIGH-ranking Taliban leader is our Scarlet Pimpernel. He is everywhere and nowhere at the same time. We huddle together at night, illuminated by the glow of a shared fag, talking about him in hushed tones. No-one even knows what he looks like.

Apart from our manic, collective obsession with this faceless Taliban guru, our lives quickly become routine, humdrum, pre-occupied with cleaning our weapons, our clothes and ourselves in that order.

We are sitting around one morning eating porridge with

the consistency of glue, discussing why we haven't been given a full physical description of what the Army calls a High Value Target. All we know is his codename: 'Objective Run Amok'.

Our hunt for Run Amok and his minions carries on 24 hours a day, occupying our every waking minute as we slog through hour after hour of 'overwatch', staring into the Green Zone, the poppy fields and the encroaching desert which nips at their borders.

Gary is holding court. He is a wind-up merchant, usually breaking into a wide grin that forms deep dimples in his cheeks, as he slates another soldier's feeble cooking attempts or boasts of winning the 'yummy daddy' contest at his boys' nursery. As the days go by, his jokes seem to dwindle. "What's the point of being here?" he asks no-one in particular. "They won't even tell us what this Run Amok looks like! He could be walking about out there wi' us watching him every day and we wouldny even know."

"IDF!!! IDF!!!" a piercing cry from the sangar, just a few feet from where we are eating. We drop our spoons, grab our body armour and helmets and sprint towards the safety of the bunker-cum TV room. IDF stands for Indirect Fire. In this case, it was a mortar attack or a rocket fired at us. This is one of the biggest threats to us, a mortar round landing in this camp could possibly kill or maim half-a-dozen men.

Every soldier, apart from the guys in the sangars, crams into this bunker to take shelter from the mortar currently looping through the air in our direction. Sometimes we hear the metallic crump of the projectile landing, sometimes we don't. After a stifling 15 minutes in the bunker, fighting the urge to slump onto a neighbour's shoulder for a nap, we get the shout of: "All clear!" We duly troop back out to finish our cold porridge.

Life here in the killing fields of Afghanistan is 95 percent mind-numbing boredom and five percent heart-stopping terror. Another deadly mortar round flies over my head – landing a few hundred metres from my position as I come to this startling revelation. This mortar attack rips apart the sleepy mid-afternoon peace as off-duty soldiers doze in the slowly fading sunshine, hand wash their trousers and shirts in small metal basins or lie around in the shade watching the latest instalment of *Prison Break.*

A distant metallic crunch signals that bad news is on its way. I am on sentry duty, scanning the Green Zone for signs of Run Amok and his minions, when the Taliban mortar team opens up. A bang and a plume of white smoke blooms over a compound to our front. The first bang was the sound of the mortar being launched. The white smoke is a tell-tale sign of the firing point. I hold my breath and duck lower behind the walls of the main guard tower, the high explosive round taking seconds to arc through the air towards us.

After screaming the warning "IDF!" we sit hunched over like a defendant awaiting his verdict. Just an hour before, I had been engrossed in the more mundane tasks of munching a Pot Noodle and writing a letter home. Now, everyone in the camp is looking at the very real possibility of death or serious injury. Thankfully, this is a near miss, not the first and not the last of the tour. Soldiers at Ouellette are not always so lucky – several soldiers there are injured in these kind of mortar attacks.

A Groundhog Day feeling, with long bouts of boredom punctuated by these moments of visceral fear, comes to be the hallmark of this tour. Our isolated post feels like the Alamo, a British rock in a Taliban sea. From the watchtowers, you can see the occasional white Taliban flag fluttering from a crumbling compound, a stark reminder that the enemy is never far away.

As I stare out into the landscape, I am always struck by the sharp contrast of the countryside. There is no gradual change in terrain from desert to lush Green Zone. The fields of poppies and plants end sharply, then it's all desert. This area is the Taliban's breadbasket, fields of poppies here will be harvested to provide opium which will be turned into heroin that will end up on the streets of London, Manchester, Glasgow and Liverpool. All of the proceeds will help fund the Taliban.

I feel queasy, like standing on the edge of a deep precipice, when I think how exposed this camp is. The nearest back up is more than a mile away. Dara resembles a tiny fort made of Hesco sitting facing hostile territory. We are warned that hundreds of extra Taliban fighters have been brought in from the infamous districts of Sangin and Gereshk to take part in this, the last fighting season of the last British combat tour. I visualise hordes of them sitting, sharpening bayonets on the granite hard walls of compounds, priming suicide vests, waiting for a chance to pay us a visit.

Then, we spot Run Amok. Or, to be precise, Paddy

Burns sees him. Paddy is a twenty-something fusilier with a head shaped like one of the Easter Island statues or a 50 pence coin, depending on who you ask. He is known as 'Fat Burns' back at barracks, but a combination of desert heat, Army rations and hours in the gym is chiselling away at his physique. It seems that every day, he loses more weight.

Burns, staring out into the wilderness when he is on 'stag', aka sentry duty, sees something unfamiliar in a compound off to his left. A fighting age male is carrying a long barrelled rifle, known in this game as a 'prestige weapon system', a hallmark of a high-ranking insurgent. Intelligence briefings have informed us that Run Amok likes to wear a digital camouflage vest while carrying an M16 rifle or something similar. Could this be him?

Grabbing the binoculars, Burns can feel his blood pumping in his neck. He hones in on the bearded man moving around in a compound a few hundreds metres from our razor wire perimeter. He pulls his machine gun up into the shoulder, ready to take a shot, using a scope to keep an eye on him.

He tries to get word to Queeny in the ops room, should he fire, killing possibly one of the biggest threats to our safety, a Taliban fixer who doubtlessly orchestrates the attacks on our outpost? He hesitates, confused. He, like every one of us, has been briefed to death on our so-called Rules Of Engagement. These restrictive rules dictate when we can or, crucially, cannot kill the enemy. Every soldier has to be a potential lawyer, weighing up when to pull the trigger, making split-second decisions under extreme stress that could end someone's life or see him put behind bars.

Under these rules, a Taliban fighter can fire at us, drop his weapon then start walking away in the opposite direction. We can do nothing but watch. In this scenario, if it's not Burns' 'honestly held belief' that his life or his comrades' lives are in immediate danger, he must impotently watch as the enemy strolls away. These rules kicked in as President Obama's troop surge began in 2009. They were designed to placate Afghan President Hamid Karzai, who was responding to local elders' justified outrage over the deaths of civilians from NATO air strikes and ground operations.

A legal case in 2013 highlights the life or death decisions that are routinely made on the frontline in Afghanistan. Royal Marine Alexander Blackman was sentenced to life in prison for murdering an insurgent in Afghanistan. Blackman, age 39, from Taunton, Somerset, will spend at least 10 years in prison.

The judge and board at the court martial heard how Blackman's promising career had been shattered in a "momentary" lapse of judgement. His high-profile trial, during which Blackman was referred to as Marine A, was the first time a member of the British armed forces had faced a murder charge in Afghanistan. Two other marines were cleared.

Back at Dara, no-one wants the blood of innocent civilians on their conscience. Troops, however, feel this kind of bureaucratic double-think is costing them dear. Many of my Dara muckers feel they are trying to fight a war with one arm tied behind their backs. Each Taliban fighter that's allowed to escape is one more terrorist free to attack us, to fight another day, to plant homemade bombs. An American general sums up the thoughts of the soldiers at Dara: "We handcuffed our troops in combat needlessly. This was very harmful to our men and has never been done in combat operations that I know of."

Burns doesn't take the shot. A sound like the sky ripping apart heralds the arrival of a US Black Hawk helicopter. Heavily-armed troops, rumoured to be US Navy Seals, lean out of the side doors, weapons poised, scouring the ochre landscape for any sign of Burns' man. They never find him. As Burns trudges into the ops room, looking like he is about to burst into tears, Queeny, fag hanging out the side of his mouth, gives his verdict: "Ach, see you! How did ye no' take a shot? Yer a fuckin' pussy!"

According to my limited military experience, Burns makes a good call, he is right not to take a shot. Is it Run Amok? The camp is divided on the subject, but if nothing else it gives us a new topic of conversation as we enjoy an evening meal of spam fritter curry.

We never find out what happens to Run Amok. Our camp motto is: "We are like mushrooms, kept in the dark and fed shit." For all we know, he is still out there now.

CHAPTER 13

SURVIVING

"Night comes to the desert all at once, as if someone turned off the light"
– Joyce Carol Oates

IT feels like the end of the world. A massive Biblical sand-storm sweeps towards us, like a sudden tidal wave of sand, ready to wipe us off the map. The tawny clouds billow more than 100 feet into the sky, blotting out the midday sun. As the surging, writhing mass swarms towards Dara at an alarming pace, I keep thinking of the desert scenes in the horror action movie *The Mummy*.

Not only do we have to contend with the Taliban, we also have to engage in a daily fight against the elements. Sand invades our ears, nostrils, eyes, socks and boots. It turns my feet into what looks like raw hamburger. My first letter home demands a steady supply of blister plasters. This huge blast of powdery fine sand turns the air red before completely blocking the sun, cutting visibility to zero. Day becomes night in a few seconds.

At first, this freak of nature is a laugh but it quickly becomes clear that the Taliban might use the sandstorm to overrun us. We scramble into defensive positions as the wind whips the choking clouds into our eyes. I grab a rag to cover my mouth, trying not to choke on the particles. Gary isn't as quick to cover up. As he shouts instructions, his teeth have been turned browny black by a mouthful of sand.

I run up a pile of sandbags and the remains of a Hesco barrier to look over the perimeter wall. Peering into the dust clouds, I'm barely able to see a few foot in front of the razor wire, our fragile last line of defence. Minutes or possibly hours creep by, but the storm refuses to die down. Radio intercepts, known as 'Icom chatter', picks up the Taliban talking about using the storm as cover to overrun a small camp. As it turns out, the small camp that they are talking about is ours.

Is this for real, or is it a diversion? No-one really knows. However, the Taliban are no fools, they know we can pick up on their radio communications. Sometimes they use it to their advantage, to spread propaganda or misinformation to put us off the scent of what they are really up to.

My hands begin to tremble and ache. It dawns on me that I am gripping my rifle so tightly that the circulation is being cut off. My knuckles are white as dry bone as a 'terp runs around throwing bottles of water to us as we perch over the

Hesco, facing out in all directions.

My mind wanders as the time drags past. I imagine this must have been similar to what World War One felt like: crouching or standing in a 'stand to' position, waiting for the Germans to come scrambling at you through the barbed wire. Short for 'Stand-to-Arms', the process of 'stand to' was observed every morning and evening by both sides of the war in the trenches, especially on the Western Front.

Each man was expected to stand on the trench fire step, rifle loaded, bayonet fixed. Most enemy attacks were mounted either before dawn or shortly after dusk under cover of darkness. German and British commanders took great care to make sure troops were alert at these dangerous times. Little has changed.

Once the storm eventually blows past, the threat of being overrun quickly subsides and we are stood down. As we dust off our weapons, we swap stories about how sand got into the most unexpected bodily nooks. As suddenly as the storm hit, the camp returns to normality. Some soldiers head to the kitchen to start preparing dinner while others change into shorts and t-shirt to hit the makeshift gym.

We start off the tour with nearly 30 soldiers but this drops as the weeks go by, with injuries, people getting sick from diarrhoea and vomiting or going on rest and recuperation. I was nearly taken out by diarrhoea and vomiting, or D and V as we call it, in the first few weeks at Dara. Our austere living conditions mean that we are fighting a constant battle to stay fit and well. Bottles of sanitising hand gel are all over the place, while a bowl and jerry can of water sit near the

wooden toilet cubicle, aka the Thunderbox, where we duti-
fully fill our sani-bags.

After three hours on stag, it's my tent's turn to cook and
clean. It's just gone 7am as I empty the bulging crap bags
into a black bin liner before heading out to the burns pit to
douse them in diesel before setting them alight. The smell is
overpowering. I start feeling light-headed but it could be the
foul smells or my desperate, overpowering need for sleep.
Corporal Teru, a rugby-mad Fijian who towers over me, is
directing our efforts to make breakfast.

Sweat forms on my brow as the temperature starts to
rocket as the day wears on. Our creaking gas stove blasts
away, adding to my comfort as I try to shell and prepare
dozens of eggs for an omelette. My stomach is in turmoil,
bubbling away, causing me to grab a sani-bag at what seems
like two-minute intervals. Teru roars: "Hey shitey!" as I
run off again. An hour of this is taking its toll. Each trip is
followed by a round of hand washing and sanitiser gel.

I definitely have diarrhoea but no vomiting. Gary takes
one look at me in the kitchen, before asking: "You alright?"
Colour has totally drained from my face and I feel distinctly
faint. Teru spies me and sends me to my bed space for a lie
down. I toss and turn for hours, half sleeping, half awake. I
need to get better though because Queeny has told us that
anyone with D and V gets sent back to Ouellette to recuper-
ate. There's no way I want to go there, it's too much hassle,
too many officers, too many rules. I'm going to do my best
to stay put at Dara.

It's the one and only time I am ill at Dara although my

stomach is ropey from time to time. Anti-diarrhoeal tablets bulge from my kitbag. Later, I find out that Queeny was hours away from punting me out of Dara. Luckily, I perked up just in time.

Severe stomach cramps, rations, warm water and the sanitation reduce each of us to infants when it comes to toilet habits. One day that I will rather forget sees me losing any semblance of dignity. I am alone in a sangar on guard duty when my stomach liquefies, spasming, threatening to empty its contents right here, right now.

Our two sangars are fortified sentinels that peer outwards, never sleeping. They must be manned 24 hours a day. As the months wear on, we do three hours on stag followed by four hours off throughout the day and night. To leave your post when on stag is a total no no. In days gone by, you could be shot for deserting your post. If I leave my sangar now, a horde of Taliban fanatics could sneak up to the camp and take us all out. Sleeping on stag or leaving your post, is the ultimate soldiering taboo.

So, I am trapped here with the desperate, mounting urgent need to evacuate my bowels. It feel like my insides are clenching then loosening in clammy waves. Do I break the ultimate taboo, bolting for the refuge of our wooden cubicle, clutching a sani-bag? The possible consequences of deserting my post are unthinkable. I could use the radio to ask someone to come and relieve me but that will take way too long. Squinting into the afternoon sunshine, through my yellow-tinted ballistic glasses, I scan around the sangar for a receptacle to dump my guts.

I am reduced to grabbing a black bin bag, full of empty water bottles. Crouching down, steering my backside over the bag, I make sure I can't be seen. As the explosive diarrhoea kicks in, firing a slurry of brown liquid into the bag, my stomach groans. A feeling of blissful relief washes over me. I tie up the neck of the bin bag, sticking it at the entrance to the sangar. A fistful of hankies serves as toilet paper. After a couple of hours, another soldier turns up to relieve me. I make sure I furtively grab the bulging bin bag on my way out, making a quick detour to the burns pit.

My stomach cramps cease, giving me time to muse over my surroundings. Our wee camp is like the United Nations. We have Scots, obviously, English, Fijians, Mauritians, St Lucians, Zambians. We all get on fairly well, most of the time. If Queeny is the camp's daddy, big Teru is the camp big brother. He is hard to ignore: he speaks in a Fijian lilt fused with a Scottish accent, chatting away in his native language with his countrymen before dropping in the occasional "bawbag" or "belter". A fearsome reputation follows him around him like a shadow. He grabbed a soldier by the shirt collar and 'ragdolled' him around the gym at Glencorse on the day we left for Afghanistan over a perceived slight.

He apparently likes me but he shows it in the same way as a child. A punch on the arm as I walk past, a bit of sparring. Since he is a 6ft 5ins, 20-stone rugby-playing machine, these encounters leave me literally battered and bruised. He is quick to lose his temper which, in these conditions, is a worry. An English soldier, who is attached to us for a short time, jokingly asks Teru if he has been eating all the rations after we are told supplies are running low. Teru, brow creased in a complete rage, follows the soldier into the TV room. He is narrowly talked out of bouncing him off the walls.

He is also deeply religious, ending every night reading the bible by the light of his head torch. He's also a bit of a prankster. I have lost count of the times I find large stones or other rubbish tucked under my pillow or folded into the bottom of my sleeping bag. He chortles like a schoolboy every time I find his 'wee presents'.

Other camp personalities include Mr Motivator aka Brian McAllan, so-called because of his love of bossing people about in the gym. Brian's Army career is turbulent, to say the least. He's a capable soldier who's well into his thirties so he could, at least, be a sergeant by now. He has, however, been busted down the ranks more than once. The story goes that he went out on the lash to watch a football game, got hammered, then neglected to turn up at work the next day as his unit was heading out to Iraq. He is now a mere lance corporal, one rank above me.

Garry John Urie, who developed our machine gun skills back at Glencorse, is here. He is the unofficial camp barber, ready to grab the electric clippers and dish out a haircut at a moment's notice. He never seems to get down, he's always full of what we Scots call "the patter", the banter, the chat. He is also a massive Paolo Nutini fan, going to the extreme of getting his song lyrics tattooed on his forearms. He belts out *Candy* and *New Shoes* at every available opportunity. Importantly, he also turns out to be a good cook.

SURVIVING

Peter comes from the sun-kissed island of St Lucia. He uses Scottish slang, calling everyone large or small "big man", with a Caribbean accent. He has been on tour before, apparently having a few close calls. In one firefight, he crouched behind a bush, listening to the rounds snapping through the branches, inches over his head. As he plays chess, with a toothpick dangling from his mouth every night, he looks unflappable. He's a good guy to have around.

Fellow campmate Davie McCabe, from a former ship-building town, just outside Glasgow, loves his football. He even has the Celtic FC crest tattooed on his arm to prove it. He must be in his mid-twenties, his chestnut brown is starting slowly to retreat from his scalp. His high-pitched, giggly laugh is infectious. After a while, I go out of my way to get him laughing when we are in the sangars. An angry-looking, puckered scar from a stab wound on his back is a shadow, perhaps, of a darker time in his life.

Essoo is another Commonwealth soldier, an adopted 'Jock'. Hailing from Mauritius, but of Indian descent, he is built like a whippet. Knots of muscles on his legs criss-crossed with veins testify to his passion for running. The camp is too small for a proper running track but this doesn't stop him. Even in the peak of the midday heat, he dons his shorts, trainers and body armour to trot between the two sangars, completing hundreds of laps. I am amazed to discover that he's well into his thirties, having served with the marines in his native country. He is getting so thin it looks as though his legs may break on the rubbly path.

I'm amazed that such a diverse group of people gets on

so well in such trying circumstances. Up the road at Ouel-lette, they aren't as lucky. A brawl breaks out between a black soldier and his white comrade over allegedly racially abusive comments. Details are pretty vague but something must have happened. Within days, Zambian Joe is sent down to us at Dara to keep him away from the soldier he fell out with. Some weeks later, Joe goes up to Ouellette while his nemesis – a sniper called Regi – comes down to work with us.

This tour is the beginning of the end. The drawdown, which will see all British troops out of Afghanistan by the end of 2014, starts here with us. Government ministers have also announced that reservists will be the backbone of the British Army from now on. For these reasons, Defence Secretary Philip Hammond is paying a visit to our area – and he wants to meet Gary Carling and I.

After coming off another three-hour stint of stag, we spend our downtime cleaning weapons, cleaning ourselves, hand washing socks and underpants, cooking, cleaning and gener-ally taking care of the camp. Queeny leans out of the ops room: "Haw, youse two stabs! Get yer kit, yer going to Ouel-lette tae meet a feckin' VIP."

I tighten the slack on my belt, pulling my trousers in tighter. They keep threatening to fall down as the days creep by. Sleep deprivation is a major problem for me. After just a few hours of snatched sleep, I still feel totally drained. I should feel excited about a break from the routine, getting a chance to meet a top politician, getting away from this cramped camp. However, I am too tired to really care.

SURVIVING

Heat and the terrain are starting to take their toll on everyone. Fastening my ballistic underpants, designed to protect a soldier's pelvis and family jewels in a bomb blast, we get ready to leave along the rocky trail to Ouellette. A convoy of Mastiff armoured vehicles will pick us up, shuttling us to meet our VIP. A water bottle and my rifle are never more than a foot away from me at any time. We are constantly told to drink up to 10 litres of water a day to combat the real threat of dehydration. Temperatures are in the high 40s.

Clambering from the back of the Mastiff after a bumpy ride from Dara, I feel like I'm drowning in a monsoon of sweat under this carapace of body armour and helmet that weighs more than 20kgs. No matter how much water you take on board, you still feel thirsty. I lose more than two stones in weight as I count the days to my eagerly anticipated R&R, or I&I for 'Intercourse and Intoxication' as it is dubbed by the troops.

Hours tick by. We are told to wear headdress, rolled up sleeves, clean-ish combat trousers. All done to impress our guest. More than four hours after we arrive at Ouellette, Gary is smoking his fifteenth cigarette of the day as I sip the first cold can of juice that I have consumed in a month. We are sitting in the shade of a shelter knocked together from bits of plywood flung up between two ISO Containers. A company sergeant major sticks his head around the corner, prompting us both to sit bolt upright. "Stand easy, boys" he says. "Mr Hammond isny comin'. Ah'll sort oot yer transport back to Dara."

It turns out that there were security concerns over his visit.

He flew in aboard a chopper but as there was no Apache gunship to watch the surrounding landscape, his security team apparently thought it was unsafe. We came here for nothing. If I wasn't so tired, I would be furious that we came here, driving over ground that's notorious for being laced with IEDs, for a visit that never takes place. Lives are put at risk for nothing.

We grab our rifles and daysacks, trudging through sand with the powdery, fine consistency of snow. I see Bobby as we walk up to the vehicle park where we will grab a Mastiff to take us back out to Dara.

He towers over his pals, who amble along beside him. Spotting a free Portaloo next to a Hesco wall, he dashes over. I pause, wondering if I should wait for him to come out to say hello and see how he is getting on. 'Nah. I'll pass through here again soon enough, no doubt. When I have got more time I'll give him a shout then', I think.

It is the last time I ever see him.

CHAPTER 14

NEVER FORGET

"It is said that time heals all wounds. I do not agree. The wounds remain. In time, the mind, protecting its sanity, covers them with scar tissue and the pain lessens. But it is never gone"
– Rose Kennedy

MY knees turn to water, ready to pitch me face first on to the wooden planks on the floor of the sangar. Just a few hours ago, only a mile or two from my position, a huge roadside bomb rips through an armoured vehicle killing my pal Bobby and two of his comrades. Brian McAllan is at the foot of steps leading up to the sangar, shouting up the news. He stumbles over Bobby's surname. "The third guy is called Bobby Harrington, or Herrington. It's just came over the net from Ouellette," he says. "Was his surname Hethering-ton?" "There was a Bobby Hetherington up there. He was a reservist like me," I choke, unable to comprehend what seems to be happening.

My mouth is bone dry, even though I have already drank four litres of water since I came on duty. This is the visceral, gut-wrenching news that every soldier dreads. The fact that Bobby, like me, is only attached to 2 SCOTS for this tour, would explain the doubt over his surname. We are new faces at this battalion so maybe that's why people don't know his name. A glimmer of hope hits me, like a ray of sunshine through grey clouds. *Maybe it's not him? Perhaps there is another guy with a similar name? It's all been a mistake?*

I know I am kidding myself, trying to escape the horrible reality. Bobby will not be going home. It feels like I have been punched in the stomach. I can't even sit down, I have to stand staring out into the desert, the Green Zone, the Taliban graveyard just a few hundred metres away. This entire situation feels surreal and overwhelming. My jobs as a *Daily Record* reporter and a reservist make me fully aware of the dangers of this country. As both a reporter and a soldier, I am all too aware of the grim death toll in Afghanistan.

I have seen all the pictures of soldiers killed in action but I never, ever dreamed one of these tragic deaths would be so close to home. This had been a day like many before at our tiny outpost: sweaty, claustrophobic and routine. Earlier, I had felt like a medieval knight donning armour as I yet again got kitted up to go on duty.

This, however, turns out to be anything but a normal day. Bobby, Corporal William Savage and Fusilier Samuel Flint died when their Mastiff armoured vehicle hit an improvised explosive device on a routine patrol. Thinking back to my

Band of 'brers': Smiles break out as it's time for the sentry shifts to change over at Dara. Soldiers were on guard 24 hours a day – keeping an eye out for the Taliban. 'Brer' – Glaswegian slang for brother – was a common word at Dara; (below left) at the start of another bout of 'stag'

Desert views: (Above right) A sunblasted landscape taken from a vantage point at Dara. Other than Route 611, there were no real roads in the area. Desert merged suddenly with the Green Zone, creating a sharp contrast and a productive area for the Taliban; (above, bottom right) a view out toward Fob Ouellette. Note the coils of razor wire. As the tour wore on, children would grow bolder, trying to pull out the metal poles and wire with their bare hands

Flying the flag: Scotland flags were everywhere at Dara. This particular specimen was draped over the mosquito net above my bed for the entire tour

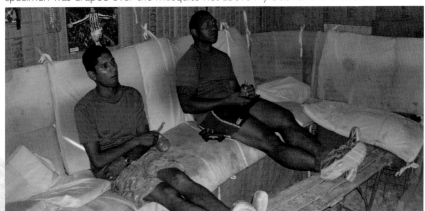

Chilling: The supposedly mortar-proof bunker at Dara doubled as the recreation room with a TV and Playstation. Fifa football tournaments could get fairly boisterous

Resting up: Taking a break after going to the gym

R&R: (Top) Enjoying a beer in Cyprus after being delayed for 24 hours on our way for Rest and Recuperation

Back at Dara: (Above) The camp in all its glory – looking like a Brazilian favela

Scoff's up!!! Cooking – as well as stag – was one of the main duties at Dara. Here I'm rustling up a mean Malaysian beef curry thanks to the sauce sachets sent from kind folk in the UK

Embrace the suck: 'Embracing the suck' – or stoically getting on with the job, could have been the camp motto

Run Amok: It became a running joke that one of the High Value Targets (HVTs) in the area – codename Run Amok – could have been walking past Dara's towers every day, so poor was the description of him; (below left) communications between different parts of the camp were not always up to scratch; (right) looking out towards a series of crumbling compounds – many of which, though dilapidated, were still lived in

Gym time: Working out helped keep fit and relieve the tensions of camp life; (above right) taking a seat, next to the sandbags which sprung up around the camp as the tour wore on and the IDF attacks continued

Sign of the times: A message that popped up in one of the sangars reads: "Help Me! Let's all go home and pretend this never happened"

The Great Pineapple Robbery: Something as innocuous as the disappearance of a tin of pineapples from a ration pack could cause a fight as people's tempers wore thin

Collapsing the camp: Breaking up the kitchen was one of the first tasks as Dara was demolished as part of the British withdrawal

Through the looking glass: Keeping a look out for the 'absence of the normal and the presence of the abnormal' was part of the camp routine; (below) manning a GMG – Grenade Machine Gun. Full personal protective equipment had to be worn when above the Hesco as the sniper threat was high

Final hours: On the last day at Dara as the camp is pulled down. Note the locals arriving in the background; (left) with Garry John getting a snap at Dara at a key moment in the British campaign – the beginning of the end of British involvement in Afghanistan

Kick it: Even in the camp's final hours, there was still time for a bit of messing about

End in sight: (Top) An ANCOP soldier watches as local people start to flock towards the camp as bulldozers move in to level Dara; (above) bulldozers and soldiers from the Royal Engineers make short work of the defences at Dara as the author and his unit stand guard

Dara days: Towards the end of the tour

visit to Ouellette, both of us laden with body armour and ammunition, I feel a shiver of regret that I did not wait to chat to him when he went into a Portaloo.

I stagger down from the sangar in a daze at the end of my shift. The atmosphere is muted, people seem to have been told that I knew Bobby well. I get the impression that I'm getting the kid gloves treatment. Teru and Gary Carling are pottering about in the kitchen, trying to go about their business as usual but everyone is thinking about the deaths and the horror that the families will endure. A knock on the door from an Army officer wielding an ID card could come at any time of the day or night. It heralds the life-shattering news that a son, brother, boyfriend is not coming back.

My mind is in turmoil, the whole situation feels surreal. How can this happen? I had seen him just days before. Later, we are given the full details of what happened. They were on a patrol in a Mastiff vehicle along Route 611 when they hit a massive IED. The blast throws up the back end of the vehicle, blowing off an axle, before crashing back to the ground. Intelligence reports suggest that more than 100kgs of fertiliser went into the bomb. Bobby, William Savage and Samuel Flint were sitting at the back of the wagon, bearing the brunt of the explosion.

As the reality of the horror sinks in, among the grief and shock, I start to feel a creeping sense of guilt. It could easily have been me in that vehicle. This naked self-interest shocks me. I should be thinking of my friend, his comrades, their families. Instead, I am plagued by a variety of conflicting emotions, including relief that I wasn't in the stricken

Mastiff. Everyone thinks like this but I feel shame for having such nakedly selfish thoughts at a time when others have just made the ultimate sacrifice.

Queeny is uncharacteristically serious when he sees me sitting outside my tent. He knows Bobby was a friend of mine so grabbing his fags and lighter, he ushers me to one side, away from the hustle and bustle of the camp, to have a chat. I tell him how I'm feeling: sad, tired, tormented by a bizarre sense of relief. He reassures me that it is normal to have what some call "survivor's guilt". The reality of the war in Afghanistan is that any one of us could have been in that blast. The truth is that there is no real frontline.

Our only solace lies in the fact that Bobby, Corporal Savage and Fusilier Flint died doing something they really wanted to do. I know, without a doubt, that Bobby was desperate to serve in Afghanistan. My Army career mirrored Bobby's in so many ways. At every step of my training and deployment, he had been there.

At dusk, a memorial is to be held for the three guys. Queeny asks me to read a bit from Psalm 23: "The Lord is my shepherd; I shall not want. He maketh me to lie down in green pastures: he leadeth me beside the still waters. He restoreth my soul: he leadeth me in the paths of righteousness for his name's sake. Yea, though I walk through the valley of the shadow of death, I will fear no evil: for thou art with me; thy rod and thy staff they comfort me. Thou preparest a table before me in the presence of mine enemies: thou anointest my head with oil; my cup runneth over. Surely goodness and mercy shall follow me all the days of my life: and I will dwell in the house of the Lord forever.''

He says I can talk about Bobby at the end of the memorial, paying tribute to him in my own words. I want to talk about how we bonded through our shared Army experiences, how we endured the dreaded 'gas chamber', how I wiped tears and snot from my face outside the chamber before collapsing in laughter as he emerged from the chamber coughing in a blur of mucus. We had so many bonding experiences and I am glad that I shared those laughs with him.

Night falls suddenly like a cloak over Dara. We put our head torches on, walking out to a space just within the front gate. Soldiers in the sangars stood silent, watching over us as we say a few words to mark our comrades' deaths. I think of Bobby's best mate and fellow reservist, Russ MacLean, who is out at Ouellette. He and Bobby were inseparable.

Unknown to me, Russ penned a tribute to Bobby which is hitting newspapers across the UK in an MOD press release confirming his death. It reads: 'I first met Bobby on a TA exercise in the south of France in the summer of 2009. I instantly bonded with him due to his infectious and riotous laugh, which made even my most feeble jokes seem to be stadium stand-up comedy.

'Following the exercise we became firm friends; outwith the TA, enjoying many legendary nights out as our bromance flourished. Like everyone he met, he endeared himself to my fiancée, Jen, and my daughter, Grace. He had an almost spellbinding captivation over small children who would go from shyness, hiding behind the sofa, to presenting various toys and long monologues about soft play and CBeebies.

Grace would always be delighted to hear that Bobby was coming over for a visit.

'Bobby, like myself, had a passion for infantry soldiering and pushing yourself to physical and mental limits. He certainly helped me get through demanding exercises with his constant stream of morale. He loved soldiering and was heartbroken when a hernia operation delayed his ambitions of becoming an officer at Sandhurst, which no doubt he would have completely excelled at.

'Bobby was my best friend. He was the life and soul of the party and one of the kindest and friendliest people I have ever met. He was always at the end of the phone or across the table at a pub if you had problems you needed to talk about. He was delighted to be an usher at my wedding after I told him I was getting engaged. When my pregnant fiancée had her scan last week and we found out it was a girl, Bobby was the first one I told and he was delighted.

'My heart truly goes out to his family, who will be as distraught as I am. He had a loving and caring family, along with his girlfriend, Maeve, and my thoughts are completely with them. Love you mate.'

In the same document, Major Stephen Dallard, who commanded Bobby's company, says: 'Private Hetherington immediately made an impression on me. Strong, fit and intelligent, he quickly grasped the complexities of pre-deployment training and demonstrated a real aptitude for soldiering. He became a key character, loved for his jokes, an infectious laugh and for his genuine and warm character. He willingly put his life in harm's way as his company supported the Afghan security forces. He truly touched the lives of all who got to know him; I have yet to meet a more perfect example of what the Army Reserve has to offer the wider Regular Army. A true friend to those serving with him, Private Hetherington will be sorely missed.'

At Dara, when it comes to my turn to talk about Bobby, I can't manage it. My voice breaks, faltering as I try to say a few words at the end of the impromptu memorial service. I just blurt out: "He was a great guy and he will be deeply missed", as Davie McCabe gives me a reassuring pat on the back. After the ceremony, I'm told that I will be able to go back to the relative safety of Camp Bastion to attend his repatriation service. There, the remains of the three men will be flown back to the UK. Next day, I am told that I won't be allowed to go. Another soldier from Bobby's company at Fob Ouellette will take my place.

In a way, I'm eventually relieved that I am not allowed to leave my post at Dara to go to the repatriation ceremony. I doubt I would have been able to hold myself together. The pace of operations here is relentless. Within minutes of the service, it is time for me to go back on duty again.

Walking up to the sangar for another three hours of watching the Green Zone and the deadly desert all around, I hear the haunting call to prayer from a nearby mosque as I think of Bobby's family. The notes of the muezzin's call echo across Dara, seeming to reverberate off the camp's walls.

It's haunting, sombre tone makes me think of life and loss. I remember losing my mum and dad as if it were yesterday. Now, families across the UK will have to cope with an unimaginable hole in their lives. I can't even begin to imagine what it must be like. This tour of duty and its aftermath will resound with them for the rest of their lives.

I take solace from knowing that Bobby, William Savage and Samuel Flint may have died but their names and memories will endure forever. Their comrades will guarantee that.

CHAPTER 15

FIGHTING SEASON

*"Ironically enough, the only people who can hold
up indefinitely under the stress of modern war
are psychotics. Individual insanity is immune to
the consequences of collective insanity"*
– Aldous Huxley

HIS screams are like a pickaxe to the brain. "Help me!
Somebody help me!" Until now, apart from the generators'
relentless droning, there had been total silence. Peering out
towards Route 611 as it shimmers in the midday heat, I
almost drop my rifle in panic, straining to see what is going
on behind me.

Paddy Burns is on fire. Flames explode up his arms, his face
is frozen in terror, flapping his arm around to put out the
flames. This only serves to fan the blaze. Bits of burnt skin
and shirt fly off as he waves his arm, screaming in agony. He
is out at the burns pit, under our watchful eyes in the sangar,

where he had been trying to ignite a few rubbish bags.

Ross Burton, a shaven-headed Glaswegian who has to stand on a block of wood to see over the sangar walls, knew this was going to happen. We both watched earlier as Paddy fiddled about with the jerry cans of petrol that sit in the shadow of our sangar. He filled an empty water bottle with the top cut off, full of petrol. We noticed this, with Ross warning him: "Hey, watch what you are doing. You are meant to use diesel to light the burns pit." Pressure in the jerrycan popped the lid off, squirting petrol up Paddy's shirt. "Careful, you are going to go up like a Roman candle," I tell him, leaning out of the sangar.

Our warnings fell on deaf ears. He held the water bottle, while lighting the petrol with a lighter. There's a boom as he is wreathed in flames. He runs round in jagged circles, eyes pleading for help. He then sprints down from the burns pit, towards the sangar before tearing into the kitchen and eating area. He has not stopped screaming once, not even pausing for breath.

His cries have now stirred the camp, with people gathering to see what's causing the commotion. Out of sight of us, Paddy is still running around, writhing in agony. Essoo, who had been busy washing his socks, dashes over, rugby tackles Paddy, slamming him to the ground so he can give him first aid.

Some well-intentioned soul grabs a jerrycan of water, throwing its contents over him to douse the flames. Unfortunately, the water has been sitting in the overpowering sun all day. Paddy howls, wrinkling and writhing like a worm in bleach as the scalding water hits his ravaged flesh. Eventually, they manage to stabilise him enough to dress his wounds. He is so seriously hurt that he is given morphine to ease his pain.

We stand about in the sangar, helpless, unable to leave our posts to give any assistance at all. At first, I thought it was a joke. 'Paddy up to his usual tricks', I think, trying to raise a laugh. As time passes, it is clear this is no joke. I hear them running about in the ops room, sending a 'nine liner', a request for an immediate medical evacuation by helicopter. Then I notice that Ross is doubled up with laughter.

I don't know if it's stress, sleep deprivation or an extreme reaction to our pressure-cooker environment and Paddy's accident but Ross is in fits of laughter. He is bent double, slapping his thighs, almost unable to speak. "What was that all about?" he manages to say. I start laughing too, it feels like a pressure valve. "Jesus Christ, do you think he's alright?" We can still hear him roaring, although his cries have died down a bit.

Minutes later, a couple of Mastiffs arrive at the front gate to take Paddy back to Ouellette. He is crying in great gulps and has to be half-dragged, half-carried into the back of the vehicle. His arm is held out to one side, wrapped in what looks like cling film.

An American 'Pedro' helicopter swoops in to Ouellette as another Black Hawk chopper patrols overhead, ready to pounce on any Taliban foolhardy enough to try to attack. These rescue helicopters are unsung heroes in Afghanistan, manned by elite paramedics. They boast two miniguns, capable of spewing out thousands of bullets a minute. They provide around-the-clock combat search and rescue and casualty evacuation here, ready to save the lives of stricken troops, Afghan soldiers and civilians. They are given the 'Pedro' call sign after a fleet of rescue helicopters that saved thousands of lives in Vietnam.

Later, we are told Paddy has suffered third-degree burns. He is being treated at Camp Bastion before being sent back to the UK. We won't see him again any time soon. His fate makes me think: there are so many ways to die or get seriously hurt in Afghanistan. We all know the risks. We could lose our lives to a sniper's bullet, or be blown up by the blast from a rocket-propelled grenade. However, Afghanistan, can also injure you in ways you never even imagined. Camp jokers immediately christen Paddy as 'Burns Pit Burns' in honour of his accident. It will be more than a year before he can return to work after treatment at the Defence Medical Rehabilitation Centre at Headley Court in Surrey.

Our numbers are dwindling. Another soldier, who I will call Jay, has vanished back to Ouellette, never to return. He earns the contempt of the whole camp for finding any excuse to be sent back to his pals at the bigger camp. An adopted Scot, originally from the north of England, this soldier is dogged by the most seemingly insignificant aches and pains. One day, he gets a boil on his leg so he wants to be sent back. After Queeny forces him to return, he gets a spot up his nose which he says needs the urgent medical attention of experts at Ouellette. He is also notorious for doing as little work as humanly possible, trying to drop to the back as soon as a vehicle patrol arrives with our supplies, which have to be lugged off the back of Mastiffs in excruciating daytime heat. Queeny, never one to mince his words, says he is "the worst soldier I have ever seen".

When Jay disappears for the final time, we are told to pack up his stuff to send it back to Ouellette. A group of soldiers, like a plague of locusts, descend on his gear. His clothes are tied into knots that will take hours to undo, strawberry jam is poured into his training shoes, any perishables such as melting bars of chocolate are dished out among the troops.

Fewer soldiers means more food for the rest of us but it also means less people to go on stag. Everyone left behind now has to spend more time sweating it out in the sangars. As a result, there's little sympathy when Jay's kit gets ravaged.

Within days, the camp is rocked by news from home. Thousands of miles away, in the middle of London, a soldier is hacked to death in broad daylight. We hear the news via the Internet and the TV news which we watch religiously, shaky signal permitting. Lee Rigby is murdered by Islamic terrorists as he walks back to barracks in Woolwich.

Jambo, one of the youngest soldiers at Dara, tells me about the horrific killing in London as he climbs up the metal ladder to join me in the main sangar. Local men, dressed in grey and black shalwar kameez that look like overgrown pyjamas, are heading towards one of the local mosques. They are shuffling along in the growing dusk as I watch. Strangled tones of the call to prayer reverberate from a battered old loudspeaker. We watch this pattern of life, day after day. No-one approaches us and we certainly don't approach them.

Jambo is normally upbeat, bubbly, boasting about his efforts to "smash the gym" to develop his budding six pack. Tonight, he looks pale and drawn. "Fuck sake, man, have you heard what happened? A soldier was walking along the street and two guys ran him over, stabbed him and tried to chop his heid aff!" It's hard for me to process the information, so surreal does it sound.

I feel sick. What the hell is going on at home in the UK? After my stag is over, I head into the ops room, clutching my tablet, to scour the Internet about the murder. It's all too true. I have to read the news reports several times. A grainy video shows people walking past as Lee lies in the street. One brave woman confronts his attackers as one of them rants and raves, while a witness films the horrific incident on their phone.

Clutching a bloody knife and a meat cleaver, the killer speaks: "The only reason we have killed this man today is because Muslims are dying daily by British soldiers. And this British soldier is one. It is an eye for an eye and a tooth for a tooth. By Allah, we swear by the almighty Allah we will never stop fighting you until you leave us alone. So what if we want to live by the Sharia in Muslim lands? Why does that mean you must follow us and chase us and call us extremists and kill us?

"Rather you lot are extreme. You are the ones that when you drop a bomb you think it hits one person? Or rather your bomb wipes out a whole family. This is the reality. By Allah if I saw your mother today with a buggy I would help her up the stairs. This is my nature. Through many passages in the Koran we must fight them as they fight us. An eye for an eye, a tooth for a tooth. I apologise that women had to witness this but in our lands women have to see the same.

"You people will never be safe. Remove your governments, they don't care about you. You think David Cameron is going to get caught in the street when we start busting our guns? You think politicians are going to die? No, it's going to be the average guy, like you and your children. So get rid of them. Tell them to bring our troops back so we can all live in peace. So leave our lands and we can all live in peace. That's all I have to say. Allah's peace and blessings be upon you."

His words haunt me. We came here to fight terrorism in its own backyard, to make sure Britain stayed safe. Yet terrorists now freely walk about in broad daylight in our country, killing our comrades. A few of us stay up talking about the murder into the small hours by headtorch. A shadow of doubt about this whole Afghan adventure passes over us. It's not a good feeling.

Books keep me sane. My Kindle eBook reader keeps my mind active, while daily sessions in the gym keep my body ticking over. Despite being surrounded by sand and bullets, I am engrossed by a novel called *Yellow Birds,* about the invasion of Iraq. John Bartle, a private soldier in the US Army, narrates the story which documents his friendship with fellow soldier, Murphy.

Author Kevin Powers was a soldier in Iraq for two years, serving in Mosul and Tal Afar, so he knows his stuff. He was also a poet, which shows through in the sheer quality and power of his writing. Reading makes the time pass by more quickly. I usually steal a prime spot underneath the metal framework of the main sangar, where someone has set up a threadbare hammock. The shade is bliss, as is the chance to get away from everyone else for an hour or two.

I devour another book called *Allah's Mountains* about the Chechen mujahideen, some of whom are rumoured to have come to Afghanistan to fight alongside their Taliban brothers in arms. These Chechens have a reputation for ruthlessness and are first-rate fighters as many of them were trained by Russian special forces.

I make the mistake of discussing my reading with Jambo one night as we slouch against the Hesco for sentry duty. He nearly chokes on his mouthful of Haribo as I tell him about these Chechens. "Jesus," he says. "I hope we dinnae see any of these bastards oot here or we are all for the high jump."

Life inside the camp's razor wire is dominated by the gym. No matter the time of day, or the temperature, someone is out there on the plywood platform banging out reps with the dumbbells or grinding out mile after mile on the cycle machine. Everyone seems oblivious to the old saying that "only mad dogs and Englishmen go out in the midday sun."

Queeny even devises challenges for us. Slightly pot-bellied with hunched over shoulders, he doesn't look the greatest physical specimen but he takes great delight in seeing us suffer. His dark brown eyes glint like a shark closing in for the kill, as he sits drawing up a chart. "Rrright, troops!" he announces. "This is a league table for the Dara Challenge, everyone has tae dae it. Nae exceptions!"

We each have to go as fast as possible on the rowing machine for two minutes, then we immediately trot over to the bike machine to go flat out there for another two minutes. The distance we cover on both machines is recorded by Queeny on his table. It sounds easy. How bad can it be? I watch several men buckle as they come off the bike, red faced and struggling to walk in a straight line. While Queeny goes looking for his fags, I dive down to the other side of the camp, looking for something, anything to do in the kitchen to keep out of the way.

My ploy doesn't work. "Haw Stewarty ya stab! Get back there and get your shot!" Queeny tells me as he peaks around the corner of the kitchen. Thrashing away on the rowing machine doesn't feel too bad but then the cycling kicks in and I am exhausted. My distance on both machines is logged and I get a respectable placing in the league table. Collapsing on a couple of sandbags, I gulp tepid water from a battered bottle, vowing "never again".

Queeny even has a go at recreating the TV game show *The Cube*. He takes on the role of Phillip Schofield, shepherding each person through each event. In the TV show, contestants have to complete deceptively easy-looking tasks in a glass cube for cash. In our version, we do it under the blazing sun to waste a few hours.

He re-creates some of the games from the show. In one event he uses an old bit of wire strung from the Hesco walls. We have to move a metal hoop around the wire without letting the hoop touch the wire. Contestants also have to step over barriers while blindfolded, and throw a ball over their head trying to get it into an old bucket. It's a big hit so Queeny say it will be a weekly event. However, after a few days and several mortar attacks at all hours, our initial interest fizzles out.

Outside the wire, the landscape is surprisingly lively. In parts of Helmand, the desert is known as Dasht-e Margo, the Desert of Death. This patch around us, though, is teeming with life. The main focus for locals is the mosque. Men throng there at prayer times, while women are conspicuously absent. One day, a massive bomb blast comes out of nowhere. We hear it but can't see any smoke or dust kicked up by the impact. It sounds like a J-Dam or Joint Direct Attack Munition, a bunker-buster bomb used by the Americans. It rocks our camp, rattling the fillings in my teeth but the men in their sombre, loose-fitting clothes barely look up as they stroll towards the mosque.

Watching this 'pattern of life' is our daily task. In Army jargon, we are looking for the 'absence of the normal and the presence of the abnormal'; anything out of the ordinary should be relayed up the chain of command. On an average day, boys who are too young to have started growing beards play a bastardised version of cricket. It seems to revolve around throwing rocks at your opponent's head as he flails around with a stick. They are close enough that we can see their shaved heads, grimy faces and the small pieces of glass dotted over their skullcaps, glinting in the unforgiving sun.

Their rough game is interrupted constantly by men riding ramshackle motorbikes and battered white Toyota Corollas. It seems that the roads of Afghanistan, if they can properly be called roads, are littered with old white Toyotas. Some enterprising Afghan must have bought a job lot of them in the eighties as they seem to be pretty much the only type of car on the road.

Unlike the media image of downtrodden Afghan women clad in burkas and walking slavishly behind their menfolk, the women here usually sport bright, almost garish, dresses. Their chiffon head scarves flutter in the wind, half hanging off their heads as they collect brushwood for their fires. Mirrored decorations on their Dayglo pink and yellow dresses glint like stars in the night sky. Puffy pyjama-style trousers round off their ensemble. Bling is definitely in here, in this corner of Helmand.

These women also do not take any nonsense. I watch a mother, who is in her twenties or thirties, punch a young boy for lobbing a stone in her general direction. Life is tough in Afghanistan – we notice a withered woman, who looks to be in her eighties but could be around 50. She is almost bent double with arthritis but is feared and loathed by the local kids. She seems to live alone, ready with a big stick to chase kids away if they stray too close to her compound.

Animal life is everywhere. Camels, donkeys and goats flood our field of view day and night. They scream, bray and roar, which is especially disconcerting on a night stag when you are alone, waiting for Terry Taliban to use the cover of night to creep up on your sangar. A desert fox prowls around our camp, trying to intimidate the feral ginger cat that has taken to raiding our kitchen in the early hours.

One morning, I wake up to find that a family of baby desert

rats have gnawed through the Hesco walls before setting up home in my clothes. A few babies, so new to the world that they are still blind, nestle in the hood of my smock. We scoop them into paper cups before, humanely, throwing them over the fence.

It's now the poppy harvest season so men walk bent over like a half-shut knife as they carry their burden of dried stalks and stems. Shepherd boys sit on their haunches watching as they lumber past.

Back inside the camp, we feel a growing sense of unease as the fighting season looms. Local Taliban fighters impose a curfew – all locals must be indoors by 9pm or they will be tied to a tree and shot. Streets and compounds look deserted well before the curfew kicks in. Obviously, the Taliban's word is law in these parts.

Once the harvest is brought in, the fighting season will start in earnest. A group of soldiers arrive one day from Ouellette to give us a rare intelligence briefing about what is happening in our area. A Taliban offensive, dubbed the 'Spring Demonstration', is about to start. This is the spectacular kick-off to the insurgents' fighting season.

Two new suicide bombers are now operating in the area, we are told. We have already experienced several mortar attacks but there will be more on the way. Taliban chiefs call this new operation 'Khalid bin Waleed' in honour of a seventh century Islamic general known as the 'Drawn Sword of God' and a companion of the prophet Muhammad. These guys certainly know their history.

Launching the offensive, the Taliban issue a typically

bombastic statement: 'We once again call on all the officials and workers of the stooge Karzai regime to break away from this decaying administration in order to conform to Islamic commands, national interests and protection of yourselves, and to choose a life of prosperity living alongside your own people in an atmosphere of peace and security.'

It's around this time that I am standing in the smaller of our two sangars when I hear a distant thud. Looking around, I then hear a bang and a cloud of smoke rising from what appears to be the centre of Ouellette. A mortar has found its target. At least two soldiers are wounded. I learn later that a soldier has his testes torn open by shrapnel, a wound that makes me wince at the thought of it.

At night, a small camp which sits a mile further into the Green Zone seems to be attracting attention from the Taliban hordes drafted in for the summer season. Red tracer rounds light up the night sky like a scene from *Star Wars*. Afghan forces based there fire randomly back into the dense foliage surrounding them. The dull metallic thud of machine guns and other heavy artillery seems to wax and wane like the tide. They get smashed night after night as we watch slack-jawed, thinking we could be next.

Taliban chiefs regularly use children as tools in their war against British and US forces. In just one year, the UN logged 316 cases of underage recruitment by the Taliban. In 2011, eleven children, including an eight-year-old girl, were killed carrying out suicide attacks. Everyone at Dara knows that, especially in our corner of Afghanistan, kids aren't always bystanders.

Children, such as the skinny shepherd boys who tend massive flocks of goats, seem to be becoming bolder. At first, they gave our camp a wide berth, glancing occasionally up at our sangars as they walk across our panoramic views. Now, they come ever closer. As they run on sinewy legs as nimble as a mountain goat, they also seem to become more defiant, watching us intently from the foot of the hill that our camp sits on.

I am not surprised when someone spots three shepherd boys, no more than 10 years old, hunched over something, just a few hundred metres from our razor wire. They are scared off after a soldier fires a mini-flare above them, screeching into the blue sky over their heads. It turns out that they were making a model of our camp, presumably to pass on to their Taliban masters.

I am not the only one here thinking that my rest and recuperation can't come quickly enough.

CHAPTER 16

MORE GOODBYES

*"Never say goodbye because goodbye means
going away and going away means forgetting"*
– JM Barrie

IMAGINE Christmas, New Year and your birthday rolled
into one. You still aren't even close. R&R is finally here. I
will get to go home, to civilisation, to friends and family for
two fun-filled weeks. Showers, flushing toilets and fresh food
will no longer just be a figment of my fevered imagination.

The clock is ticking, though. After all the travelling at the
start and end of my leave, I will be lucky to get 10 days at
home. I pack my gear up at Dara in a daze. I ram trousers,
shirts, shorts, everything into my large black issue kit bag.

I come off stag at 5am. In less than an hour, Gary Carling,
a quiet Fijian soldier called Bolatiki and I will be picked up in
a Mastiff vehicle to be taken back to Ouellette to begin our

journey home. I should nap for a while but I pace around, drinking stewed tea, too worked up to sleep. I never thought that this day would come.

Once the two Mastiffs arrive, we waddle out to meet them. Shouting cheerio to the guys in the sangars, we wade through ankle-deep sand, throw our bags into the back then squeeze in. When we are in the sangars or going outside the wire, we have to wear full Personal Protective Equipment (PPE). That means helmet, body armour, gloves, safety glasses, ear protection and a ballistic nappy. All this gear plus weapons and our bags means it's a very tight fit in the back of the vehicle. Seats are no bigger than a dinner plate along each side of the armoured vehicle. It's not yet mid-morning and the heat is infernal. My glasses fog up, sweat dripping from the lenses.

Thankfully, we don't have far to go. After a few minutes of being thrown around like an egg in a can, we reach the gates of Fob Ouellette. This is just the first stage on our way home, making me realise just how remote our tiny encampment is at Dara.

A few hours later we are ready to board a Chinook helicopter which swoops into Ouellette to take us to Camp Bastion, where we will then get a flight to the UK. This base is one of the hottest landing zones in Afghanistan, where pilots are most likely to be shot at. Choppers, unsurprisingly, don't like to stay on the ground for long.

We have to grab everything – daysacks, black kitbags, rifles, before sprinting for the ramp at the back of the chopper. It's a mad scramble to get on board. It's a far cry from strolling onto a civilian aircraft to be greeted with a glass of champagne by a smiling stewardess.

We strap ourselves into the canvas seats, making sure our rifles are pointed down the way. An errant round could bring the Chinook crashing down. There were two rows of seats along each side of a narrow aisle. We sit huddled together, staring directly into the faces of the soldiers opposite. It's not the time to moan about the lack of room although my knees are nearly up at my chin. The cramped conditions are the main feature of the aircraft although there's also the roaring noise which manages to penetrate my Army-issue ear defence, as do the aviation fuel fumes.

Our journey is punctuated with swoops and dives. At one point, we are flying parallel to the ground, banking wildly in a series of evasive manoeuvres to confuse any Talib waiting to fire at us. After 20 minutes, we arrive at Camp Bastion where we file off at a slightly more sedate pace this time.

We get on a bus that takes us to our transit accommodation: basically, a 20-man tent that has seen better days but it at least has the blessed relief of air conditioning. We ditch all our gear then go for a shower. Bastion's showers are in a large Portakabin-style unit. They aren't the best but after months of standing under a leaky shower bag or using a sliced open water bottle to wash yourself, it's bliss.

Next up, a visit to Kentucky Fried Chicken. Bastion has a number of fast food joints but we opt for KFC as it's closest, only a mile or two from our tents. We haven't been near any women for months so it's quite startling to see female soldiers wandering about, going to the gym or browsing in the shops that seem to specialise in Haribo and Pot Noodles. I now know what a convict feels like as he walks out of the jail gates, trying to get his head around his new life in civilisation and a sense of normality.

As great as it is to be away from OP Dara, I can't stop thinking about the place. Will there be more mortar and rocket attacks? Will my bed space still be there or will I be shunted into another part of the camp? Maybe the tour will be cut short and I won't need to go back?

Going back to Dara looms over me like a rain cloud on a clear horizon. We pass a couple of days at Bastion before our flight back to RAF Brize Norton. We land at RAF Akrotiri in Cyprus for a brief refuelling stop when things start to go wrong. Gary has gone off to the Duty Free shop to load up on last-minute fags when the tannoy screeches into life.

"Sirs, Ma'ams, ladies and gents…" I can't even bring myself to listen to the rest of the message. We're told we won't be going home tonight, something about a mechanical problem with the plane. A tidal wave of groans and curses echoes around the departure lounge, which in places looks like a relic from the 1970s.

After hours of hanging around, we get on another bus which is to take us to our home for the night. A 15-minute drive takes us through the base, up to a hillside dotted with crumbling whitewashed accommodation blocks. We could sit around moaning about the fact that we are losing a day of our precious leave.

Instead, like every soldier on that flight, we go looking for the first place that sells beer. None of us have any civvy clothes as for some reason, which was never explained, our clothes were taken off us, bagged up and kept at Bastion on the way out to Dara at the start of the tour. None of us have seen them since.

We sit on a tiled terrace outside the accommodation block, drinking Grolsch beer and enjoying the sunshine. A bin has been rinsed out, filled with ice and beer to serve as a cooler.

Next day, we are up at the crack of dawn nursing fuzzy heads to get the bus back to the air terminal. The waiting area looks like a refugee camp, with bodies sprawled out all over the place. A sandy-haired soldier, with the merest hint of sunburn, lies on the floor with his head resting on a bright yellow and blue vinyl mat which marks the edge of a children's soft play area. After an hour or two of hungover dozing, we are off. Time to board.

We land without incident at Brize then get on yet another bus, which drops some people off in Oxford before taking us to Heathrow. As we tear along country lanes in rural Oxfordshire, the afternoon sun is mellow and warm. The driver turns up the radio and *Rebel, Rebel* by David Bowie blares out. Its rocky, upbeat vibe fits the mood perfectly.

Arriving at the gleaming chrome and glass paradise that is Heathrow's Terminal 5 after three-and-a-half months at Dara is like landing on a different planet. We are wearing uniform and headdress, standing out among the hordes of leisure-suited tourists and well-heeled business types.

Walking through the terminal, I do a double take as I see an unexpected familiar face. Fiora, one of the *Record's* picture editors, is just getting past security after having her handbag checked. I smile and wave. She hesitates, unsure of this uniformed person waving like a maniac. It takes a few seconds for her to recognise me despite the fact that when I was in the newsroom I would see her almost every day.

She is down in London for the tennis at Wimbledon. My burnished skin and the fact that I have lost almost two stones in weight made me almost unrecognisable, she said. She wishes me well and we head off in different directions.

"Who is that?" Bola asks. Bola is a solid, reliable guy. He is an indiscriminate age, perhaps in his thirties. Like nearly all his countrymen, he is a rugby fanatic. He also has a daft sense of humour, shouting: "Sssssttteeeeevie!" at inopportune moments. I was fuming one night after he once tried to lock me in our makeshift wooden shower cubicle at Dara.

I explain that Fiora is a work colleague from my civilian job. He nods, off in the direction of the shops. I vowed to Lynda that I will get her perfume here so we wander off in search of the duty free.

We are like fish out of water among the gleaming shelves, groaning with Gucci and Prada bags in Harrods and the rows of ornate-looking Fortnum & Mason hampers. Our uniforms are coated in salt, the gritty residue from our constant sweating in Afghanistan. It has formed in dappled white patches, bleaching the backs and arms of our shirts. We never had time to do a proper washing in Bastion.

I can't really notice it but I know I must stink. The desert has a kind of acrid, dry, stale smell that lingers long after you have left the place. From the corner of my eye, I notice a pair of snooty-looking women in layers of make up, wearing fur coats. They look at us as if we are a pair of Vikings arrived in their village to rape and pillage. I spend the best part of £100 buying a bottle of Chanel Chance perfume before heading towards our gate.

An old man with kind eyes, grey hair and wire-rimmed glasses stops us. I'm half expecting him to ask us for directions but he asks where we have come from, where we are off to and what our white hackles represent. It's always old boys, old soldiers, that talk to you when you are in uniform. It's happened to me countless times now, at service stations, shops, fast food outlets. Most people just gawp and stare or look faintly intimidated. He shakes our hands, wishing us all the best. 'Once a soldier, always a soldier', I think.

I say my byes to Bola and Gary before I get on my connecting flight. They are on a flight to Edinburgh while I am flying into Glasgow. I keep looking at my watch. I am a day or two into my precious leave and yet I am still not home.

Arriving at Glasgow, I collect my bags before heading through a set of automatic doors into the main part of the airport. Lynda sees me, running over to give me a hug. She looks the same, just the way I remembered. I was worried about coming back in case she had changed. I have never been away from her for such a long time. Until now I had only been away from her for a day or two at most, when I had travelled abroad for a work trip.

She holds on to my hand, looking genuinely glad to see me. I feel euphoric, my pulse racing, although I also feel that if I was to sit down, I would sleep for a year. I let Lynda drive home as I don't fancy driving straight away. It's been a while so I want to ease myself back into it.

A lot of the guys at Dara have planned big foreign holidays for their R&R. I wanted the opposite, to just stay at home and vegetate. On the way back from the airport, we went to our local supermarket so that I could stock up on all the goodies I had been missing.

I feel slightly dazzled and overawed as I look around. For months, I have been lucky to get an old battered can of luke-warm Coke but here there are rows of garishly coloured cans of juice stretching as far as the eye can I see. I have a few months wages in my bank account as there isn't anything to spend your money on at Dara so I could go on a mammoth spending spree. Instead, I meekly grab a few cans of Red Bull and head for the checkout.

Three days later, after I have unpacked and settled back into home life, we go on a long weekend to a posh hotel in central Scotland for a break. It feels weird driving my car. I'm not sure whether this is due to the fact that I haven't driven for months or whether it's because I only bought my car days before I left for Afghan.

Sitting in an Italian restaurant for our evening meal, I can't help checking my watch, eyeing the date and time. "What's wrong?" Lynda asks. The days are flashing past.

Lying in the massive bed in our hotel suite, I work out that I will only get about nine days at home. I already have less than five full days left. I can't sleep so I get up, grab my phone and walk into the lounge. Logging into Facebook to see what my Army mates are up to, I find some old photos of Bobby, Russ and I in training.

We are standing in a damp-ridden hut in Warcop training area in the north of England, looking incredibly unhappy. Our sour expressions poke out from underneath layers of camouflage paint that's smeared across our weary faces. It was taken a year before we deployed. As I flick through my phone, I find his mobile number still logged in my contacts book. It's hard to believe he is gone forever.

I am dreading going back to Dara but his death puts my unease in perspective. At least I have the chance to come home, even if it is for a short time. His loss seems surreal. I sometimes get the feeling that it was a bad dream, that it can't possibly be true, but then I realise it is only too real. Even though it was beyond my control, I also feel guilty for missing his repatriation and his funeral service.

Days go by, and Dara looms ever closer. Thinking about going back makes me depressed so I try to keep myself occupied with days out, visits to friends and family. My eyes are always drawn to my watch, though, wishing I could freeze the date and time.

Guys who had completed a few tours warned me about this. Russ, who served previously in Iraq and Afghanistan, told me that going back to Afghan after R&R was actually far worse than heading out at the start of the tour. At the start, you are quite optimistic and looking forward to getting out there to do the job. Ignorance is bliss, as they say, as you don't know what you are getting into. After R&R, however, you know exactly what you are heading back to.

The day finally arrives. Lynda drives me to the airport as I sit in silence feeling like a condemned man on death row.

She parks up in a multi-storey car park, walking me over to the airport terminal. We don't talk much. She seems to be holding up well while I feel almost in a stupor at the prospect of leaving again.

My flight is called. Lynda bursts into tears as I kiss her goodbye yet again. I know she is even more worried now after Bobby's death. His loss was very close to home for all of us. It brought home how bad things could get.

I try not to drag out our farewell. Short and sweet is the order of the day. Straightening my headdress, I ask Lynda if my uniform looks ok. I'm feeling self-conscious as I am the only one here in uniform. The rest of the lads were flying down from Edinburgh.

Lynda waves, wiping streaks of mascara from her face, as I walk down a long corridor into the departure area. Holiday-makers in an eye-popping array of garish colours stand in a long queue, waiting to go through customs. Many of them are openly staring at me, seemingly goggle-eyed at the sight of an Army uniform.

Eventually, it's my turn to go through the metal detector. A female customs officer pulls me to one side, apologising as she asks me if she can inspect my bags. It turns out my rifle cleaning kit shows up like a beacon on the x-ray. I forgot all about it. Sitting in the departure lounge minutes before my flight, I call Lynda on my mobile. I don't want to go back, I tell her in a confessional tone. She tells me that no matter how awful it is, I should remember that I have been through worse in my life. Thinking of my mum and dad, I pick up my bags and head for the plane.

CHAPTER 17

HEADS DOWN

"You can cut the tension with a cricket stump"
– Murray Walker

IT takes me weeks to get back to Dara. My flight to London is uneventful. I meet Bola and Gary within minutes of my arrival at Heathrow. We then rush to pick up hire cars for the hour-long drive out to Brize Norton. No sooner have we got the keys than a young soldier in our group gets a text saying our flight to Afghan is delayed by at least 24 hours. A few calls and a quick search online confirms it – we are stranded at Brize for a day.

Eventually, we get our flight out to Bastion. That's when my travel woes really start. We are booked onto a Chinook heading out to Ouellette but as we stand on the flight line, we are told the flight is off. More aimless days at Bastion. Then, a US Marine flight from Camp Leatherneck, which sits next to Bastion, is scheduled to take us out. As night falls, I get to within inches of the odd looking tilt-rotor aircraft which flies like a plane but can land and take off like a helicopter. Suddenly, a female American officer taps my shoulder and says there is not enough room for me on the flight.

A few other soldiers and I trudge dejectedly back to the air terminal, humphing all our kit, asking each other what the hell do we do now? After a few hours, transport is organised to take us back to our tents at Bastion. I stagger into the nearest tent, lob my bags and body armour in a corner and slump on a bunk bed. I don't even want to go back and yet now I need to battle just to get out there. I will end up spending more time travelling and hanging about at Bastion than I did at home.

Days later, I manage to get a flight out to Ouellette. Ross Burton, the fellow Dara inmate who was with me when Paddy Burns set himself alight, greets me at the flightline. His stubbly, small head is brown like a berry. He isn't long back from a holiday to Turkey for his R&R. He looks as happy as I feel about going back to Dara.

Sweating, lungs burning with the infernally hot air, Ross and I stumble off the Chinook at Ouellette. A fair-haired sergeant major tells us we are staying there overnight as they don't have transport to take us down to Dara. First, though, we have to work. We have to help carry out 'area cleaning'. Metal ISO Containers at the back of the camp have to be gutted, rubbish burnt and the back end of the camp picked clean to prepare for the eventual collapse of the base as troops withdraw.

We spent the next eight hours with half a dozen other unlucky souls bending over to pick up old water bottles, fag ends, broken wooden pallettes and every type of rubbish imaginable. A battered red ISO Container full of decaying rations in festering cardboard boxes smells so bad that some of us actually retch.

By dusk, the job is done, the place looks immaculate. We head to our refuge for the night. Soldiers have already started breaking up the camp with a view to pulling out later in the year so we won't even have a tent to sleep in tonight. We grab a couple of camp beds, setting them up against some Hesco walls which have a bit of shade. We are the only two soldiers in what used to be a tented area where nearly a dozen men once slept. The place has the feeling of the Marie Celeste, with water bottles sitting half drunk next to empty fag packets on a plank of wood that served as a shelf. Chesty women in frayed *Zoo* magazine posters look down, doe-eyed, at the chaos from the walls.

The next morning, at the break of dawn, we are driven back to Dara. My bed space is still where I left it. Someone has zipped up the mosquito net over my bed after they piled my welfare parcels on it. Dozens of parcels, laden with shower gel, sweets, newspapers and goodies of all sorts, have arrived when I was back home. When these parcels arrive, it feels like Christmas Day.

We gather at the benches across from the kitchen area when a couple of Mastiffs bring down our mail. This usually happens after a Combat Logistics Patrol or CLP, a long snaking convoy of vehicles, has been to Ouellette. Sometimes, a Chinook will drop off a few bags as they fly into Ouellette. Then, they are brought down to us.

Lynda sends me stuff all the time. When I was home on R&R, I went to the supermarket to stock up on supplies which she could then drip feed to me over the coming months. Small bottles of Pepsi, chilli sauce, fruit gums, fruit squash and anything to liven up our tepid drinking water were must-buys. I also bought Oxo cubes and piles of cooking sauce sachets to brighten up our rations. When a pile of parcels is brought in, I can spot her distinctive hand-writing on the brown paper wrapping a mile away.

Fellow soldiers from the Army Reserves send me treats as well. My most bizarre request to them was for permanent marker pens. We have to put our initials on our food and water bottles or some rogue will just go into the fridge and take it. The effect on morale of the goody parcels really can't be overstated, especially out here in what soldiers call the boonies, the wilderness, Apache territory.

I feel like a child every time some parcels arrive with my name on it. At the start of the tour, it took one or two deliveries before I started to get parcels. I felt totally crushed every time there was nothing there for me. I asked Lynda what the delay was when I was on the welfare phone one day. She sobbed as she told me she hated sending them out to me as it just reminded her how remote I was. Thankfully, she got over this and became a prolific parcel poster. I sent her a stark email that sums it up: 'Got your parcels. Thanks. They make me feel loved.'

Parcels and letters take anywhere between two to six weeks

to reach us. By then bags of Haribo sweets and fizzy cola bottles have melted into a big congealed, multi-coloured jelly mess. We eat them anyway.

My heart was warmed by the number of parcels that were sent by people we never knew and never would know. Groups like Support Our Soldiers and Treats for Troops send out parcels all the time. We divide them up among the soldiers. I was always moved when they had a note from an old woman in Maidstone or Bromley or some other place that I had never even visited. She had taken the time and effort, spending her own money, to send me sweets, tooth-paste and other luxuries that were hard to come by out here. I make a point of writing back to these people.

An old soldier, who now runs a military fitness company, rallies his troops and we start receiving scores of parcels from his recruits. One box contains a drawing and a hand-written note from a nine-year-old boy wishing me well. I stick it to the Hesco next to my bed so that I can see it first thing in the morning.

Coming back to Dara, I notice a real change in atmo-sphere. Some guys don't use the gym as much after R&R. They seem lacklustre, keener to count down the days until they can get out of here for good. My favourite spot in the hammock under the main sangar starts to get a bit crowded. It is like a prison sentence, counting the days until you can get your life back.

In Vietnam, soldiers served for a year. Troops with 99 days or less to go of their tour were what was known as 'short'. I read that short-timers counted down those final days in a variety of ways. Some carried a short stick with notches, wrote on helmet covers or used special calendars similar to paint-by-number pictures. We only have to do six-and-a-half months in this hole but we have our own methods of counting down the days.

Hand-drawn calendars pop up everywhere. On the metal pole frames of the sangars, on steel girders holding up the sangar roof, on the side of the ISO Container ops room. Gary Carling has his own version. A *Where's Wally?* calendar takes pride of place at his bed space like a garishly coloured shrine. Every day on sangar duty, I carefully mark down the days on a calendar carefully scrawled on a large block of wood. For a time, it feels as if it's Groundhog Day with the days just not passing at all. For a while, I stop even looking at the wood block calendar as it just pisses me off.

Post-R&R, tempers are definitely fraying, including mine. Queeny pulls me up for wearing non-issue boots so many times I lose count. He is a grizzled veteran, a career soldier, who tells everyone that "getting shot at and blown up is over-rated". Yet he turns into a grinning, nervous schoolboy when any VIPs decides to visit Dara.

When a sergeant major and the commanding officer are coming down to visit us at six in the morning, Queeny rouses everyone, even the guys that have just collapsed into bed after stag. He makes us all wear long-sleeve shirts, combat trousers and boots despite the fact that if we are not on guard duty, we usually wear shorts and flip flops. The hierarchy at Ouellette are totally aware of our casual attire as they can see us when we are off-duty, lounging about, on their powerful security cameras.

He goes into full blown sycophant mode when they arrive. He is not the only one. Teru may be a 6ft 5ins bruiser but even he comes over all gooey when officers arrive. He is heard purring: "Oh yes, sir, do you like rugby? Yes, rugby is wonderful" as he launches a charm offensive on a young, bemused-looking junior officer.

Gary Carling and I are totally transfixed by this display of exaggerated fawning. We are told that this happens because senior ranks can make or break your career. If they don't like you, you are doomed. Either way, we just torture those one or two rough, tough soldiers who suddenly turn into servile careerists at the first sign of a heavy rank slide.

One day, after another volley of abuse for wearing non-issue boots, I snap, giving Queeny both barrels. "Look", I say, "I bought these for £150 because they are comfortable desert boots and they do the job. The issue boots I got ripped my feet to shreds. I had massive blisters and had to limp about. What difference does it make out here anyway? I am not the only one wearing non-issue boots, by the way!" He looks slightly miffed, puffs on his fag and walks off to continue his game of chess.

We also seem to be running out of water with worrying frequency. Every couple of days it seems, we are told that the water is rationed so we can't shave or wash our clothes. Late one night I am filthy, covered in a film of grime and sweat. We are running low on jerrycans of grey water which we would usually use to wash. I decide to use bottled water. No sooner have I stripped off to wash myself at a basin than

I am spotted.

Shane McNee, a sergeant from the recce platoon, has been attached to us from the start of the tour, spending most of his time in the ops room. He looks Italian, with a heavy growth of stubble and jet black hair. He is easygoing most of the time but loves to flaunt his military knowledge. I am not in the mood for him tonight.

"Haw!" he says. "Whit are you daein'?" I reply with: "What does it look like?" The conversation slides downhill from there. He tells me what I already know: that the water is rationed, that we aren't due to get a resupply for a few days. I respond: "Well, it's not rocket science, you need to get on the radio and tell them we need water." I had lost count of the times we had been told that some vehicles from Ouellette were bringing down water. We would haul open the doors of the Mastiffs to find there were only half a dozen jerrycans, enough for a day or two. On bad days, they would turn up with no water at all.

I finish washing and walk around the Hesco partition to my bedspace, tucking my wash bag into my black holdall under my camp bed. Peter, a tall St Lucian, grinned at me before lunging over to give me a high five, saying: "Well done, big man."

Unlike the others who spend less time in the gym, I'm determined to work out as much as possible. It passes the time and gives me an outlet for my pent-up frustration at being stuck here for another few months. At one point, it seemed as though everyone was taking some sort of fat burning pill or protein shake. Even spindly armed Queeny had a go at Op Massive, hitting the gym for hours, lugging around heavy weights and taking protein supplements. Long into the night, you could hear weights clanging, people puffing away on the bike machine or sighs of exertion as a soldier did pull ups off the metal skeleton of the main sangar.

That was before R&R kicked in. Things now seem more sedate. When I was back in the UK though, I was hitting the health food shops on a daily basis. I now have a stockpile of protein powder, pre-workout drinks and energy bars. If nothing else, it will augment my dismal diet here.

At first, I'm a bit sceptical about the muscle building supplements but after taking them religiously for a few weeks, they do seem to work. On a previous tour, I am told, a notoriously daft soldier from this battalion took loads of protein supplements designed to build mass and bulk up the body. He, however, neglected to do much in the way of exercise so he just put on about three stone in flab.

I even try Insanity, a high intensity circuit training-style workout. One of the guys has it downloaded on his iPad so we can be found perched around it, doing flutter kicks, mountain climbers or squats. Temperatures in the late 40s make this workout even more insane than it needs to be. One or two of the boys who were a bit chunky at the start of the tour now look positively gaunt.

I try anything to keep myself occupied, especially if it keeps my mind off that damn calendar.

CHAPTER 18

ARMY PATTER

"Swearing was invented as a compromise
between running away and fighting"
– Peter Finley Dunne

"GET out yer gonkbag, start scrubbing yer Gat then go round to that full screw and see if he's got more dhobi dust." Those first two lines are incomprehensible to most people but it's how we speak at Dara. Getting home for a while to normality before plunging back to our rocky outpost makes me realise that we use a different language out here.

British Army slang is full of jargon, archaic Indian words and arcane terminology that most people just wouldn't understand. Our lingo becomes even more mind bending when you add earthy Scottish 'patter' and a liberal dose of profanity to the mix. It makes me fully appreciate that a soldier really is part of a sub-culture with its own values and norms, which looks down its collective nose at 'soft civvies'. Language is a key part of that. For the record, that first sentence means: "Get out of your sleeping bag, start cleaning your rifle then go round to that corporal and see if he has any more washing powder."

Insults and foul language fill the air at Dara like motes of dust in an old library. A newspaper office is a robust, occasionally intimidating atmosphere so my ears were used to the odd bad word or the occasional angry outburst. However, nothing could prepare me for Dara. Swearing was like drawing breath, the 'f' word used like a punctuation mark.

Insults are fired around morning, noon and night. You have to quickly develop a thick skin. As a reporter, I am used to sometimes being sworn at or slagged off by irate members of the public. Other people, however, don't fare so well. A chubby-cheeked soldier, going by the unfortunate nickname of "Pudsey", is sent down to us to work on our camera systems. He is the mastermind behind the raising of a hot air balloon fitted with cameras to help us keep a better eye on the surrounding landscape.

He is also overweight, a fact which does not go unnoticed. Within minutes of his arrival, he is called a "fat waster", "a fat lazy useless bastard" and a "tubby wee shite". He copes reasonably well with the deluge of abuse, even making an effort to go to our makeshift gym. His attempts to ingratiate himself with Queeny and his tormentors don't last too long though. He gives up after a while, preferring to sit watching TV in the bunker.

He also manages to piss the entire camp off when he tries to avoid going on stag, saying that he's not here to do sentry duty. As if that isn't bad enough, he is caught carrying a stiletto knife in his Osprey body armour. A night later, he is reprimanded for playing about with his mobile phone while on stag. Phones are meant to have been handed in at Bastion for security reasons and sentries are meant to be watching their arcs at all times. I fear Pudsey is not cut out for this Army life. His balloon project also ends up as a total disaster. It turns out he is not properly trained in how to deploy it. We collapse in fits of laughter as the semi-inflated balloon almost blows away one day with him clutching desperately at the tethering cable.

In Queeny's encyclopedic roll call of insults, Pudsey ranks as a "chomper". There are mongs, mutants, belters, ballbags or bawbags, bangers and chompers. One of the fire support group's officers is noted as a "belter", according to Queeny. Belters are clueless, have a tendency to flap and don't really know what they should be doing. They also tend to be further up the hierarchy.

Bawbags (scrotums) come and go. You could be a bawbag one day, then back in the good books the next. Bangers are similar to bawbags in that it's a temporary term. You could be a "total banger" for forgetting to bring a piece of kit but the label would be forgotten by the next morning. Mutants are the more awkward, gangly type of soldier that doesn't seem to know his left from his right. They tend to be seen as beyond redemption. Once a mutant, always a mutant, or so the theory goes.

In Queeny's lexicon, I am a "stab" and a "grass" or occasionally, depending on his mood, a "clipe". Stab is a pejorative, rather unimaginative, term standing for Stupid Territorial Army Bastard. He calls me a grass or a clipe, a Scottish word for tell-tale, because of my job as a reporter. Once he learns that I am actually older than him, he delights in calling me an "auld bastard".

"Mong" is by far the most common epithet. It's also the most offensive. It derives from Mongoloid, an outdated term for a person with Down's Syndrome. In Army terms, it can also be used as verb, as in "stop monging it in the sangar!" Like "retard" and "spastic", I last heard these words when I was a child in a school playground. The word "mong" grates with me so I make a point of never using it.

Some phrases do appeal to me for their sheer descriptive brilliance. One such phrase is to be "hanging oot yer hoop", or even just "hanging". Literally translated, it means hanging out of your arse or in other words, incredibly tired. You might say: "After that six-mile run, I was totally hangin.'"

"Jack" is another common, multi-faceted term. To be jack is to be lazy, leaving others to do your work. A soldier can be a "jack bastard", "jacking" on the rest of his company by being "jack". You can also be "jack" by being selfish. For example, a fellow soldier might ask you for a cigarette or a sweet but you refuse. He might say: "Aw, come on, don't be jack." It's one of the most common, noticeable phrases but no-one I ask knows its true origins.

There are loads of other terms that infiltrate every day speech. "Scoff" is food, a "sitrep" is a situation report, "stag" is sentry duty, "brews" are teas or coffees. I'm amazed that I can hear: "Send a sitrep about that feckin' scoff, ahm choking for a brew before ah go on stag", and be able to decipher the meaning instantly.

"Shimfing" and "buckshee" are another two favourites at Dara. Shimfing is like a national past time for soldiers. It's especially prevalent in some quarters in our camp. It means moaning or complaining, as in: "Stop shimfin', ya wee scrote!" I find out that it comes from the German word "schimpfen", meaning to grumble or whine. Buckshee is one that you hear quite often. It means free or spare. You could say: "The storeman gave me a buckshee belt" although given the universally acknowledged tightness of soldiers working in the stores, it would be unlikely.

There is one Army phrase that we hear all the time at Dara. Every day and night, we hear it whispered, usually accompanied by a dig in the ribs or a shove of your feet. It strikes fear and unspeakable dread into every soul that hears it. It is only five words long but it signals that you are about to be wrenched from the seductive arms of sleep, before being cruelly flung literally on to the frontline. The phrase is one that every soldier knows only too well. It is: "Pssst, mate, you are on stag."

CHAPTER 19

NIGHT TERRORS

"Fear is the mind killer"
– Frank Herbert

I HOPE we get attacked tonight. Not over-run, just a skirmish. I don't want black turbaned fighters climbing over the walls with one hand on their PKM machine guns, as their tunics bulge over bulky suicide vests. I want a stand up firefight, with a few insurgents trying to rattle off a few rounds at us as we take a bead on them from the safety of a fortified and heavily-armed bunker.

Just enough to send a signal to the Taliban that we won't be fucked about. It's 3am and everything is swamped in an inky, impenetrable blackness. My sangar faces towards Ouellette but all I see is the red light from one of their surveillance balloons, tethered a few feet off the ground.

These white blimps, which can be up to a 100 feet long, are everywhere in Afghanistan. They are a constant feature of the skies now, shimmering hundreds of feet up there in the daytime haze or as a solitary light blinking at night. They are fitted with all sorts of gadgetry, infrared and colour video cameras, and probably a lot more that they don't tell us about. They mark the British shift towards using technology for surveillance and intelligence.

Our sentinel at Ouellette is down tonight as a storm is expected to hit our area. I feel tired and restless at the same time. We have been taking IDF fire on and off for weeks. Sometimes we hear the IDF alarm at Ouellette, sometimes we don't. The alarm had been installed at Ouellette for weeks before anyone even thought to tell us about it.

We aren't getting much sleep anyway but when we do crash out for a few hours, you invariably hear the shouts of "IDF! IDF!" from one or both sangars. I leave my body armour and helmet at the door of my tent so I can grab it and run to the bunker with my eyes still shut.

It amazes me how many guys just wake up, running to the bunker with no body armour or helmet. They sit zonked out on the chairs made from old mattresses and wire mesh from Hesco in shorts and flip flops. Eventually, Queeny loses his rag, staggering in with all his gear on, once we get the all clear. "What the fuck is it with youse eh? How many times dae ye need tae be tellt?" I feel like a teacher's pet as I am about the only one with my Osprey body armour and helmet. For all his abuse, I think Queeny has a grudging respect for me. I overheard him once, slagging someone for transferring to the infantry from the Royal Logistic Corps (RLC). He said: "Fuckin' petrol pump attendants! I have got more time for the journo, at least he's been ootside the wire oot here before."

Back in the sangar, I have started chewing boiled sweets to give me a sugar rush and a meagre energy boost. It strikes me that you are always on edge out here. Even when it's quiet, you are wary. Why is it quiet? Is it usually this quiet? Are they planning something?

In the first two months of the tour alone, we are told that there has been a flurry of IDF attacks, some IED strikes, and a number of firefights in our AO or area of operations. One firefight near us lasted for 15 minutes. One day, a rogue Talib took a pop at us with what was believed to be an underslung grenade launcher, a short barrelled weapon attached to a rifle that fires a grenade over a long distance. I was sitting on a bench opposite the kitchen, eating chicken flavoured noodles, when we heard its signature pop as the round detonated. No-one batted an eyelid. I thought the noise was an old can of deodorant spray exploding in the burns pit after someone threw it away by mistake.

Earlier in the day, I was in this sangar when there was a massive IED strike two or three kilometres from us. A huge mushroom cloud bloomed over the blast site. A group of Royal Engineers triggered it. No-one was seriously injured, we are told later. Sometimes the heat just causes the IEDs to 'cook off' or explode of their own accord. You can be standing there on guard then there will be a violent boom. As you scan around, you notice the tell-tale cloud of debris and smoke in the cobalt blue sky. If it has just cooked off, all you can normally see is a few startled camels.

I put my night vision monocle up to my right eye but it's useless, I can't see a thing. These night vision goggles work on ambient light. As there is no moon tonight, they are as much use as a chocolate fireguard. Checking my pockets, I have my head torch which has a red bulb. White light should never be used in the sangar at night as it can travel for miles. Red light is less obvious. I also have a bottle of water. Even at night, the temperature is still brutal. Dehydration is never too far away. In the map pocket of my trousers, I also have a pen and notepad. A good soldier always has a pen and pad, so we were told in basic training.

Suddenly, the wind picks up. Camouflage netting stretched over the sides of the sangar starts to billow in, before the wind changes direction, whipping it around like a matador's cape. The darkness has covered the storm's arrival. As every minute passes, it gets progressively worse. My face feels as if it is being sandblasted. I pull my shirt collar up over my mouth to help me breathe.

Ten minutes after the wind has picked up, I am sitting in a total brown out. I cannot even see the other side of the sangar, no more than four feet away. I curse my luck: why did this have to happen when it's my turn on stag? Just yards away from me, there are guys sleeping, totally unaware of the drama unfolding all around them.

Ducking down behind the Hesco wall to catch a breath, I fear that I have tempted fate by wishing that we got attacked. This would be a perfect time to do it. None of us in sangar one and two can see a thing. To add to our current woes, the field telephones, clunky, green and black hulks that wouldn't look out of place in a *Dad's Army* episode, are not working properly. They have not functioned properly for some time. Why is it that these days they can cram more technology into a smartphone than they used on the Apollo moon landings, but we can't get a field telephone that actually does what it's meant to?

I just need to tough it out, remain vigilant until my shift is finished then I can go to my bed. Forget about it, until the next time. Normally, I would rest my rifle on top of the Hesco, only a foot or two from me, as I scour the area with binoculars. Not tonight though. I don't let the rifle out of my grip once.

It feels impossibly remote, as if I am standing at the edge of the world. My entire universe is reduced to a few feet in front of me. If a horde of Taliban creep up on this position, I will know nothing about it until the last second.

A flash suddenly turns the night into day, illuminating the billowing clouds of sand washing over me and my sangar. I freeze, terrified. What the fuck is that? I get it together, then duck into the Hesco for cover. My brain starts to work. A trip wire attached to a flare around our position has gone off. They are our early warning system, designed to go off when someone walks across the trip wire. Shit!

I go into hyper-vigilant mode. Time seems to slow down. I keep low, just glancing over the top of the Hesco to see if there is any movement, shadow or silhouette. The flare burns so bright you can't look at it directly. We all have loaded weapons in Afghanistan but they are not made ready. In other words, they have a magazine of live rounds fitted but there isn't a round in the chamber, ready to come out the muzzle when the trigger is squeezed. So, it's relatively safe, especially when the safety catch is on – as it should be pretty much all the time.

Now, as the flare burns ever brighter, I cock the weapon with my left hand, chambering a round. I flick off the safety. If anyone is this close, creeping around outside the wire in the middle of a storm, they aren't coming to shake my hand that's for sure. If I squeeze the trigger now, a small hammer inside the rifle will fall, striking the firing pin which then hits a small impression at the back of a 5.56mm NATO round. A very hot, sharp, pointy thing will then race out the barrel.

Out of the corner of my eye, I notice something moving about behind me, to my right. I swivel round to see Gary Carling, ashen faced. He has come down from the main sangar to see what is happening. I can tell from his face, he is thinking the same thing: is this it? Have they chosen tonight to attack?

The flare, which has been burning for God knows how long, starts to splutter and die. Still nothing. We scramble about, trying to see what caused the trip wire to go off. I cover Gary as he wanders about checking the gate, the perimeter fence, the top of the Hesco. Nothing.

"It must have been the wind," I shout to him, as I click the safety catch on. I am a non-smoker but I am tempted to cadge a fag from Gary to calm myself down. 'That's the thing about here, you never get a chance to let your guard down',

I think to myself. The words of a sergeant major come back to me: "Never be complacent. Treat every single days as if it's your first out there. As soon as you think nothing is going to happen, that is when it will all go wrong."

Later, we find out a desert fox, with a rippling thick mane of tawny grey fur, was seen wandering about in the 'Dara Dip', the rocky area between us and Ouellette. The fox was probably freaked out by the storm, bolting over the trip wire. It may even have been the strong winds that triggered it.

Finally, it is the end of my shift. I can get a couple of hours rest before we need to get up to make the camp's breakfast of soggy, slightly salty pancakes and muesli. Shattered and shaken, I walk into the ops room, tearing off my helmet and ripping open the velcro straps at the side of my body armour with a satisfying 'crrrruuunch'.

Garry John Urie looks like a man possessed. He is leaping about from foot to foot, with a mix of shock and disbelief on his face. "I canny believe it, man, canny believe it. I just canny believe it, man." It's the early hours of the morning, I have had no sleep and this is starting to freak me out. It takes me a few minutes to get him to regain his composure, settle down and tell me what is happening.

I get there in the end. He tells me how he was watching the security cameras, stagging on here in the ops room. He saw a guy, several hundred metres from our camp behaving strangely. He dropped everything else to hone in on this one guy, creeping about under the cover of darkness. He focused the high power camera on him, recoiling in horror as he saw the man furiously copulating with a donkey.

CHAPTER 20

DEATH FROM ABOVE

*"Never was anything great
achieved without danger"
– Niccolo Machiavelli*

THIS is the closest call yet. A mortar lands with a soft crump, spraying razor-sharp shards of shrapnel in every direction. I see it all from the panoramic view of the main sangar. It lands just beyond the other sangar. It's just after 5pm, still broad daylight. The Taliban are definitely getting bolder; they are also getting more accurate.

During the limbo time between the mortar being fired and the deadly projectile landing, I feel oddly calm. Afghans have a poignant saying 'Inshallah', meaning "God willing" or "if God wills it". If it's your time it's your time. There's no point worrying about it; if you are going to die, you are going to die. I am not religious but it makes sense to me. It's ironic that the Taliban probably think exactly the same way.

The threat from these mortar attacks is all too real. Two soldiers were killed at Ouellette in a similar attack to the ones that have been rocking our camp for months. Sitting on my bed using the tablet on the Wifi one night, I find a story about their deaths. Corporal Andrew Roberts and Private Ratu Silibaravi, both aged 32, were bomb disposal experts who saved hundreds of lives. They were killed after returning to base after an operation to clear home-made bombs from this area.

Both members of a high-risk search team from 23 Pioneer Regiment, The Royal Logistic Corps, died when one of the mortar rounds exploded close to them. A defence source is quoted as saying: "These two soldiers were terribly unfortunate. They were just in the wrong place at the wrong time. It was just dreadfully unlucky."

Father of three Cpl Roberts, from Middlesbrough, leaves a girlfriend, Paula Ewers. He previously completed operational tours in both Iraq and Afghanistan and represented his regiment at boxing and cross country. His girlfriend Paula is quoted: "Andrew truly was a hero and I'm so proud of what he achieved, he was such a special, kind and caring person. I was blessed to have spent the past two-and-a-half years with Andrew. He made me and my son Josh so happy. I have lost my soul mate and my best friend. The memories I have of our time together I will hold in my heart forever. Sweet dreams my hero, all my love always."

His children Jessica, six, Kyle, five and Kayla, three, said:

"For our brave Dad who went away to build sand castles and stop the bad men hurting people. We love you to the moon and back. You are an angel in Heaven now looking down on us all, we wish yesterday had never happened and you were still here to phone us and take us out. You were the best dad, we remember all the fun things we did, we will never forget you and will love you forever. You are our hero and we will pray for you always."

Pte Silibaravi, originally from Fiji, had also served previously in Afghanistan and Iraq and played rugby for his regiment. The news story went on: 'The use of mortars by the Taliban in the past has met with limited success and very few casualties. But after this latest incident, intelligence officers will now be assessing whether this attack represent a new departure for insurgents.'

An inquest into their deaths raises safety questions about Ouellette. One of their comrades says: "I felt the protection at FOB Ouellette could have been to a higher standard. It is a shame it took an incident like that for something to be done." In my experience of Ouellette, things have certainly improved, with more hard cover and tighter rules on the wearing and carrying of body armour.

This article also says our area, called Nahr-e Saraj or the Upper Gereshk Valley, depending on who you ask, remains one of the most dangerous and contested areas of Helmand. From December 2011 to May 2012, five British soldiers have been killed in bomb and gun attacks while serving there.

The suicide bomber threat is also ever-present. Taliban leaders have drafted in two known fanatics to our area to plan and carry out suicide attacks. In an attack on another base, the insurgents drove up in a car laden with explosives, blowing a massive hole in the Hesco and razor wire. Heavily armed men, clad in suicide vests laced with high explosives, followed behind in a human wave trying to overrun the base. They nearly managed it.

Before, during and after the most accurate mortar attacks on us yet, the locals are totally unfazed. When we are attacked, I expect them to scoop up young children, disappear into locked compounds before the action kicks-off. They never do, though. We are all scrambling about trying to identify the firing point but the locals calmly go about their business as usual.

Outside a collection of compounds to our north, boys, no older than the age of 12, play a bizarre game with ropes. They have made a circle around them from their sandals. Two of them then stand in the circle trying to flick each other with the lengths of thick rope. It all looks vicious. A crowd of old men, with beards down to their chests, watch with faces like stone masks. No-one seems to even notice or care that the Taliban has just tried to kill us up here at Dara.

It is clear that the Taliban are ingrained here, part of the landscape here as much as the sand dunes and the poppy fields. In a way, that makes our job easier. Since we have no interaction with the locals, we know that anyone coming near us is likely to be a baddy.

During the celebrations for Ramadan, local kids, with adults lurking in the background, crept closer to our wire. At night, they started burning tyres. Was this a signal? All we know is that the Taliban consider Ramadan a great time to die. Very auspicious, apparently. Any jihadis who martyr themselves at that time are guaranteed a place in Paradise.

At night, we randomly fire flares into the sky. They explode hundreds of feet up in the sky, turning night into day before drifting eerily down to earth. There are more mutterings about the Taliban trying a night-time attack. A battery of heavy guns and mortars at Ouellette also fires illumination rounds all over the area with a satisfying metallic thump that we can feel as much as hear.

One day, we watch an Apache helicopter strafe a position about half a mile from us. They run back and forward, hammering the ground with strafing runs. Ripping, rending the air with its heavy machine gun. Hellfire missiles tear a compound apart, filling the sky with ribbons of smoke and dust. A guy who monitors the radio and the Taliban icom chatter tells us the chopper was taking out an insurgent mortar team. We later also hear that the attack was a case of mistaken identity. The chopper might have actually taken out a farmer carrying watermelons home. I never find out the real truth.

A drowsy day in the sangar is shattered by the crack and whip of rounds whizzing past our heads. I jump down from my perch on a metal scaffolding which runs around the side of the Hesco inside our cocoon. It is only 9.30am in the morning and the rounds whipping past us sound very close. I am in the sangar with Tony, who has done a couple of tours before and knows his stuff. He is crouching under the Hesco wall, head tucked into his chest, trying to see where the fire is coming from.

"It's like fightin' fuckin' ghosts," he says. A day or two later, in the same sangar, something very similar happens. This time it is easy to see where the firing is coming from. The Afghan National Civil Order Police (Ancop) are getting smashed to bits as they drive along Route 611. The Taliban must be firing at them from the crumbling, disused compounds dotted along the sides of the road.

There are dozens of police armoured vehicles and trucks but still, the Taliban have a go. You may not agree with their politics but you can't knock their bottle. A man in uniform is standing at the back of a Humvee vehicle popping rounds back up the road in the direction they have just came. A crack and a whizz means that some rounds are coming down our way. Are they Taliban bullets or Ancop whipping by us? It would be ironic to be killed by the very people you are there to help.

Our allies in the Ancop are taking a hammering. I hear from people that have been sent back to Ouellette with diarrhoea and vomiting that their casualties are often taken through there. Guys have given a hand as they are brought in, bleeding, ripped to shreds by an IED.

Ancop are considered to be the elite of the Afghan police. Coalition chiefs created the force as a friendlier, more open, better-educated unit which would form the kernel of the police of the future in a country that is dogged by corruption and weak central government. They are supposed to bridge the gap between the Army and the police, almost a para-military force who are able to move across the country.

They are even organised on military lines with battalions, brigades and companies.

They are not soldiers though. In Marjah district, Helmand, in 2010, they were sent in to fight well dug in Taliban positions. Their training, leadership and lack of heavy weapons meant they were not up to the task. Ancop units suffered heavy casualties. They were also criticised for setting up illegal checkpoints to tax residents and using drugs, according to reports at the time.

They are supposed to be the storm troopers of a new Afghanistan, setting the bar for the development of Western-style policing. However, it hasn't quite panned out that way. In the early days of the Marjah operation, US Marines sidelined an entire Ancop battalion after one-quarter of the 179 police officers tested positive for drug use. Many officers were also Tajik Afghans, ethnically different from the proud, predominantly Pashtun population in Helmand.

As I watch the Ancop officers batter off rounds in every direction, it dawns on me that they are almost as much outsiders here as we are. We don't have any Ancop here at Dara, they are all based inside a camp within a camp at Ouellette. I read somewhere that for many of these more sophisticated, ethnically different Afghans, being here in Helmand is a step down. They see Helmandis as country bumpkins, yokels, hillbillies – but dangerous ones at that.

We watch one night as an Ancop Humvee is blown to pieces by an IED on Route 611. Through the green hue of the night vision gear, we watch the whole battle unfold. Taliban fighters follow up the blast with a storm of small arms fire. They will be busy at Ouellette tonight, taking care of the wounded. It's clear that the Taliban see the Ancop forces as the soft underbelly, the weak link in the chain. As a result, they are taking a hammering nearly every night.

Death swoops down out of the skies one night. It is yet another night in the sangar, so dark I can hardly see Bola a few feet away from me. A rumble like distant thunder suddenly erupts from somewhere out there. We have no idea where it's coming from or what is causing it. The indistinct noise comes closer, evolving into a distinctive "whocka whocka" noise. It's clearly a chopper of some sort. Good news as, thank God, the Taliban don't have helicopters.

We see a Chinook appear on the horizon, through the NVGs. The dark green speck gets bigger. It's coming from our far left, travelling over the tiny Afghan base that seems to get smashed every night from surrounding Taliban forces. I watch the Chinook, rotors thumping as it heads closer. I can now see the wheels on its undercarriage.

Hold on, it's getting really close to us. Engines whining, rotors chopping, it swoops down towards us. The noise is so loud that I can't even hear my own voice when I shout across to Bola. Everyone in the camp must have heard it but as I peek down the stairs into the camp, nothing is stirring.

I instinctively duck as the chopper looks as if it is about to land on our heads, ripping the reinforced roof off the top of the sangar. It thunders past, missing the top of the sangar by a few feet. Bola and I laugh nervously. Jesus, what was that all about? It would have been nice to have been told that a helicopter would be coming in. The Chinook roars away towards Ouellette but strangely it doesn't land there. It looks as if they have landed nearer the 611.

Later, we are told that it was the SAS out on a covert raid. It felt close in the sangar but those guys know what they are doing. What a way to go? Wiped out in a sangar by the British Army's most elite regiment. We never get to find out what they are up to on their night excursion. It's possible a Taliban facilitator was woken up in the middle of the night with a dig in the ribs as he was surrounded by a group of black clad ninjas.

This is a risky place for reasons I could never even have imagined. Sometimes, though, the threat is not always outside the wire.

CHAPTER 21

INSIDER THREAT

*"It is easier to forgive an enemy
than to forgive a friend"
– William Blake*

HE is the enemy within. Peter is singled out by Queeny for getting too close to one of the interpreters. Peter is one of the cleverest, most easy-going soldiers here. Yet, he could get kicked out of Dara for fraternising with the 'enemy'.

It seems like a bad joke. We could lose one of our best soldiers. All over nothing. Queeny is furious over the amount of time Peter is spending with one of the interpreters, seeing this as evidence that he is about to 'go rogue'. The whole episode seems ridiculous especially when the interpreters are our allies, the very people we are there to help.

This is Peter's second tour of Afghanistan. He dived into

a ditch, listening to bullets whistle inches past his head on the last tour. He is one of the most switched-on guys we have here, yet he is facing the prospect of being sent back to Ouellette for the heinous 'crime' of playing chess with an interpreter. Queeny seems to get on well with Peter although I think the banter sometimes goes too far. When Queeny wins at chess, he insists that Afro-Caribbean Peter has to be his slave for the day. It works both ways, though, as Peter apparently gave caucasian Queeny a disparaging look once, muttering: "Ah, you people" meaning, "Ah, you white people." The famous Army banter.

It's all meant as a joke, but what isn't funny is Queeny's treatment of the "'terps" as we call them. In his eyes, if he is feeling generous he views them as exotic, suspicious and untrustworthy. At worst, he sees them as hostile outsiders in league with the Taliban. I can't understand it, assuming at first that the whole chess-playing debacle is a wind up.

After speaking to a few others, I find out that this is definitely not a joke. Queeny is worried about the amount of time Peter is playing chess with a young, wavy-haired terp called Sayeed. They do spend a lot of time playing chess but that's because they are good at it and enjoy playing. Let's face it, there's not that many options to keep yourself amused at Dara. You have to grab them where you can.

They sit early in the morning or late into the evening in the dining/recreation area opposite the kitchen under the shade of a wriggly tin canopy. There is nothing covert or suspicious about the pair. They don't sit huddled together, plotting. Sayeed speaks perfect English so they occasionally chat away but more often than not, they sit engrossed, staring at the chess board trying to decide the next move.

We do have a very high turnover of terps here. One of them looks like an Elvis impersonator that has gone to seed. He has thick black hair, slicked back off his face and a slight paunch. He is also in his mid-to-late thirties, older than most of the interpreters we get. The rumour is that his dad is high up in the Afghan army or police. He looks about as happy to be here as we are.

In the early days of the tour, we had a lanky terp with collar length hair who was as thin as a cadaver. He seldom spoke to us, only mumbling a "thank you" at meal times when we dished out spam fritters or curry. He was with us for no more than a month or two. When he went, there were whispers that he was found to have mobile phone sim cards on him. Sim cards can contain dodgy incriminating contact details. Phones and their sim cards can also be used to detonate roadside bombs.

I spoke to another terp who sported long hair, a bushy beard and Oakley wraparound sunglasses, looking to all the world like a special forces soldier ready to plunge behind enemy lines. He wasn't especially religious so I asked him why he had the beard. His answer was telling. "I am keeping the beard for when the Taliban are back in power," he said.

I feel sorry for the terps, as I fear they may be thrown to the dogs once we leave. Some 600 Afghans who worked as interpreters for the British Army will be given the chance to move back to Britain once the withdrawal kicks in. Visas will be offered to half the terps working for the armed forces and the Foreign Office. God knows what will happen to the rest.

Only certain terps will get visas for themselves and their 'immediate dependents' to come to Britain for a period of five years, along with free travel. Those eligible will have had to serve for at least 12 months 'outside the wire' where British troops have been fighting the Taliban. Those who do not qualify for emigration to the UK will be offered the choice of 18 months' pay or money for training and education for up to five years if they want to learn a skill or take an IT course. If they feel their lives are in danger they can report threats under the UK's intimidation policy, which offers relocation to Britain in 'extreme cases'.

I read that 94 per cent of respondents had received threats since they started working for the British. Fewer than three per cent of interpreters said they will feel safe in Afghanistan when UK forces withdraw. Twenty interpreters have died since 2001 – five were abducted and murdered by insurgents. Canada, Australia, New Zealand and the US have all granted Afghan interpreters the right to asylum. If anyone deserves to come to my country, it's these people.

Queeny doesn't share my respect for the terps. Their main job is to monitor the radios, listening in on Taliban communications. Their handlers are a couple of English signallers attached to us. They tend to keep themselves to themselves but they still manage to rile him. We have been told to look out for changes in their demeanour such as extreme nervousness, becoming more devout or mumbling, as signs they may be going 'rogue' by preparing to attack us.

The terps' space is next to the kitchen, where they sit or

lie sprawled out on grimy off-white mattresses, listening in to the intercepts as the pasty-faced soldiers with them sit watching movies on their laptops. They seem to knock off at a certain time of day which seems weird as I am pretty sure the Taliban still operate outside normal office hours. Mullah Omar doesn't run a nine to five operation. I raise my concerns but get roundly ignored.

I am not sure what caused Queeny to see Peter as a possible insider threat. The idea seems laughable. Maybe cabin fever is starting to kick in, with months of living on top of each other beginning to take its toll?

Peter's brow furrows as he tells me about his run-in with Queeny. "I can't believe it, man. I don't want to get kicked up the road to Ouellette." He seems as shocked as I am. We all know the risk though. Fear of 'green on blue' attacks is all too apparent. 'Green' in this case represents Afghan forces and 'blue', meaning Nato troops, is shorthand for an insider attack. They are another weapon in the Taliban's armoury of "asymmetric warfare".

They know they can't win an open firefight so now they use roadside bombs. As coalition troops get better at beating the IED threat, the Taliban hit back with the insider attack. Since 2008, there have been 142 coalition deaths after Afghans turned on their allies. Another 163 coalition troops were injured in such attacks.

Five British soldiers were killed in one of the worst green on blue atrocities in 2009. A rogue Afghan policeman blasted troops that he worked alongside, without warning. The officer, known as Gulbuddin, was being trained by the

British soldiers at checkpoint Blue 25 in Helmand. He went on the rampage with his AK47 before fleeing. His motive has never been established although the Taliban claimed he was one of their own.

These attacks are also very close to home. As I mentioned in a previous chapter, a soldier from this battalion was shot dead at close range by a rogue member of the Afghan army while playing a football match on Remembrance Day in 2012. Captain Walter Barrie was playing alongside members from the Afghan National Army (ANA) at his base when he was gunned down. The gunman was dressed in full ANA uniform when he walked up to the pitch and fired nine shots at Capt Barrie. He was highly regarded at his old battalion so scores of 2 SCOTS soldiers turned out for his funeral just before we left to start this tour. Maybe this influenced Queeny's thinking but it still made no sense as Peter is one of us, a key player in the team.

Once it is clear that the terps are a permanent feature for the entire tour, Queeny insists that all our weapons are centralised in a makeshift armoury in the ops room. Normally, we would keep our rifles beside us, even when we slept. He thinks they are better off in the ops room under the watchful eye of whoever is on stag. He also makes us have a roaming sentry, a soldier that wanders, armed in full body armour, around the camp to make sure the terps stay down in their side of the camp. This move is supposed to stop them going mad, grabbing a rifle and going on the rampage.

Queeny seems to loathe the terps for reasons that no-one can fathom. He rages when the Muslim interpreters ask for more water to wash themselves before they pray. He also fumes when they say that for religious reasons they can't eat pork. "Fucking clowns, just gie them fuckin' spam, they should be grateful," he says in earshot of a bemused-looking interpreter. He seems to be on a one-man mission to turn the terps against us by isolating and harassing them. His worst outburst is still to come.

Mercifully, after Queeny sits down with Peter for some 'face time', the problem disappears. As suddenly as the drama flares up, it evaporates. Peter stays. I don't know what is said but everything goes back to normal.

Sitting in the sangar one night, Peter and I look out into the Green Zone as the daylight fades. Bright orange tracers whip across the night sky, throwing up sparks as they smash into Hesco walls or compounds. Observation Post Zumbalay, a tiny outpost like ours, is under attack again. The Taliban seem to surround the place before smashing it with heavy weapons night after night. There is so much gunfire that it's hard to tell what is coming from the enemy and what's being fired by friendly Afghan forces. In some ways, it's a microcosm of this whole conflict. Sometimes, it's hard to tell who are the good guys and who are the bad.

Peter was always one of the good guys. He is taciturn tonight. When I ask about the outcome of his run-in with Queeny, he just looks thoughtful, chewing on a toothpick. So, what's the score I ask him? Business as usual, he tells me, as we stare out into the unforgiving Green Zone.

CHAPTER 22

FINAL FORAY

*"Secret operations are essential in war, upon
them the army relies to make its every move"*
– Sun Tzu

NO-ONE wants to die with the end in sight. A massive blitz into the Green Zone is planned to disrupt the mortar teams that have been blasting away at us for months. Enthusiasm for this adventure is at an all-time low. We are nearing the finish line so everyone views this op as a potential disaster.

It makes no sense – why now? We have been getting IDF for ages. Dara was actually built to stop the Taliban using this rocky hill as a firing point to rain death on Ouellette. They have just modified their tactics, firing from the villages and compounds or the Green Zone.

It feels like being on Death Row. Days of waiting, pacing

about Dara, with this mission hanging over our heads like a guillotine. Are we going on this op or not? When will we find out? What exactly is our job going to be? As per usual, there are lots of questions but very few answers.

Day and night have long lost their meaning as we stag on relentlessly. Three hours on, four off, all day and night. We are bleeding, as the Army phrase goes. The boys are definitely bleeding. We look like a ragtag mob of dead-eyed zombies as we shuffle about, eating our spam and noodles washed down with tepid water.

Now might not be the best time to go for a wander about the Green Zone. Ramadan and Eid, two key events in the Islamic calendar, passed without incident. Young boys and men in the area did seem to get a bit more boister-ous, burning tyres and wandering about at all hours. After a gang of tyre burners got a bit too close to us for comfort, a sergeant fired a flare at them. The ball of white spitting fire had the desired effect as they ran off in all directions. A firework roaring at your face tends to focus the mind.

The pattern of life is the same. People working the fields, the muezzin calling the faithful to prayer throughout the day and night. I watch a small family, who live in a ramshackle compound at the foot of the hill that Dara perches on. They are by far the closest people to us. I'm told this is because they wanted to live, literally, under our protective shadow. A woman with jet black hair and a baby permanently strapped to her hip, seems to be the no-nonsense matriarch. She wears what appears to be bright coloured saris as she collects firewood or cooks. There's no hint of the burka here that the

Taliban supposedly force their womenfolk to wear.

Her daughter is a toddler with a shock of brown hair, like a troll doll. She runs around with a grubby t-shirt on, trying to grab the tails of dogs or goats. It's rare to see the man of the house, although he does occasionally make an appearance. He can be seen, bearded and wearing the ubiquitous shalwar kameez, as he tends his goats in a pen made from branches, twine and old bits of barbed wire.

I am not one for sentimentality or romanticising poverty but I envy the simplicity of their lives. No office politics, no bills, no hassle other than feeding and looking after your family. It amazes me how little we really need to live. I learned that out here. I can't help but wonder what will happen to this wee family that has lived in our shadow for so long. What will happen when we leave?

Finally, we are told what is happening with this op into the Green Zone. A group of snipers will come down to Dara as we provide overwatch for the foray into the area around Taliban Town 1, 2, and 3. We hear through the Dara rumour mill that the 2 SCOTS hierarchy has refused to allow its men to go out in the vehicles. Most people on the ground view this op as a badly planned adventure. For once, the battalion's senior officer seems to agree. Soldiers from other units will provide the manpower as we watch over them from our vantage point at Dara.

It sounds like the assault on Leningrad. A few days later, the throbbing rumble rolling across the dunes signals that the op is underway. Scores of armoured vehicles, like metal boxes on caterpillar tracks, thunder from the 611 into the

Green Zone. They roll past the compounds that are now such a familiar part of our landscape, leaving a huge plume of dusty sand in their wake. If the Taliban didn't know they are coming, they sure do now.

Our area is too dangerous to wander about on foot so this is a vehicle patrol. These rumbling behemoths are Warthogs, an ugly name for an ugly vehicle. They are the British answer in the spiralling race to outwit the Taliban's bomb makers. They build bigger bombs; we then design bigger, better vehicles in response.

These 19-ton wagons replace Viking and Vector vehicles, which were taken out of service after a total of 12 soldiers died in them. Lieutenant Colonel Rupert Thorneloe, the commanding officer of the Welsh Guards, was among those killed while travelling in a Viking. He became the most senior officer in the British Army to die in combat since Colonel H Jones in the Falklands.

It's meant to be one of the safest vehicles in theatre at the moment. It is better armoured than the Viking, and has been equipped with state-of-the-art counter measures against bombs and mines. They boast improved electronics, and seats which protect crews and passengers more effectively in the event of a blast. It is also faster, enabling it to get away from attacks more easily. I still don't want to get in one though.

Dozens of vehicles plough into the Green Zone, manoeuvring over ditches and across bridges as they sweep through into bandit country. Their route is like a big sweep, a circuit that takes them through the tiny hamlets that border the irrigation canals that criss-cross our area.

An operation of this scale would normally take a month to plan but this one is organised in a week-and-a-half. Three or four shots pierce the morning air, rattling off in the general direction of the vehicles. This is the Taliban's way of saying: "We are still here and we won't go away or be intimidated", rather than a sustained barrage of well aimed, heavy fire.

After roughly six hours, the vehicles loop round, cutting past the ragged flags of the local graveyard on their way back to the 611 and Ouellette. No-one died and there were no injuries. We get a briefing from Queeny telling us that they found three tons of fertiliser and eight or nine items which could be component parts of IEDs.

There's a healthy dose of scepticism at Dara about the reasons for the op. As we sit around the trestle tables next to the kitchen, drinking cups of tea in the gathering gloom, there's a muted atmosphere. Some say that since we are in a rural area, there could be a legitimate reason for having fertiliser. Also, a torch bulb, a battery or even black insulating tape could be classed as a "potential IED component" if needs be. Doubtless, this will be painted as a huge victory. A young soldier pipes up: "This op only happened 'cos some of the high heid yins got mortared when they were up at Ouellette on a visit the other week."

The day after the op, we get mortared five times. Perhaps the Taliban are thumbing their nose at us. I can't help but feel they are trying to send a message – you come into our territory and you will suffer the consequences. We spend the day running backwards and forwards to the reinforced bunker as the IDF alarm wails away at Ouellette.

We breathe a collective sigh of relief that the op went off without incident. Was it a success or a waste of time? As with many things in Afghanistan, it's too hard to tell.

CHAPTER 23

THE END IS NIGH

*"Fixed fortifications are monuments
to the stupidity of man"
– General George S Patton*

A BEDRAGGLED man lumbers towards us, staggering like a drunken tramp, his long shirt bunched up and looking suspiciously bulky. "Get the fuckin' terp up here nooow!" a soldier screams. The man in our sights could be a suicide bomber wandering up here to wreak havoc. In a split second, he could trigger a suicide vest and take us all with him.

This is our most vulnerable time and the Taliban know it only too well. Only a few weeks before, a suicide bomber had blown a hole in a base's perimeter defences before a wave of insurgents flooded into the camp, taking advantage of the bloody chaos.

"Lift up that shirt! Lift it up!" we scream in unison. After a few puzzled glances and the terp's help, the bearded man lifts his loose fitting pyjama-style top to reveal his wiry, hairless torso. No suicide vest, thank God.

It feels like the Alamo. We sit sweating it out, besieged on all sides by swarms of local men and boys who have been pelting us with boulders for days. They know we are leaving. Our tents have been hauled down so we are sleeping under canvas ponchos to shade us from the piercing sun. The temperature drops, but only to the low forties, as we start to collapse the camp.

This is history in the making, the beginning of the end. The withdrawal of thousands of British troops in Afghanistan, the end of more than 10 years of combat starts here, now. It is, however, too panicky to sit back and savour this pivotal moment in the Afghan campaign.

Every curious local is a potential walking improvised explosive device. It has been twitchy over the last few weeks. For months, most of the locals gave us a wide berth, not coming anywhere near us but that's all changed now. Kids and young teens have been using slingshots to bombard us with rocks. They slam into the sheets of bullet proof glass in the sangars, shattering the reinforced panes.

The Taliban's use of children as scouts is well known and now there are kids everywhere. Boys, with tousled hair and grimy faces, try to pull out metal posts that secure our perimeter fences. These children are so poor that they are desperately ripping out massive rolls of vicious looking razor wire from our perimeter fence, oblivious to the blood pouring from their hands.

Older fighting-age males stand in the background, impassively waiting to see what will happen next. People are flooding towards our camp now as sentries are posted on the walls. We feel impotent as we are warned not to fire warning shots, or even mini flares to keep people back. Danish tanks are brought in as a show of force to stop the place being over-run. They fire flares in a vain attempt to keep the human tide back. One of the flares screams over our Hesco walls, nearly hitting a soldier in the face as he walks back to his cot bed.

"When are they coming down to pick us up?" I ask no-one in particular as I stare out at a wall of faces, edging nearer our walls. The end can't come soon enough for me. Our last day here has been postponed and put back so often, we all thought this day would never come. We would get to within sight of the finish line only to be told that our plans to withdraw back to Bastion had been changed at the last minute. Queeny would say: "Right troops, the dates have changed again, we are no' goin' noo." I would have cried at the soul-destroying news if I had any energy left.

I feel like I am stuck on a treadmill, running at full pelt but not actually going anywhere. Our move is long overdue. Tempers are fraying. Logging on to Facebook and writing emails was a nightly ritual for us before retiring to our lightweight sleeping bags for another sweaty night under the stars, but the Wifi is now long gone. Sleep deprivation and stress manifest themselves in odd ways. In this pressure cooker environment, small things that wouldn't normally raise an eyebrow became major sources of tension. Smokers faced a daily battle to try and eke out their cigarette supplies. Water is often rationed, making washing difficult if not impossible. A furious row erupts over a can of pineapple chunks. The tin vanishes from the cool box, leading to a witch hunt to find the culprit. No-one admits it.

In the last few days, Teru has pulled me up for talking while on guard duty. "Hey you, shut it," he barks at me. "Keep your eyes on your arcs, watch what's happening out there, I don't want to die with the end in sight." I can't argue with that. Queeny also loses it as we are getting bombarded with stones. "Haw you!" he tells the terp, "tell them to pack it in or we'll fuckin' fire rockets into their mosque and burn the place doon!"

The fact no-one ever comes to blows here is testament to the professionalism of the soldiers. For weeks now, we have been eating 24-hour rations, boil in the bag delights such as chilli, spaghetti or even gurkha curry. I actually prefer this scoff. Gone is the stress of cooking for 20 other guys. It's every man for themselves as we boil water in a massive pot over a cooker made from bent chicken wire and Army issue solid fuel blocks.

Looking back on our last few weeks here, I am amazed how the atmosphere turned a tad homo-erotic. One night, I walked out of my tent, turned the corner and saw two soldiers walking, holding hands. They laughed it off, "it's just a carry on". I wasn't the only one to notice the change. Gary Carling was also surprised by how some rough, tough infanteers suddenly began whitening their teeth, plucking their eyebrows or squeezing each others' spots. I had heard about the same thing in all-male prison environments, with vehemently heterosexual men finding their feminine sides.

I'm convinced that prisoners probably enjoy better conditions than we do. At least inmates have their own personal space, their own TV and toilet. Our small gym packed with dumbbells, kettlebells and powerbags has been a lifesaver but it, too, is packed away into an ISO Container before being taken to Ouellette.

I have been worried about the security here for some time. Our camp gate, which is the main access point in the most remote camp in Afghan, is a flimsy square of wire and canvas held together with cable ties. It is months into the tour before an anti-vehicle ditch is dug in around the base. For some reason, which no-one fully understands, our grenade machine guns and 50 cals are packed up and sent to Ouellette while we are still languishing here.

Our home for the last six months is crumbling before our eyes. The main 'super sangar' is already gone. Engineers demolished the fortified tower under cover of darkness to avoid sniper fire. Bulldozers drove back and forth all night, throwing choking clouds of sand, just inches from our heads. As we tried to sleep last night, we were all thinking the same thing. What a way to go! Mangled by a bulldozer right at the end of your tour.

Suddenly, the sky starts to shake. A metallic cacophony seems to be coming from all directions. A black, sinister-looking Apache helicopter suddenly rips through the air, just feet above our heads. I've seen an Apache before but never this close, carving through the dips and crests around our base. It's an awesome sight, an airborne 'show of force' to deter the locals and Taliban from doing something stupid. A crowd of children bolts back to the safety of their compound.

But still they come. Hordes of people throng the hilltop, grabbing at wire, pulling at fences. After a long tour guarding Route 611, a vital lifeline, our final job is to protect the engineers as they tear the place apart around us. It's proving far from easy.

A female dog handler and her canine comrade is brought down to help. She proves to be as ineffectual as the rest of us. Hours pass painfully slowly as I stand on top of the Hesco walls, rifle tight into my shoulder, eye looking through the sight, watching as fighting-age males continue to appear among the crowds of young boys surrounding the camp.

As I scan the compounds around us, looking for enemy firing points, I am still moved by the unrivalled landscape. Staring out of Dara is like looking into a mirror on the past. This place is almost Biblical, a bleak desert landscape that would not be out of place in an Old Testament parable. Camels, donkeys and goats swarm among the sun-blasted dune and crumbling homes.

"When are they coming down to pick us up?" someone shouts in Queeny's general direction. He just looks dazed. A senior officer turns up to see what is going on. He chats to me to boost morale. "Yes, there is a heightened suicide bomber threat at the moment," he says. "The Taliban are co-ordinating the locals coming up here. We have to be on our toes." Brilliant.

He disappears not long before the Quick Reaction Force, a special unit of soldiers that respond to emergencies, are sent down to back us up. They zoom down in a fleet of Mastiffs, spreading out over the hillside. Locals back up but they don't disperse. After stalking around for a while, the QRF soldiers head back to Ouellette.

However, the threat is far from gone. As the hours tick by, more people appear, coming ever closer to the camp again. This is precisely the worrying change in the pattern of life that we are always warned about. Then, a ripple of tension runs through the crowd around us. Two Ancop soldiers arrive, shouting in Pashto. The crowd quickly back off.

One soldier with a flak jacket but no helmet appears to lose his temper, shouting and gesticulating at a group who don't move off quickly enough. He raises his AK47 rifle, firing in the air. Still unhappy, he then fires again in the direction of a young boy. A puff of dust kicks up, just yards away from the child. "Jesus," Gary Carling says, "did ye see how close that was?" They stomp around the perimeter of the camp, grim faced, throwing rocks at locals who pluck up the courage to creep back towards the camp. It's clear the local population fear these Ancop men. They speak no English but sometimes make gestures at us, but no-one knows what they are trying to say.

As swiftly as they appeared, the two Ancop men vanish. Looking towards Ouellette, I see them wandering over the hills, rifles slung over their shoulders as if they are on a Sunday stroll. "It must be chai time," Teru says.

The crowd comes back with a vengeance. We take turns

on what's left of the walls trying to keep them back. We were supposed to get picked up at 6am but it's well into the afternoon. As the day wears on, we end up huddled in a corner, in the shadow of the small stripped out sangar, now roofless with no protection. This husk is the only shelter we have.

'So, this is what the beginning of the end feels like', I think, as I slump under the weight of my body armour at the foot of the sangar. It feels more like the fall of Saigon rather than a glorious tactical withdrawal.

After hours more of interminable, unexplained delays, we pile into a Mastiff vehicle to make the journey over the track connecting us to Ouellette, the first step on our way home. Every day here seemed like a marathon but this is a milestone. As for today, no-one died and that's the main thing. It wasn't another bad day in Helmand.

Sitting at the back of the wagon as we move off, I can't help but notice that this is the same type of vehicle that Bobby died in. He was also sitting at the rear, next to the doors. I shiver despite the excruciating temperature. My head is wrenched from side to side as we hit the dips and furrows in the track. Looking back at what's left of Dara, I see a shaven-headed boy of around eight years old. He is clutching my old chipped mug, emblazoned with the black, red and green of the Afghan flag. I left it sitting on a small wall of Hesco where my bed once was.

He is grinning, holding the mug up to the light as if it is the crown jewels.

CHAPTER 24

OFFSKI

*"The first virtue in a soldier is endurance of
fatigue. Courage is only the second virtue"*
– Napoleon Bonaparte

MY guts shake with the blast. The concussive blow of the
IED seems to rattle through each and every bone in my
body. I feel it as much as hear it. The metallic thoomp leaves
me pitching and yawing as if I am on a storm-lashed ship.

It reminds me of the sensation of being thrown around that
I had when I was on a train that hit a woman. I was travelling to Edinburgh on an express train a couple of years ago
when the desperate lady decided to end her life. I felt the
train veer from side to side as her body battered along the
bottom of the carriage. This moment has the same feeling
of horror, disbelief and total helplessness.

OFFSKI

There's no Hollywood special effects here, with a burst of technicolour flames amid choreographed pyrotechnics. Just a roiling tawny cloud of sand enveloping the battle tank as it lumbers into place. One minute it is there, the next it is gone. The Danish tank has just been taken out by a booby-trap bomb on a trail leading to Dara, the very same track we went over less than 24 hours before.

It is the final day of the tour. I am on guard at Ouellette, facing the site that was once Dara when the IED rips through the afternoon stillness, wrecking the Leopard tank which has been sent out to watch over the old Dara site, making sure the Taliban don't use it as a vantage point to smash us up here at Ouellette. We were the last patrol to use that rutted track as we abandoned the camp to hordes of local people tearing away at the Hesco and razor wire.

Half a dozen Danish tanks arrived at Ouellette a few days ago to go out over the Dara dip, their huge guns facing into the Green Zone. Their mission was to watch over us, a show of force to deter the Taliban. It worked in the sense that no-one was killed during the collapse of Dara. It seems, though, that the Taliban weren't put off from trying to take out one of these armoured behemoths.

These 52 tonne tanks have sights that are so accurate they can reportedly put a shell through the door of a Taliban compound with 95 per cent accuracy at a range of two-and-a-half miles. However, as this attack shows, they aren't invulnerable to attacks themselves.

These Danish soldiers inside the tank are coming towards the end of their tour, just like us. The Danes are pulling

259

out of Afghanistan. At around this time, their soldiers were also ending their 12-year involvement in the war. Denmark originally planned to withdraw its troops by the end of 2014 but decided to speed up their drawdown in line with their British and American allies.

Their homeland is divided over the war. Denmark is one of the countries that have carried the toughest load in Afghanistan. Many of their countrymen see their service as invaluable, protecting the streets of Copenhagen and other towns and cities from the efforts of Al Qaeda and their allies.

But politicians such as Zenia Stampe, the defence spokeswoman for coalition party Radikale, say the war is a mistake, that soldiers were sent on the "wrong" and "impossible" mission of introducing democracy to Afghanistan. Their campaign cost the lives of 43 Danish soldiers and resulted in total costs of approximately 15 billion kroner, or £1.6bn. Another 211 Danes were injured in Afghanistan. I just hope the guys inside the tank haven't joined that death toll.

After what feels like a lifetime, the hatch of the tank opens as a soldier looks through the wafting clouds of dust. Out of the corner of my eye, I can see a rescue force is being scrambled to help the soldiers and recover the crippled tank.

After a minute or two, there is the sound of an air horn from inside the camp. A soldier somewhere presses the pneumatic device which is used as an IDF alarm. This camp now thinks it's under attack. People start running for shelter, thinking mortars are about to start raining down.

My vantage point in a guard tower means that I know this is a false alarm. I radio the ops room telling them about the

IED strike, and the need to signal the all clear. There is no mortar attack today.

Another Danish tank clanks out to help his stricken comrades. No-one is injured. Inches of armour have done their job, protecting the soldiers from the blast. They escape shaken with cuts and bruises but it could have been far worse. The tank seems badly damaged. Its front end is bent and mis-shapen, as though it has smashed into a wall at high speed. One of the tank's track is split and blown off, lying black in the sand like an old burnt tree trunk.

It later emerges that the bomb may have been planted by a child under the cover of darkness. The blast again re-emphasises how much worse things could have been. I can't get it out of my head that we drove over the exact same spot just the day before. My Dara mates and I could have been in that blast. Until you are completely out of harms way, no-one can afford to let their guard down in Afghanistan. A soldier's eternal optimism, that "it won't happen to me" just does not apply here. A sergeant major mate's words came back to me: "Treat every day in Afghanistan as if it's your first. Never get complacent."

After sentry duty, I trudge back to my bed for some much needed rest. I am working with Gary Carling, my old Dara gym buddy Sean Neil and Mauritian Essoo. We are tasked with taking guard shifts in the sangars while the rest of our Dara mates clean out ISO Containers and humph kit. I eat a cold ration pack of beef and cassava which smells like dog food. It makes me want to gag but I eat it anyway. The cookhouse at Ouellette is long gone, dismantled and packed up. So, we have to fend for ourselves. There are no tents here now either so we have set up our dilapidated, ripped cot beds against a Hesco wall, covering them with a couple of ponchos to give us some shade.

I am desperate for a wash before I try and sleep. My skin feels as if it has been scoured by the unforgiving sand. Gary tells me the wash point is just around the corner so off I go, wrapped in a towel, wearing flip flops and clutching my washbag. Five minutes later, I arrive at what was once the shower area. All of the showers, bowls and mirrors have vanished. I am forced to wash using tepid bottled water in the middle of a dusty track with armoured vehicles driving past. Amazingly, passing soldiers don't even raise an eyebrow as I lather up in the fading sunlight.

Walking back to my bed space, I get covered in sand again, defeating the purpose of getting washed in the first place. No matter how hard you try it's tough to try and stay clean here. It's like painting the Forth Bridge. You wash and scrub and by the time you towel yourself down, you are already covered in a greasy film of sand, grime and sweat.

Our wee cubbyholes are deserted. Gary must be on duty in one of the sangars. Essoo and Sean might be up at a joint operations office which works with Afghan forces. The sunshine is calming down but it's still too hot to sleep so I jump up on top of the Hesco walls, clutching a paperback I have been trying to finish for weeks. The title *Inferno* is quite apt given the hellish temperatures we get out here.

I am right in the middle of the camp, well away from the perimeter defences, so there is no sniper threat here. I can sit on the top of the Hesco wall, minus body armour and helmet, without fear that I'll get a bullet through my skull.

I'm reading Dan Brown's latest book as a form of pure escapism. I would never normally read his work but in Afghanistan, his far-fetched tales of cryptography, secret societies and convoluted murders are just what I need, chewing gum for the eyeballs. Opening the book, I notice the pages seem loose. Flicking through, they start to come away in my hand. The glue in the book's spine is melting.

Time for bed then. I clamber down off the wall, laying my lightweight sleeping bag out on top of my cot. A shrill, piercing noise grabs my attention. Standing bolt upright, I twang my head off the bungee cords that attack my poncho sheet to the Hesco. *The IDF alarm. Christ.* I roll my eyes upwards, noticing the sky as blue as an electric spark. At least if this is my time, as the medics work on me, I can stare up in the sky and imagine I am somewhere more pleasant.

Snapping out of my daydream, I grab my body armour and helmet and start to leg it. We have been given a guided tour of what's left of the camp so I know where to find the bomb proof shelter. I make it to the welfare room-cum -bunker. It's reinforced steel beams and Hesco roof mean it will survive a direct hit from any Taliban mortars or rockets. The stomach tightening prospect of imminent death or life changing disfigurement is replaced with the old familiar boredom of 'hurry and wait'. Soldiers slump around in various states of dress, from full uniform to shorts and t-shirts waiting for the all clear. Eventually, the all clear comes and we slope off back to our beds to chill out.

I am still too wired to sleep so I dig out an on old bluey that I was in the process of writing to Lynda. A bluey is the slang name for Forces Free Air Letters, blue aerogrammes that don't need a stamp. I have a sticker that I bought in the cavernous American PX store at Bastion that has been languishing at the bottom of my black kitbag since I went on R&R. It has a yellow ribbon and a heart on it, with the words 'Missing You! From Afghanistan'. I stick it the top right-hand side of the bluey.

I start writing, telling her how glad I am to be going home for good, how much I have missed her, how much I have missed some good miserable Scottish weather. She has been asking me whether I will go out again to Afghan so I try and reassure her that this is it. There'll be no more jaunts to this place, that's for certain. I also tell her how I plan to take us away on a holiday, perhaps to New York since we loved it so much when we went there a few years ago. I even hint that I may use my operational bonus cash to get her that expensive diamond ring she is constantly bending my ear about. I smile as I read over the letter, she will like that. Putting the letter into my daysack, I make a mental note to post it before I get on the flight to Bastion.

After an hour or two of snatched sleep, I'm woken up with a nudge and the immortal lines: "Pssst, mate! You are on stag." Groaning, I grab my weapon, getting my gear on for my last sangar shift. Clambering up the wooden steps to the tower, I see through the murk that my sangar buddy is one of the dog handlers I have seen wandering around camp. We pass the hours in idle chit-chat although he does open his heart, explaining how his girlfriend, also a soldier, has fallen out with him after he was seen chatting to another female soldier. I tell him that, at Dara, we never had that problem. No women came near us for the full tour.

Later on, a couple of illumination flares are fired up over the no man's land between us and the surrounding compounds. A couple of figures are spotted, skulking around, running from some dead ground. Even with the green all seeing eye of the NVGs, we still can't see them.

My last shift ends mercifully quickly. I head back to our wee encampment where Gary is packing up his gear. It's just after 3am so we have a few hours before our flight but it's better to get up to the flight line as soon as possible. There's no way we want to get bumped off this flight.

My back's breaking trying to haul all our gear. We are all wearing full 'battle rattle' for the flight: helmet, Osprey body armour with chest, back and side ceramic plates, ballistic glasses, hearing protection, three tiers of pelvic protection including anti-microbial lycra boxers and a Kevlar 'combat nappy' to safeguard your bits.

Sitting in a massive, empty white tent that serves as our version of a departure lounge, we sprawl across the floor or flop on a couple of battered wooden benches. It's not long now. A few of the old Dara faces start coming through the door. We all look shattered but who cares? Going to Bastion has never felt so good.

We move out to the helicopter landing site, forming two lines ready to sprint on to the back of the Chinook. Gary gives me a thumbs up, I grin back. There's a lot of backslapping. Ross thumps me on the back: "Oooh, Stevie boy! This is it! We are offski, outta here, on our way home, son!"

The thunder grows closer. Then we see the helicopters swooping down to us. As the Chinooks flare up, blasting sand and grit across our backs, I can't help but smirk as I tuck my chin into my chest. We trot up the ramp at the back of the chopper, dumping our bags in a big pile in the aisle at our feet.

Looking over my shoulder through the tiny circular window, I grab a glimpse of the sun-blasted, featureless chunk of rock and sand where Dara used to sit. Smiling again, I am struck by the fact that there's a great irony at work here. When I was in Camp Bastion at the start of the tour, I hated the place. It encapsulates everything I loathe about the Army: the barracks bullshit, rules about rules. You can be pulled up for not having a torch on at night, soldiers must wear a high vis belt after a certain time, troops have to wear full uniform and head-dress pretty much all the time.

There's so many reasons I don't like Bastion.

Now, though, I can't get there soon enough.

CHAPTER 25

HEATHROW IN THE DESERT

*"Farewell has a sweet sound of reluctance.
Goodbye is short and final, a word with
teeth sharp to bite through the string that
ties past to the future"*
– John Steinbeck

"HEY, get they fuckin' boots aff! It's issue boots when you are cuttin' aboot here." And so it begins. I am just back in Bastion a few hours and I am reprimanded from a grumpy colour sergeant for wearing non-regulation boots. I've been on the frontline for six months but that makes no difference.

I toy with the idea of ignoring him. Queeny has also been having a go at me about these boots so I could make a stand. Opting for a quiet life, I dig my old Meindl boots out of my bergen and start wearing them. Anything for an easy life. In a week or two, I'll be home anyway.

Someone else gets pulled up in the cookhouse for not having ties in the bottoms of his trousers. Wearing them with ties, which are green bits of elastic with hooks at each end, tucks the trousers in and is considered smart. Wearing trousers that are loose is considered untidy. I play the game.

Anyone who has been involved in the military knows there can be a lot of daft rules: "Don't walk on the barracks grass". "Sleeves must be rolled up/down depending on the time of day, month etc". My favourite was the old, "no hands in pockets" rule despite the fact that the issue smock has fleece lined pockets, specifically designed to keep your hands cosy while on exercise.

Well, all of the old rules and regulations are being enforced with a vengeance now that we are back in Bastion or "Remf-land" as some of my mates call it. Gary sums it up: "All of this guff about boots and discipline and aw that, is supposed to get us used to 'barracks routine'. That's fair enough, but you and I don't normally live and work in a barracks so it isny routine for us." He laughs: "Anyway, I'll leave you tae tell Queeny that."

I feel almost untouchable as it's almost over. We are up at dawn every day now for PT, which consists of a run around the roads that criss-cross Bastion. It feels good to get to actually stretch my legs after months of being cooped up at Dara.

Getting up at 5.30am doesn't feel too bad. I dive into short, t-shirts and trainers before we form up outside our tent. It's just a straightforward gallop for four miles or so. Near the end, a sergeant stops us so we can divide into pairs in a sprint to the finish line.

After we get a shower, it's off to the cookhouse for a proper breakfast. The whole camp is a lot quieter than when we passed through here at the start of the tour. Some of our unit's guys have been held up at Ouellette, handing over the base to the Afghans.

We hear that the transfer was far from smooth. There was a delay as the main group of Ancop troops didn't show up on time. Supposedly, the Ancop weren't too keen to take over the camp. Tempers reportedly flared, weapons may have been brandished. A soldier, who was up there at Ouellette, tells me the place was in the process of being demolished as the Afghans just did not want to hold on to it.

Sitting in Heroes cafe, a slick welfare facility with flat screen TVs and pool tables in the heart of Bastion, I am catching up with the news online on my tablet when I stumble across an MOD press release about Ouellette.

It stands in stark contrast to what I'm told about the eventual fate of Ouellette. It reads: 'In a further demonstration of the increasing capability and confidence of the Afghan National Security Forces (ANSF), British troops have handed over control of Ouellette to the Afghan National Civil Order Police (ANCOP).

'The base, which is situated on Route 611 in the district of Nahr-e Saraj, had been home to UK Armed Forces since July 2011. Its transfer is part of an ongoing base reduction programme which is expected to leave just four forward operating bases in central Helmand in addition to Camp Bastion by the end of October 2013.

'The handover comes as British forces no longer routinely provide support to Afghan forces in Nahr-e Saraj District which was marked by a ceremony held by Afghan officials. Security for Route 611 is now entirely conducted by the Ancop who will retain the base as part of their force structure in the area. Base reductions are discussed closely with the local Afghan forces to ensure the best solution as part of the ANSF's enduring presence in the area.

'Route 611 is a crucial link between northern Helmand and the provincial capital Lashkar Gah. Security along the route is key to the freedom of movement for locals, which in turn promotes governance and economic development.'

'Task Force Helmand commander Brigadier Rupert Jones hails the handover as a soaraway success and "another indicator of the progress of the Afghan security forces as a whole that we have seen across central Helmand this summer". He adds: "As we come to the closing stages of what is typically the fighting season it's a good moment to reflect on the reality that the Afghan National Security Forces have done exceptionally well. They have very firmly held the momentum in Helmand over the insurgent all the way through.'

I know people that will certainly take issue with that assessment. I never get to the bottom of what happened to Ouellette. Is it still even there? My journalistic instincts tell me that the campaign in Afghanistan is clearly as much a propaganda war as anything else.

I meet Russ later that day. He is staying in the tent next to us and the other Dara soldiers. Our tents are huge, like long hospital wards situated under canvas. Beds line each side of the tent. Each man has a cot bed and there's no bunk beds for a change. There's also very little privacy but at least there is air conditioning.

We decide to get on the decrepit shuttle bus that trundles around Bastion to take us to the so-called Blue PX for a burger. It doesn't take long to get tired of the cookhouse so the change will do me good. I feel fed up and just want to get home. A night out on the tiles, or as good as you can get in a huge alcohol-free military camp, will perk me up.

It's good to see Russ. I think he appreciates the chance to get the chance for a chat with Gary and I away from the babble of the younger, regular soldiers. Inevitably, our talk gets around to Bobby's death. He tells us about the repatriation, how well it went, how he struggled to keep it together during the ceremony.

A few months ago, we were all sitting, like this, in a takeaway with Bobby talking about the tour, what it would be like for us, how we would cope and our plans for coming home. Now, he is gone. I still find it difficult to comprehend. I never thought that the war would come so close to home.

In Afghanistan, death or disfigurement is never that far away. It's also very random. A guy can stand on a pressure plate IED that doesn't go off but then minutes later, his mate stands on the same device and ends up losing his legs. I know a soldier who triggered an IED but the main charge was far behind him so the bomb killed his pal, embedding pieces of his mate's splintered bones into his own flesh.

A few nights later, I'm lying in my cot bed, reasonably comfortable even though the metal framework feels as if it's on its last legs. I've just started on my latest eBook on my Kindle when a soldier sticks his head through the tent door: "Here Stevie, you have to go along to the vehicle park, I think Queeny has pinged you tae clean the Mastiffs."

Surely some mistake? Is he getting revenge on me for wearing non-issue boots or does he genuinely think I am what he calls a "grassing journo", worthy of his contempt? Who knows? I am past caring, I'll do whatever I'm told. A few other soldiers, looking like condemned men, are gathered in the darkness at the side of the huge hulking Mastiffs.

It's just after 9pm and we spend the next 10 hours washing the wagons. We drive to a wash area with ramps so we can get underneath the wagons with high pressure water hoses. As far as I can tell, we are just moving the dust and grit around, rather than getting rid of it. During a tea break in a nearby Portakabin, a gangly lance corporal looks at us, dripping sweat and grime. "This is shite," he says, "but we are aw just semi-skilled manual labourers, that's aw."

I crawl back to my tent just as some guys are getting up, getting changed into their PT gear for the obligatory dawn sprint around the camp. Mercifully, someone has seen fit to grant us an exemption from this run due to our all-night, vehicle-washing endurance test. I'll never moan about having to wash my car again.

I cocoon myself in my sleeping bag, stick in my iPod earphones, then drift away. It's bliss to be left alone for a while. I am out cold for a good few hours. When I wake up, it's mid-afternoon. Time to wander over to the American PX for some shopping. We haven't done that much actual work since we got back to Bastion, and that suits me fine.

The American PX is a massive, air conditioned hangar with loads of rubbish you don't need. There's all kinds of militaria: pistol holsters, desert boots, Shemaghs, sunglasses in every shape and colour. They seem to cater to a particular kind of over zealous National Guardsmen from Texas who would be labelled a 'kit monster' in the British Army.

I spend most of my time in the candy section or the toiletries aisle. I get half a dozen packets of a kind of American sweets that Lynda loves. They are called 'Hot Tamales', a spicy, cinnamon flavoured hard candy. I enjoy the languorous feeling of aimlessly wandering about with no hassles.

Gary and I wander over to the Green Bean cafe next door for a latte and a muffin. He isn't much of a shopping fanatic on these trips. "Every penny is a prisoner," he says. After our drinks, we decide to go to the American military DFAC, or Dining Facility, for our evening meal.

I much prefer the food in here. You also receive two cans of soda for free. Result. I manage to consume a Philly cheese steak that's bigger than my head, which is followed by a mound of cherry chocolate ice cream. I've never been that big a fan of fizzy drinks but the freezing cold Pepsi tastes like liquid heaven after six months of drinking tepid, faintly slimy bottled water.

Apart from the odd flurry of activity, which generally involves emptying or filling ISO Containers that are so hot you can't stay inside them for more than a second or two, the days are relatively free and easy. I even begin to enjoy the dawn running frenzy.

Soon enough, it's time for us to catch the flight back to the UK. The reservists are leaving here a week or two earlier than the main body of troops. It's something to do with contracts, or the length of time that we are allowed to stay in theatre or some other arcane military rule but I don't want to ask too many questions in case the powers that be change their minds.

My kit is packed and ready to go, hours before we need to be at the flight line. Gary has done the same. We wander over to a line of containers that sit to the far end of our transit tent accommodation.

A Fijian soldier who runs the stores is there waiting for us. We hand in our weapons, bayonets, morphine syringes, the lot. He locks them away, shutting the ISO Container with a dramatic clang.

This makes it real: we are going home now.

Inside our tent, everyone is back from evening scoff so the place is packed. We walk around each bed space saying our goodbyes, shaking hands, using our time to have a last minute piss-take of each other.

I'm delighted to be heading home but there is a twinge of sadness too. It took ages for me to get to know these guys, to be part of the in jokes, the slagging, to be trusted. Now, I will never see some of them again. I will almost certainly never work alongside them.

As I lumber towards the tent door, with my bergen on my back, my black kitbag in one hand and my daysack in the other, Garry John dives up from his cot to give me one last pat on the shoulder.

"Well, brer," he says. "What did you think of your tour?"
I tell him: "I loved it, but I hated it too."

CHAPTER 26

THE FINAL HURDLE

*"Home wasn't a set house, or a town on a map.
It was wherever the people who loved you were,
whenever you were together. Not a place but
a moment, and then another, building on each
other like bricks to create a solid shelter you
take with you for your life, wherever you may go"*
– Sarah Dessen

IT was billed as an outrageously big piss up with the odd
punch up or two thrown in to spice things up. A drunken
barbecue followed by sun bathing and diving into the clear
blue Cypriot sea. I had heard so many raucous tales about
'decompression' that I was starting to looking forward to it.

Decompression is the British Army's version of Butlins,
designed to let soldiers unwind and de-stress before they
return to the normality of the UK. Only the Army could
come up with the concept of 'enforced fun' or 'mandatory

relaxation'. It is like a holiday camp minus the laughs. We even have our own Army version of redcoats – soldiers tasked with watching over us while sporting lurid red polo tops and natty shorts.

My hopes of a riotous romp across Cyprus are quickly dashed. If this is a holiday, it's the most regimented holiday I have ever had. Everyone just wants to get home. 'It's only a pit stop', I keep telling myself, 'try to enjoy it'. This is the time when you are supposed to look back at the tour, assess everything that's happened and prepare for getting your life back. I feel we have already done that. To me, it just seems like another box ticking exercise.

It does give me some time to think about whether or not I will go back to being a Reservist soldier or whether I will just leave the Army. I am tempted to sign off as completing the tour was my one and only goal. I put those thoughts to one side. That's a decision for another day, not now.

A couple of hours after we arrive in Cyprus, our group of roughly 50 soldiers are herded on to buses before we stop off to grab some breakfast. Then we are bussed to another venue for a series of safety briefings. We get changed into suitable beach attire for our day of fun. Next, it's back on the buses again as we are taken on a long ride on winding roads perched on scrubby hillsides. We arrive tired and bleary eyed at a secluded beach for our day out.

Anyone who wants to go for a dip in the sea has to perform a swimming test consisting of a few hundred metres swim out to a floating, diving platform, then back to the shore. Gary goes for it while I vegetate on a sun lounger. Boredom starts to kick in after a while so we opt for one of the organised activities – horse riding.

A coach takes us out to the stables, where a 50-something English lady talks us through the rigours of riding a horse. My off-white, sad-eyed horse looks totally uninterested as I bound up a couple of wooden steps before climbing into the saddle. All the pulling of reins and nudging him in the ribs with my legs is pointless. He seems determined to do his own thing.

I know I'm supposed to be a rufty tufty infantry soldier but I discreetly ask the young woman who is steering us around the paddock to come along to guide my horse when we go out on the tracks. I don't want to end up in traction thanks to a disobedient horse.

It turns out that rather than being an errant, rampaging force of nature, my horse is an ageing nag that is set in its ways. If it sees some bushes to chew on, it meanders off to the side of the path to have a munch. My resistance is futile.

I enjoy the chance to do something that I've never done before. However, I also make a vow never to do it again in a hurry either. Back at the beach, we are served loads of fresh fruit, salad, soft drinks and ice cream. I can now really start in earnest to gain all the weight I've lost at Dara.

Gary and a few other lads go for a swim so I fall into a surprisingly deep sleep on a sun lounger. Waking up an hour or two later, I can feel the subtle sting of sunburn kicking in. Ah well, at least I will have a tan to show off when I get back. It's ironic that I was sensible enough to stay out of the sun for six months in the Afghan desert, but then end up looking like a lobster after one day in Cyprus.

As the sun starts to drop, we get back on the buses to drive to our home for the night, Bloodhound camp. It sits in splendid isolation up in the hills, with foreboding looking fences presumably to deter us if we decide to go on the rampage before making a dash for Ayia Napa.

We had a barbecue, which wasn't a real barbecue, with the food just prepared in the cookhouse and laid out before us. Then, there was a comedian. We sat in a large auditorium, nursing our cans of beer, as he took the mickey out of officers in the audience.

A strict four can rule was in force. We had to buy vouchers for the beer, which were then stamped when we went to the bar. No room for bucking the system. After the comedian, a mediocre pub band came on. At the end of the night, a few younger soldiers hung about outside the large grey warehouse-looking structure which was our entertainment venue for the night. They chain smoked cigarettes while moaning about only getting four beers. Maybe someone will try and bolt for Ayia Napa after all.

I go to the welfare suite, lined with comfy chairs, computer terminals and newspapers, so that I can email Lynda. I am barely in the door when a burly man in a red shirt tells me that they are shutting down the PCs as the place is closing for the night. *Superb*. I remember I have now got my iPhone back anyway and just text Lynda to say I am safe and well. I can worry about the roaming data charges at a later date.

We are sleeping on bunk beds in a big, breezy 20-man dormitory. One thing I won't miss, when this is over and done with, is the lack of personal space. For the decompression staff, it must have been a good night. No-one drowned, collapsed or went AWOL. It is all reassuringly dull.

Gary goes outside our whitewashed block for a fag. Over the chirping crickets, I can hear him chatting to a blond-haired Paratrooper who is staying in the block next to us. They start to talk about Bobby. Our neighbour from the Parachute Regiment knew Bobby well, they went to university together. I can't sleep so I nip outside to join them.

"It always happens to the good guys," the Para says. He echoes my shock and disbelief. He sounds quite bitter, too, upset that he didn't achieve more during his tour. He fumes at the fact that Bobby was taken by an invisible enemy. They strike and then they are gone. It's like fighting ghosts and shadows, he says.

We set the world to rights for a long time, it could be 45 minutes, it could be an hour or more. When I eventually climb into my top bunk, I finally get it. Decompression has done what it was supposed to. It has served its purpose, giving us a breather, a chance to reflect, to talk about what has gone on. Maybe, it isn't a waste of time after all.

We wake up with just a bus ride and a few hours on a plane between us and the chance to get our lives back. We arrive in Brize Norton, collect our bags with the minimum of fuss, then dash on to the coach for the last leg of the journey. I was hoping that we would catch a shuttle flight from Heathrow up to Edinburgh, but it is not to be. We are getting yet another bus.

There's a bit of a carnival atmosphere on the coach.

Everyone is bright-eyed and grinning like a five-year-old on Christmas morning. After an hour or so, we pile into a service station to stock up on beer, crisps and snacks, but mostly beer. A few renegades crack open the duty free they bought in Cyprus. Some bright spark comes up with the idea of adding rhubarb and custard-flavoured boiled sweets to his bottle of Smirnoff blue label to make an infused vodka. I fear this is going to end in tears one way or another.

A few hours down the road, everyone is chatting away. Music is blaring out from an iPod docking station. It feels like we are going on holiday. A Mancunian officer, with a luxuriant moustache, comes to the back of the bus. He says: "Listen lads, enjoy yourself, just don't get totally ruined, alright?" A wave of laughter ripples around the bus.

We stop off in the north of England for a burger at another service station. Everyone is fairly tipsy as they wander around the concourse. On the way back to the bus, I see a few soldiers standing smoking. Our vodka connoisseur is a few feet away, silently looking at the ground. A second later, he lurches forward, takes a few jittery steps and plunges headfirst into the bushes that line the car park. Without saying a word or betraying a flicker of emotion, a soldier stamps out his fag, picks him up and half drags, half carries him on to the bus.

It's after 3am when we arrive at Glencorse barracks in Edinburgh. A piper is there to pipe us into the camp. A few soldiers are waiting to help us with our kit, shaking our hands, saying "welcome back". We have to stay here as there are a few hours of briefings to be endured in the morning.

A couple of hours sleep then we head to the cookhouse for the powerpoint presentations. The theme seems to be: don't drink and drive, don't waste your op bonus on booze and definitely do not beat your wife/partner/girlfriend. We all agree that there must have been some horror stories in the past for the MOD to insist on this arse-covering exercise.

After an interminable few hours, we are given the green light to head for home. To my horror, I am told that none of us qualify for a free travel pass for the train as we thought we would. No transport has been laid on to the station either. It feels as if we have served our usefulness so now have to fend for ourselves. Eventually, we manage to get a minibus for us and our kit before mutiny breaks out.

We head off in our separate directions at Edinburgh Waverley station. Gary and some of the others are swallowed up by the crowds as they head off to get on the Stirling train while I head for the Glasgow express. I get a nice double seat, spreading myself out. I get out my tablet to use the train's excellent Wifi signal. It feels great to be connected after spending so long at the edge of the known universe, or at least that's how it seemed at the time.

At Dara, Facebook was so slow because of the temperamental Wifi, it was painfully difficult to use. Now, I take the chance to catch up. Some of my fellow Dara inmates have turned into an Internet phenomenon.

A newspaper story on my news feed reads: 'A Facebook campaign has been set up to find the lost love of a Scots soldier. Corporal Garry John Urie, from Paisley, met the girl of his dreams while on R&R from Afghanistan. But a combination of boozing and a poor sense of direction while partying on Ibiza meant he lost all contact with the girl. Friends of the lovelorn soldier, back fighting the Taliban in Helmand, decided to take action to locate the missing girl.'

The article goes on: 'The Dear Garry John Facebook site has more than 1000 likes, with well-wishers promising to spread the word for the 29-year-old. A pal said: "We went to Ibiza basically to have fun because Garry John and his soldier mates need some proper R&R to split up the tension of their time in Afghanistan.

'"Garry got dumped recently and he really fell for this girl in Ibiza and kept going on about her so we thought we'd take some positive action. Garry was embarrassed at first but he has warmed to it and we are hoping to track the girl. She is around 22 and a cute blonde from Cumbernauld or somewhere around Lanarkshire or Glasgow."'

The report says that he doesn't remember much more because he was so bladdered. The romantic encounter happened on his second day in Ibiza. Garry ended up at a pool party and after catching the eye of the girl, he sang *Loving You* by Paolo Nutini in front of everyone. He shuffled off home with his friends, with the intention of popping back to the hotel later. But he was too drunk to remember and only found out the name of the hotel, the Marco Polo II, after she'd flown home. Only Garry John could get so wasted that he meets the love of his life, but can't remember her name or where she comes from. It's hard to stifle a laugh among the sombre-looking commuters.

Then BOOOM!! A huge metallic bang suddenly reverberates through the carriage, causing me to involuntarily duck. The sound reminds me of the IED strike on a Danish tank just a week or two before. Everyone else looks unaffected, reading their magazines or newspapers, looking out of the windows or listening to their iPods. This, after all, is Scotland and not Afghanistan.

Looking around, I see that the ear piercing bang which has just shredded my nerves is caused by the train's trolley dolly dropping a metal drinks tray as she dishes out sandwiches and cold drinks. No-one else even seemed to notice. I decide to pop my earphones in to listen to music and maybe get some sleep. Rooting through my daysack, I find my letter to Lynda. I forgot to post it at either Ouellette or Camp Bastion. I tuck it into my map pocket for safekeeping.

I meet Lynda in George Square in the middle of Glasgow, a few streets away from her work. She has been given a half day off work to pick me up and take me home. She sees me across the street, waving and smiling. I dodge across the late-afternoon traffic, grabbing her in a hug. It feels as if I am truly home now.

It starts to rain, the first rain I have seen in more than six months. She looks at me as if she is about to cry, saying: "Are you really ok? Do you think you have been traumatised?" I just laugh, rain streaming into my eyes. "I am fine, absolutely fine." I don't feel overwhelmed, just relieved that I am back. I know she has read all the Army pamphlets about looking out for changes in her returning soldier, monitoring me for the first signs of mental breakdown. "Take it slow – be patient and communicate", she has been told in the military guidebooks. I even occasionally catch her watching me out of the corner of her eye as we walk down the street.

When we get into her car, I give her my letter. She hugs me, saying: "Don't ever leave me again." She reads the letter, smiling at my plans for us. Each line is full of the holidays we are going to take, the nights out we will have and my plans for OUR future. A line in the letter says: 'When I come home, that's me back for good.' This makes her shine.

As we sit in her small hatchback, the rain gets heavier, turning to hailstones in a matter of minutes. The hail batters down on the car roof, splintering into small pieces. It sounds like stones shattering a sangar's bulletproof glass.

"Afghanistan became part of each person who fought there. Each of the soldiers who went through this war became part of Afghanistan – part of the land that could never absorb all the blood spilled on it"
– Artyom Borovik

TWO MONTHS LATER

MY life has gone full circle. Wearing my civilian uniform of a suit, shirt and tie, I am back working as a journalist. It's a clammy mid-November afternoon as office workers, shoppers and tourists line the streets, jostling for a better view.

Soldiers from my battalion, 2 SCOTS, my mates among them, are about to march through the centre of Scotland's biggest city to mark their homecoming from Afghanistan. I could have joined my comrades for this event in the middle of Glasgow but I didn't fancy the weeks of preparation, the square bashing, polishing and uniform tweaking, that would have gone into making this run smoothly. I opted to go back to my civilian job, sooner rather than later, following my obligatory period of post-operational leave.

Sweat forms in the small of my back thanks to the over-cast, unusually humid weather. God knows how the boys felt wearing their full Highland regalia: highly polished brogues, thick khaki jacket, Glengarry with a cockfeather and the all-important woollen kilt.

As soon as I got to the side street where they were forming up, preparing to step off, I saw a few familiar faces. There was bold Brian, waving as he nudged Davie McCabe and wee Ross. They giggled like schoolboys when they saw me waving. I arrived just as the regimental sergeant major was getting ready to give the order: "By the left, quick march!"

My stomach lurched with pride and nervous anticipation as the pipes and drums kicked in, even though I was only there to write about the march for the newspaper. The entire battalion was here, making for an impressive sight. The battalion's colours stood out in their gold brocaded glory. The military anorak in me remembered that this unit is the only one in the Army to have three colours. These flags are festooned with some of the unit's 200 battle honours, more than any other in the British Army, from Blenheim to Anzio.

Watching the troops march through the city is a fascinating experience. I keep glimpsing faces that I know only too well from my six-month stint at Dara. As I walk alongside the parade, I find myself falling into step as a sergeant major screams "left, right, left, right". As the march weaves its way towards George Square, I feel a fleeting pang of regret that I have not taken up the battalion's offer to march in the parade. Then I shrug and smile, remembering my horror of drill and polishing brass insignia, deciding I had made the right decision after all.

As the troops file into the City Chambers for a swanky civic reception, I bump into some of my old comrades in arms. Garry John, Davie and Ross and I share a few laughs reminiscing about our long, uncomfortable nights at Dara, staring into the twilight as we provided security on Route 611. I could tell they are eager to get all the gear off and, no doubt, get to the pub to celebrate.

Roughly 400 soldiers took part in the parade, but I keep thinking of the guys who did not come home. For many families, this is a time of homecoming, a time of celebration but also a time of relief. Now, they can stop worrying about getting a knock on the door at any time, day or night, from a man in a suit, clutching his military ID card.

Sadly, the families of Corporal William Savage, Private Robert Hetherington and Fusilier Samuel Flint will have to deal with the aftershocks of this tour for the rest of their lives.

At the parade, I heard lots of well wishers shouting: "Well done, you all did a great job out there!" But, did we? Did we make any difference at all on that tour, or any other for that matter? Our campaign in Afghanistan has been accused of 'mission creep'. Britain went there at the start to help catch Osama Bin Laden, preventing him and his cohorts from making Afghanistan a safe haven for international terrorism.

Years later, he is found and killed, not in Afghanistan, but in Pakistan, a so-called ally. Some heavyweight commentators, such as Carlotta Gall and the late Richard Holbrooke, the US special envoy for Afghanistan and Pakistan, have even commented: "We may be fighting the wrong enemy in the wrong country."

Herrick 18 marked the end of an era. My tour was the beginning of the end, the start of the withdrawal of British forces from Afghanistan. When the bulk of our troops return from Helmand at the end of 2014, it will be the end of a century or more of unbroken warfare by British forces.

The year 2015 will have the distinction of being the first since at least 1914 that British soldiers, sailors and air crews have not been engaged with some enemy somewhere in the world. Since Britain declared war against Germany in August 1914, not a year has passed without its forces being involved in conflict. It is an unenviable statistic.

There have been two world wars, large-scale conflicts in Korea and Iraq, and small-scale actions in Africa, the Middle East and Asia. There have been operations in defence of empire, cold war skirmishes, post-9/11 support for the US, and the euphemistically titled Troubles in Ireland.

My comrades were making history in Afghanistan – overseeing the destruction and handover of camps as the Army headed for the door, ending one of the toughest conflicts in decades. I felt privileged to have been there to witness, first hand, such a momentous period in our history. Personally, I am unsure what, if anything, we achieved over there. This single truth leaves a bitter aftertaste when I think of the sacrifices made by soldiers and families.

At Dara, we certainly never won any hearts and minds. A key component of any counter insurgency, such as Afghanistan, is winning over the locals. It has become a truism trotted out by armchair military theorists. There was precious little wooing of the locals at Dara or Ouellette. Afghans were out there in the poppy fields and the compounds while we watched them from behind razor wire and sandbags. Or drove past them in heavily-armoured convoys.

Britain's mission in Afghanistan morphed again from hunting Bin Laden to nation building. Before long, rebuilding the nation, ravaged by decades, if not centuries of warfare, became the focal point of the campaign.

Before I went to Afghanistan in 2009 as a reporter, we were given a briefing by officials from the Department for International Development on how much work was being put in to rehabilitate Afghanistan. We were blitzed with graphs and glitzy PowerPoint presentations showcasing an impressive list of achievements: maternal mortality has halved since 2001 and life expectancy for Afghans is at its highest-ever level. Afghanistan's government revenue has soared to $2 billion. The country also boasts "a written constitution, a democratically elected government and a system of local democracy".

In 2013, no-one even seemed to mention the rebuilding mission. The focus was on putting the time in, then leaving as quickly and cleanly as possible. When I stared out from Dara as a soldier, the landscape seemed unchanged for centuries. It could have been the 21st century or the 11th.

There seemed to be very little regeneration in this remote part of Helmand, where it was most badly needed. Afghan president Hamid Karzai has criticised the West for shortchanging his armed forces. I did notice Afghan troops used Humvees, long since discarded by the US military for heavier, better armoured vehicles. Afghan forces also lacked the expensive counter IED devices that the British and Americans routinely used. As a result, they have been battered by the Taliban's use of roadside bombs.

It was galling to be in the middle of a tour of duty in Afghanistan fighting the Global War on Terrorism, or GWOT, only to hear that a serving soldier was hacked to death by terrorists in broad daylight in the streets of London. We were meant to be in Afghanistan to stop terrorism festering there, and yet it was obviously alive and well at home.

Three months after I left Afghanistan, David Cameron said it was "mission accomplished" as he visited troops at Bastion. He said: "To me, the absolute driving part of the mission is the basic level of security so that it doesn't become a haven for terror. That is the mission, that was the mission and I think we will have accomplished that mission and so our troops can be very proud of what they have done."

His statement echoed a controversial claim made by President George W Bush in 2003 about victory in the Iraq war. Weeks after the US invasion that ousted Saddam Hussein, he flew onto a US aircraft carrier and delivered a speech under a banner reading "mission accomplished". His words came to be seen as a damning indictment of American arrogance over the war.

As I write, my Army pals are left shaking their heads each night as the TV news shows that Iraq has just erupted in a tidal wave of violence which threatens to tear the country apart. Jihadists are slaughtering their enemies, then posting videos of their bloody handiwork online, as they seek to build their own religious fiefdom. Many of the soldiers I know who served there are left asking: "What was the point?" I can only hope that David Cameron's words on Afghanistan don't come back to haunt him.

I was back in the UK for just a few weeks when I read that another key coalition goal in Afghanistan seemed to have been missed. Eradicating the Taliban's lucrative opium trade was supposed to be a cornerstone of our efforts. Yet, three weeks after I got home from Helmand, I read this story on the BBC website: 'Afghan opium cultivation has reached a record level, with more than 200,000 hectares planted with the poppy for the first time, the United Nations says. A UN Office for Drugs and Crime report said the harvest was 36 per cent up on last year and, if fully realised, would outstrip global demand. Most of the rise was in Helmand province, where British troops are preparing to withdraw. One of the main reasons the UK sent troops to Helmand was to cut opium production.'

The jury is still out on our efforts in Afghanistan. As I write, 453 British men and women have lost their lives fighting the Taliban, trying to make Afghanistan a better place. For every death, experts estimate there are roughly 10 other servicemen and women who have suffered serious physical injuries. We can only guess how many others have suffered unseen, mental scars.

I just pray to God it was all worth it.

*****

IN another twist of fate, I returned to my job as a journalist on Remembrance Day, November 11, 2013. In my mind, the thought of returning to my civvy job became a bit of an ordeal as my leave drew to a close. I needn't have worried. In the newsroom, it was like I had never been away. It was ironic that one of my first jobs should be covering the battalion's homecoming parade. On my first day back, I was nervous as I walked into the newsroom but after a few handshakes, I was at my old desk, taking calls and writing stories. Then the questions started: 'What was it like? What did you do? How did you live?' I never knew what to say.

I sometimes got the impression, which is all too prevalent these days, that people thought that because I had served in the Army in Afghanistan, I therefore had to be mentally damaged. In the lift one day, I met a female colleague that I had worked with for years. Off the cuff, I mentioned jokingly about getting flashbacks to Afghanistan due to the sunny weather. She immediately looked crestfallen, nodding sympathetically as if I had just revealed my hidden, inner torment. I should have found it funny. Instead, it just annoyed me that so many people were ignorant about Afghanistan, specifically, and the military, generally.

My military experience was a rewarding one. It was like running a marathon or climbing Everest: an experience to be enjoyed and reflected upon afterwards, not at the time. I loathed it at the time but now, I am glad I did it. I strongly believe that military service, rather than making soldiers psychologically ill, actually improves your mental health. The average member of the public too often thinks that someone who has served in Afghanistan or Iraq is seconds away from either pulling out a machine gun and strafing passers by or collapsing in a sobbing heap. Not everyone that goes to Afghanistan ends up with Post Traumatic Stress Disorder (PTSD). It sounds blindingly obvious but some people don't grasp that simple fact. Almost every veteran or serving soldier I have ever met, including some with PTSD, are incredibly mentally robust, able to deal with pretty much everything life throws at them.

Life on operations is trimmed down, with all the flippant rubbish of modern life cut out. It's simple when you are in theatre: you eat, sleep, do your job then repeat the process. There is no office politics, no council tax bills, no domestic squabbles. You just try to stay alive. The anti-modernity and austerity of life on ops appealed to me immensely – and still does. Now, I know why people keep going back for more. A reasonable ops bonus at the end helps too.

Soldiering gave me the chance to meet people I would not normally deal with. I hung out with people from every corner of the globe – Fijians, South Africans, Gambians, Nigerians, Nepalese. In an average day I could be chatting to an officer with a double-barrelled surname, who sounded like he was a member of the landed gentry, before going to the Naafi for a coffee with a tattooed youth with an angry facial scar puckering his translucent Glaswegian flesh.

I enjoyed the physical and mental challenge of being in the Army, doing things that you didn't think possible like carrying Bobby around Redford Barracks after an eight-mile speed march. Army training left me tired and drained, but it was a different kind of fatigue that left me feeling satisfied that I had reached another milestone in my ultimate bid to get to the frontline.

There was a feeling of culture shock when I got back from Afghanistan. It seemed strange going from a land where we lived on spam and instant noodles, sleeping under the stars, to walking around a normal city-centre supermarket with row after row of garishly coloured drinks and sweets of every flavour and variety.

It was great to be able to do small things that you normally take for granted such as going to the shops to buy a newspaper or having a cold Coke. Cans of pop at Dara were rarer than hen's teeth. Any juice had to be hidden away, with your name emblazoned all over the can, to put off any would-be thief.

At times, life after Afghan does sometimes feel a bit flat, a tad dull. Going to Afghanistan certainly puts life in perspective: a bad day here means that a story I am working on falls through, or I get a flat tyre on the way to work. In Helmand, a bad day means people go home in bodybags.

For a few months, I did notice that I sometimes went into hyper-alert mode. Driving home one evening, a car backfired with a loud bang. The sound seemed to reverberate right through me, causing me to flinch like a dog that's been smacked on the nose. Not long after, I went for a run along a cycle path near my home. As my mind wandered as I trotted along, I found myself gazing at an upcoming embankment, pondering where the best place to plant an IED would be. I don't think that means I'm mentally ill. If you have been working and thinking in a certain way for a while, it takes a bit of time to get out of that mindset.

I know one soldier pal who woke up at home in the middle of the night before starting to hunt for his rifle. In Afghanistan, you can never be more than an arm's length away from your weapon at any time, even in the shower or toilet. He was in the groggy state between the dream world and the real world. He slurred, "Where's my rifle?" and started to look under the bed. His girlfriend eased him back into bed as he gradually came to.

As I started unpacking after coming home, sifting through my kitbag lined with months of desert grime, I found a smooth grey stone that I had slipped in there as a memento. I wanted a small piece of Afghanistan to take away. I considered filling a small Ziploc freezer bag full of desert sand but ruled this out as, no doubt, it would just end up all over the inside of my bag. The stone was worn smooth by centuries of dust storms, untold years of rattling up and down sand dunes, as it slowly lost its sharp edges.

I still have this stone. It means a lot to me. As I write, it sits on my bookshelf, like an odd minimalist ornament. This wee grey rock is the only physical remnant I have of my time out there, sweating, schimpfing and working out, as the days seemed to stretch out in front of me forever. When I die, I would like the stone in the coffin with me.

You leave Afghanistan but it never leaves you.

GLOSSARY

AK47

Avtomat Kalashnikova 47, the assault rifle favoured by insurgents around the world.

Ancop

Afghan National Civil Order Police – national paramilitary force somewhere between the police and the army.

AO

Area of Operations: the area that each unit works in and is ultimately responsible for.

Apache

Attack helicopter kitted out with a dazzling array of weaponry. Much feared and loathed by the Taliban.

Bergen

Large army-issue backpack.

Chinook

Twin-rotor helicopter. The workhorse of Afghanistan.

D&V

Diarrhoea and Vomiting. Usually caused by insanitary conditions.

FSG

Fire Support Group. A mobile heavy weapons unit, usually made up of more experienced soldiers.

Herrick/Op Herrick

The military's codename for operations in Afghanistan. This book focused on Op Herrick 18.

Hexy/Hexamine

Solid fuel that looks like Kendal mint cake.

Humvee
High Mobility Multi-purpose Wheeled Vehicle (HMMWV).
Icom chatter
Messages passed between Taliban fighters on their short-wave radios.
IDF
Indirect Fire – mortar or rocket attacks.
IED
Improvised Explosive Device; the biggest killer in Afghan.
Isaf
International Security Assistance Force. The NATO-led security mission in Afghanistan made up by Britain, the US and their allies.
Mastiff
A heavily armoured, six-wheel drive patrol vehicle which carries eight troops, plus two crew.
Nato
North Atlantic Treaty Organisation.
PKM
Prestige weapon system. Usually only used by more senior Taliban.
PX
Post Exchange. US forces retail store.
QRF
Quick Reaction Force. A unit that is ready to move out at a moment's notice in an emergency.
RSOI
Reception, Staging and Onward Integration. The final training phase in Afghanistan at the start of a tour.

R&R

Rest and Recuperation. A break during a tour of duty.

SA80

Small Arms 80. The standard issue British Army assault rifle.

SAS

Special Air Service regiment. Elite unit of the British Army.

Scoff

Food.

Shalwar kameez

A long tunic worn over a pair of baggy trousers. Very common in Afghanistan.

Shimfing

Moaning, complaining. From the German verb schimpfen – to complain, grumble.

Stag/Stagging on

Sentry duty.

TA

Territorial Army. Now known as the Army Reserves.

Talib/Taliban

Student/Students. So called because many of the Taliban were schooled in strict religious schools called Madrassas.

Terps

Interpreters.

UGL

Underslung grenade launcher.

US Navy Seals

United States Navy's Sea, Air, Land teams. American special forces, similar to the British SAS.

APPENDIX 1 – ROYAL REGIMENT OF SCOTLAND STRUCTURE

THE Royal Regiment of Scotland was formed in 2006 from its antecedent regiments. It is made up of five regular battalions and two reserve battalions.

1 SCOTS: The Royal Scots Borderers, aka 1st Battalion The Royal Regiment of Scotland.

2 SCOTS: The Royal Highland Fusiliers, aka 2nd Battalion The Royal Regiment of Scotland.

3 SCOTS: The Black Watch, aka 3rd Battalion The Royal Regiment of Scotland.

4 SCOTS: The Highlanders aka 4th Battalion The Royal Regiment of Scotland.

5 SCOTS: Balaklava Company (formerly the Argyll and Sutherland Highlanders) aka 5th Battalion The Royal Regiment of Scotland.

6 SCOTS: 52nd Lowland aka 6th Battalion The Royal Regiment of Scotland.

7 SCOTS: 51st Highland aka 7th Battalion The Royal Regiment of Scotland.

APPENDIX 2 – TIMELINE: KEY EVENTS IN AFGHANISTAN

2001 October
US-led bombing of Afghanistan begins following the September 11 attacks on the United States. Anti-Taliban Northern Alliance forces enter Kabul shortly afterwards.

2002 January
Deployment of first contingent of foreign peacekeepers – the

Nato-led International Security Assistance Force (ISAF).
2002 June
Loya Jirga, or grand council, elects Hamid Karzai as interim head of state.
2003 August
Nato takes control of security in Kabul, its first-ever operational commitment outside Europe.
2004 October-November
Presidential elections. Hamid Karzai is declared winner.
2005 September
Afghans vote in first parliamentary elections since 1969.
2006 October
Nato assumes responsibility for security across the whole of Afghanistan, taking command in the east from a US-led coalition force.
2007 August
Opium production has soared to a record high, the UN reports.
2008 September
US President George Bush sends an extra 4,500 US troops to Afghanistan, in a move he described as a "quiet surge".
2009 February
Nato countries pledge to increase military and other commitments in Afghanistan after US announces dispatch of 17,000 extra troops.
2009 March
US President Barack Obama unveils new strategy for Afghanistan and Pakistan. An extra 4,000 US personnel will train and bolster the Afghan army and police and there will

be support for civilian development.

2009 August

Presidential and provincial elections are marred by Taliban attacks, patchy turnout and claims of serious fraud.

2009 October

Mr Karzai declared winner of August presidential election, after second-placed opponent Abdullah Abdullah pulls out before the second round.

2009 December

US President Obama decides to boost US troop numbers in Afghanistan by 30,000, bringing total to 100,000. He says US will begin withdrawing its forces by 2011.

2010 February

Nato-led forces launch major offensive, Operation Moshtarak, in bid to secure government control of southern Helmand province.

2010 July

Whistleblowing website WikiLeaks publishes thousands of classified US military documents relating to Afghanistan.

2010 September

Parliamentary polls marred by Taliban violence, widespread fraud and a long delay in announcing results.

2010 November

Nato agrees plan to hand control of security to Afghan forces by end of 2014.

2011 July

President's half-brother and Kandahar governor Ahmad Wali Karzai is killed in Taliban campaign against prominent figures.

2011 September

Ex-president Burhanuddin Rabbani – a go-between in talks with the Taliban – is assassinated.

2012 January

Taliban agree to open office in Dubai as a move towards peace talks with the US and the Afghan government.

2012 April

Taliban announce "spring offensive" with audacious attack on the diplomatic quarter of Kabul. Security forces kill 38 militants.

2012 May

Nato summit endorses plan to withdraw combat troops by the end of 2014.

2013 June

Afghan army takes command of all military and security operations from Nato forces.

2013 November

Assembly of elders backs President Karzai's proposed security agreement to provide US military with bases after Nato troops formally withdraw in 2014. President Karzai delays signing the deal.

2014 January

Taliban suicide squad hits a restaurant in Kabul's diplomatic quarter, the worst attack on foreign civilians since 2001. The 13 foreign victims include IMF country head.

2014 February

Start of presidential election campaign, which is marked by a rise in Taliban attacks.